SOVIET
WOMEN

SOVIET WOMEN

WALKING THE TIGHTROPE

Francine du Plessix Gray

Doubleday

New York   London   Toronto   Sydney   Auckland

PUBLISHED BY DOUBLEDAY
a division of Bantam Doubleday Dell Publishing Group, Inc.
666 Fifth Avenue, New York, New York 10103

DOUBLEDAY and the portrayal of an anchor with
a dolphin are trademarks of Doubleday,
a division of Bantam Doubleday Dell
Publishing Group, Inc.

Library of Congress Cataloging-in-Publication Data

Gray, Francine du Plessix.
    Soviet women: walking the tightrope / Francine du
Plessix Gray. — 1st ed.
        p.   cm.
    1. Women—Soviet Union.   I. Title.
HQ1662.G66   1990
305.42'0947—dc20   89-23589
                                                              CIP

ISBN 0-385-24757-5
Copyright © 1989 by Francine du Plessix Gray

To the memory of my beloved great-grandmother,
Sofya Petrovna Yakovleva

And also
to my friends
Nonna Volenko, Svetlana Makurenkova,
Elvira Novikova

with devotion and gratitude

CONTENTS

I

All Manner of *Glasnost*

A winter week in Moscow: Monolithic bastion of Father sky, cement-hued cover of brutal changelessness, for seven days it does not rain, or snow, or sleet, or shine, the pitiless cloud fortress never alters in hue or texture, temperatures hover at thirty-one degrees throughout, just chill enough for the mud-brown streets to remain treacherous . . . Murky, turbid amber of the Moskva River, cruel monotony of sky, harassed, distrustful gaze of citizens, melancholia, dejection, boreal solitude . . . Glacial gigantism of the modern city, tentacles of desolate thoroughfares converging toward the heart of Soviet power . . .

And then, Red Square, crenelated ramparts the color of clotted blood surmounted by watchtowers, belfries, sentry boxes, turrets, lookouts, all spelling perpetual siege, vigilance, despotism. . . . At its center, V. I. Lenin's rose granite mausoleum, militiamen in viridian green guarding its massive doors, gleam of their silver-plated bayonets . . .

But then, at the square's far end, St. Basil's domes blooming out like great bouquets of lapidary fruit; and as you face the russet heart of Lenin's tomb, joyous explosion of the Kremlin's churches! Bulbous domes of palest turquoise or blazing deep blue like the firmament of clearest night, exultant gilded domes surmounted by great gold crosses strung by ropes of golden chain, like hostages exiled from Byzantium.

For many years, that's where my eye found one of the few solaces from Moscow's cruel bleakness, in the Kremlin churches and in the many dozens of other churches nestled throughout the city: sky blue or tender green or tea-rosed, paschal whirls of flaking white surmounted by domes of gold-speckled cerulean, above their locked doors one could still see faint frescoes of resurrections, threatening prophets, frail Saint George, Virgin staring with terror at the announcing angel —throughout the 1970s, along with the delicate pale-hued buildings that survived the fire of 1812, they thrust like joyous flowers through the iceberg of the contemporary city's desolate cement.

Moscow's other havens, of course, were and remain the homes of friends: Those padded, intimate interiors whose snug warmth is all the more comforting after the raw bleakness of the nation's public spaces; those tiny flats steeped in the odor of dust and refried *kasha* in which every gram of precious space is filled, every scrap of matter—icons, crucifixes, ancient wooden dolls, unmatched teacups preserved since before the Revolution—is stored and gathered against the loss of memory; those homes which even in times of greatest dearth have centered about a table, about food miraculously foraged for the visiting relative or guest; those tables over which, until the Gorbachev era, one engaged in elaborate mimicries, note-passing, sign language, to escape the scrutiny of the state's murderers and spies.

Over the years, such Soviet homes, however poor, beleaguered, continued to exemplify those virtues that underlie the national tradition of *uyutnost'*: that dearest of Russian words, approximated by our "coziness" and better by the German *Gemütlichkheit,* denotes the Slavic talent for creating a tender environment even in dire poverty

SOVIET WOMEN

and with the most modest means; it is associated with intimate scale, with small dark spaces, with women's domestic generosity, with a nurturing love. It is a quality of soul my childhood was blessed with, thanks to my Russian mother and governess, and particularly my great-grandmother and great-aunt, in whose tiny Paris flat—filled with whatever few icons and china and other treasures they had salvaged from the Revolution—I spent the happiest days of my early years.

For beyond the erratic attentions of a French father, I was exclusively brought up by Russian women. They bullied me into taking my first steps, speaking my first words, surviving my first illnesses, shedding my first tears, learning my first manners, memorizing my first prayers, reciting my first lessons. They were my first loves and my first tyrants. Beneath their veneer of tenderness and Tolstoyan pacifism, the prim gentility of their White Russian provenance, there was a searing energy, an iron discipline, a formidable will to dominate, and it is in them that I first sensed the mysterious, unique power of Russian women.

Most treasured of early memories: Flutter of my Babushka's silks and mended laces as we prepare for bedtime, smells of verbena and rose water, of dried apricots and steaming *kasha*, rough edges of the cameo brooches I finger as she undresses me, her fragrant triple benediction as she puts me to bed before singing me to sleep with an old Russian lullaby . . . *Bayushki-Bayu,* the lullaby went. I realized only recently that the ancient words originally meant to "cast a spell," as in "I *spell* you into sleep"; and I wondered if this is not the mantric phrase with which Russian women have hypnotized generations upon generations of their offspring. For if I am writing this book, it is, in part, to decode the forceful spell that Russian women have had on me for much of my life; to decode, perhaps, what my subconscious had in mind a decade and a half ago, after my first brief two-week stay in the U.S.S.R., when I wrote the following meditation for the hero of my novel *World Without End:*

> . . . As he dozed off Edmund thought of all the violent women he'd seen in the Soviet Union, shouting, forbidding, force-feeding propaganda, instilling the little order there was in this most anarchic of nations or perhaps making the disorder even

more intense, women beating up their men when they led them out of bars by the scruff of their necks . . . all over the nation women were building, bullying, denouncing, censuring . . .

I began this present book twelve years after I wrote that passage, at that turning point in history—the *glasnost* era of Mikhail Sergeevich Gorbachev—when Soviet citizens had gained freedoms which were seldom assured even in czarist times: The liberty—perhaps still fragile—to sit in their homes or walk their streets speaking out their thoughts, loves, hatreds, travel plans without the fear of reprisal, to read most every form of book and missive they receive from the West, to entertain, without subterfuge, any foreign guest or relative they desire, to criticize most every form of present or past oppression; the freedom to satisfy that lust for beauty and pageantry that are constants of the Russian psyche, and to worship again in the scores of churches whose restoration and reopening have been one of the prides of the Gorbachev era.

The once monolithic texture of Soviet life has become, indeed, a wonderland of seething flux and surprises that make it barely recognizable from the U.S.S.R. of the mid-1970s: A wonderland in which the century-old slogan "Building Communism" has been replaced by such buzz phrases as "Recapturing our Spiritual Values," "Citizenly Consciousness-raising," and "Propagandize for Fuller Democracy," and in which the following marvels have become habitual:

Journalists of state-run television stations reverently interview Orthodox Church patriarchs recently returned from thirty years of European exile. In striking similarity to our own 1960s, dissenters openly sell *samizdat* publications in Izmailovo Park amid a flutter of antinuclear banners and posters announcing the formation of some new opposition party. Members of the former czarist nobility publish their memoirs in the nation's official gazettes. Many of my women friends whom I suspect to be Party members in excellent standing hang eminently visible crosses about their necks, and bring me medals of the Blessed Virgin to safekeep me on a voyage to Riga or Tashkent. Notwithstanding much public hostility and increasing government restrictions toward such ventures, over fifty thousand capitalist-style cooperatives, whose vast spectrum includes poodle-breeding and wallpaper-hanging co-ops, maid services, computer-training courses, even singles' clubs, have opened since 1987. In Moscow's cooperative restaurants—candle-lit, lushly carpeted and curtained, gleaming with fine glass and silverware, redolent with prerevolutionary nostalgia—suave tuxedoed waiters whisper, "Would it disturb you, madame, if I now bring you the main course?" And down the street, in a hotel financed by Armand Hammer, a Japanese-owned restaurant which flies in its *sushi* and *sashimi* from Tokyo presents one of the new Soviet wonderland's most bizarre sights: Blond, pink-cheeked Slavic beauties decked out in traditional Japanese kimonos and split-toe socks bow deeply from the waist, geisha-style, as they bring customers their cruets of hot saki.

It has also become a society in which all manner of citizenry flaunt their defiance of the state, and express a variety of startlingly candid and outraged opinions which I hope to make evident, through the voices of Soviet women, in the pages of this book.

One of the first questions I pose to any Soviet woman aims to decipher her views of *us*. What central differences does she detect between her community of women and ours?

Among the many traits Soviet women admire in their American peers is our lack of inhibitions, our boldness and daring.

"How I envy your inner freedom," a restaurant waitress in Moscow told me. "My generation was bred in a reign of terror, terror of jails, of reprisals, of authorities, of standing out in a crowd, of speaking our minds. . . . American women have so much more joy than we do, our lives are so much more timid, formal, constrained."

In the *glasnost* era of Mikhail Sergeevich Gorbachev, many Soviets are vociferous about the American-style freedoms they still aspire to gain.

"I demand the right to read Nabokov and Mandlestam and Solzhenitsyn the way you do!" a journalist in Tbilisi raged. "I want to be allowed to travel freely throughout the world, as freely as you! What kind of a scandalous society do I live in that does not allow a Soviet citizen to visit Venice!"

The athleticism of American women was the trait most admired by a team of factory workers in Siberia. Only two of the seven women in the group knew how to swim; they had just learned in the past year, at one of the health clubs currently being founded in many work collectives, and were now striving for "a more streamlined, American kind of silhouette" by doing thirty-lap sessions on weekends. "We hear that American women spend much of their free time *on themselves*, improving their bodies! That's an amazing notion to us."

There are, inevitably, some negative comparisons which tend to center on Americans' "sad overindividualism."

"Our sense of community is fast declining, but you're still far more solitary and lonely than we are," says actress Sofiko Chiaureli, one of the Soviet Union's most beloved stars, who has often attended film festivals in the United States. "Over here if you fell sick in the street you'd be immediately taken into someone's house; over there no one would know the difference if you died. And you're so much less domestic! We always spread the table at home for a foreign guest, it's unthinkable to take a visitor to a restaurant. American women seem to *live* in them."

Another recurring pattern in Soviet women's impression of their American peers is the youthful, daring behavior of our older citizens. My Soviet friends keep looking with wistful admiration at any American travelers over fifty years of age. One of my comrades, a thirty-eight-year-old Moscovite, was particularly awed by a group of Chicago sexagenarians in white shorts, encountered in a hotel lobby, who were traveling throughout the U.S.S.R. to engage in tennis matches with Soviet players of their age group. "How admirable that you remain so adventurous," she reflected, "it would be unthinkable for us to make this kind of a trip at that age. Here we become old at thirty-five," she added ruefully, "I am old already."

SOVIET WOMEN

But there is one aspect of American women's lives Soviet women admire and envy above all others—our men. Throughout my months of travel in the U.S.S.R. I have shared few conversations in which I did not hear lavish praise of American men's amazing "gentlemanliness" and "casual elegance," their talent as "good providers," and simultaneous invectives against the "passivity and boorishness" of Soviet males.

Leningrad fashion designer Aleksandra Sokolova, for instance, once spent two weeks in Cincinnati, Ohio, as a delegate to a women's congress. And much of her descriptions of the United States center on our men's "nobility of manner."

"Their constant smile, their gallantry—that was the most amazing and impressive part of my trip. In the streets, in their homes, as soon as they feel you mightn't like something, they say 'excuse me . . .' In comparison, our men's manners are constantly, uncouthly rude."

Even in the ultrapatriotic city of Tashkent, a group of women journalists concurred that "American men are so much more *gallant* in their behavior, and take such better care of their appearance. If a Soviet man isn't taught by his wife how to dress, how to behave, he tends to remain just boorish."

For Soviet women throughout the nation are obsessed, these days, with the decline in national courtesy. There is much talk and self-searching about root causes: Stalin's extermination of both the prerevolutionary and the Bolshevik intelligentsia, which had been traditional bearers of civility; the cynicism, the decrease of compassion, the spiraling growth of black-market corruption and racketeering, the general degeneration of morals that spread throughout the society during the Brezhnev era, now known as *Zastoi,* "the Stagnancy"; the sense of individual helplessness that grew during those years, leading citizens to boss and shove each other more rudely than ever as their only way of self-assertion.

Any foreigner visiting the U.S.S.R. will inevitably sympathize with this growing national concern with manners. One is appalled by the swinishly rude, often intoxicated waiters at state-run restaurants who, upon being asked, "What do you recommend as best tonight?" answer, "Whatever you've got at home," adding some foul profanity. Most hotels, even the select Intourist ones, are bound to have their share of some equally inebriated *nouveau riche* Central Asian farmers and merchants, who particularly prospered during the Brezhnev years; one often sees them run down the hallways throughout the night, brawling and screaming, flies unzipped, knocking at strangers' doors as a diversion, stamping out lit cigarettes on the carpeted floors.

So the obsession with finding a spouse or companion who is a decorous American-type *dzhentlemen* (one of many words which have become part of Sovinglese) has become a fetish of Soviet women. It leads to the following irony: Our own male citizenry, which for two centuries has been derided by Europeans for its uncouthness, its raw frontier manner, is presently looked on by Soviets as the paragon of chivalry and aristocratic courtesy. For although British, French, Italian, German tourists are far more abundant than ours in the U.S.S.R., one never hears any praise for their men's deportment. Only the American model will do.

Among the intelligentsia, Soviet males are trying with touching ardor to redeem their image. There is a growing fashion among them to say "Madame" and kiss women's hands in greeting. "I drink to your aristocratic eyes" (or "aristocratic hands," or "aristocratic bearing") is one of the most popular toasts at dinner gatherings. Some Soviet men's earnest efforts to open doors, to help women in and out of coats and cars, to carry their smallest parcels, transports one to pre–World War II Europe, making our most polished Western fellows seem quite rustic. And this fixation on manners must be seen in the context of a far wider nostalgia for the "cultivated person" of prerevolutionary culture. It is a nostalgia which, in turn, has to do with the current search for a more clearly defined national identity, and the renewed interest in Russian history and religion, which are some of the most striking aspects of the *glasnost* era.

"The tragedies of the past decades have created generations of males who are a totally different species from those of forty years ago," says Leningrad designer Aleksandra Sokolova. "As late as the mid-1940s, it would have been unthinkable in this city for a man not to stand up for a woman in a bus, or for an adolescent to shove his way through a tram without being reprimanded by dozens of his elders. No courses, no book manuals, can restructure them, even our contemporary youth may be lost to us—Russian men's traditional generosity,

SOVIET WOMEN

nobility of character, is gone. We are left just dreaming, only dreaming of such creatures. Now there are only a few exceptions left who are bearable to live with . . ."

Sokolova is married to such an exception, Aleksandr Sivak, a brilliant and exquisitely courteous philosopher whose particular expertise is prerevolutionary Russian religious thought, an interest his wife ardently shares. Their perspective is worth noting because the study of secular philosophy has been repressed throughout much of their nation's history. Western thinkers such as Plato, Aristotle, or Spinoza were considered subversive throughout most of the czarist era, a threat to the absolute "Truth" of Orthodox theology, and continued to be banned from university curricula for many decades of the Soviet state —a key factor in that undervaluation of the individual which may be the single greatest difference between Russian society and ours. Even Bertrand Russell's *History of Western Philosophy* (the author was notoriously pro-Soviet) had to be smuggled to the Sokolovs by a British colleague in a three-by-five-inch microfilmed copy: The text has never been available in the U.S.S.R.

It is only in the past few years of *glasnost* that Sivak has been allowed to lecture on his particular field—Soloviev, Berdyaev, and other nineteenth- and twentieth-century Russian theologians whom he has had to study for decades in utter silence and isolation. Sivak and his wife are frequent churchgoers, and gave me much insight into the Russian intelligentsia's current interest in religion. Contrary to Western clichés, which are based on the older generation of the rural population, this new religiosity may be more developed in men than in women. And it might be less connected to the reawakening of "faith" than Orthodox Church patriarchs claim it to be. The religious revival flows, rather, from the Russian Soviets' passionately renewed interest in their own history, and from their unprecedented freedom to study it.

For religion is increasingly being looked upon as the only authentically Russian national institution. It thus attracts those who suffer from that "crisis of Russianness," which, ironically, has been greatly intensified by the freedoms of *perestroika*. It is a crisis of identity made all the more acute by the realization that Russians, despite their domination of non-Russians, live less well than most other ethnic groups in the U.S.S.R.—Soviet Georgia is a case in point; that they are being taken advantage of by the very nationalities they have been oppressing.[1]

Thus religion helps to answer that prevalent self-questioning of the Gorbachev era which goes: "Who are we? We're not socialists anymore, we'll never be capitalists, what in hell are we?" Like their nineteenth-century predecessors, Russian women are far less troubled by the Hamletian "Who are we?" which plagues their more brooding, introspective men: Replying "Who cares what we are as long as we live better," women may be participating less ardently in the spiritual revival because of their more pragmatic, day-to-day approach. They are christening their children; but rather than looking on religion as a spiritual path, they tend to honor it as a tool of intellectual enlightenment, and as an invaluable reritualization which is linked to their nostalgia for bygone decorum, formality, manners.

"How much have we been allowed to know about our nation's history?" asks Sasha Sokolova. "Until two years ago we were only taught the history of the Soviet state. The freedom to rediscover the whole span of our past by learning about our religious traditions, which are the most distinct values in our history, is the most important gift Mikhail Sergeevich has offered us—far beyond the importance of any material economic advantages or reconstructions."

Her husband is the one who takes a more spiritual approach.

"Religion is what gave sense to Russian life for centuries," philosopher Aleksandr Sivak says, "and we've recently realized that our people became emptied, debased, when they were forbidden to express it. We're being drawn back to liturgy because it offers the reawakening of an *internal* culture, which is also what Mikhail Sergeevich's reforms are about."

There were over ninety churches open in Moscow as of December 1988, a great majority of which hold both a morning and an evening service every day of the week. During my earlier trip to Moscow in January of that year—it was the week of Russian Christmas on the

SOVIET WOMEN

"old calendar"—the beautiful church at the Novodevichy Convent was packed to capacity during the service: Bearded pink-robed priests waving censers in the scant dusk of candles before the gilt iconostasis, fragrant cloud of muttering and chanting and prostrated flesh, an aura of spirituality as dense and anarchic as the lichen of the ocean floor, testifying to that great craving for ornateness and pageantry that appear to be constants of the Russian psyche . . . the crowd was at least one third composed of men, and half of the worshipers were under thirty years of age.

During my stay in the U.S.S.R. that particular month, my guide had been an editor and linguist in his early forties who had an insatiable curiosity for any theological detail I could share with him. As we visited the murals of the Kremlin churches, he hungrily questioned me about the iconographical meanings of the Assumption and Dormition of the Virgin, of the conversion of Paul, of any other biblical lore I could offer him, and took fastidious notes on every shred of information I gave him.

In May of the same year, in Tbilisi, Georgia, I had to arrive forty-five minutes early for Sunday service in order even to enter the city's cathedral, the Church of the Assumption. At least half of the teeming crowd was composed of men. The majority of worshipers were couples with their young children, who by the age of eight knew all the prayers and chants by heart. I was in the company of my young Tbilisi guide, Kakha Siharulidze, who has done much research on the Soviet Union's religious reawakening. He estimates that at least nine couple out of ten in Georgia choose to marry in church these days—a striking change from his father's generation, in which no more than one couple out of a thousand dared to engage in the ceremony.

"This is so wonderful," Kakha commented as he lit candles with me to some of our favorite saints during the bejeweled gold-vested incense-filled pageant of the Orthodox service. "In the past forty years we've spent whatever fund of faith and trust we had, and our youth is replenishing that fund with their new spirituality; every human being must have a sense of the miraculous."

"What happiness, to be able to go to church again!" exclaimed a Moscow official during a Georgian dinner I attended later that day.

"I, a Party member, could never have been seen there three years ago! And now here I am, a good Communist, christening my children in church!"

She raised her glass. "A toast to Mikhail Sergeevich, a toast!"

II

Sex and Birth

The most startling example of *glasnost* I witnessed during my stays
in the Soviet Union occurred at a doctor's office in the same city—
Tbilisi, Georgia.

It occurred in the office of gynecologist Archil Khomassuridze, one
of the angriest of the many angry citizens I have recently met in the
Soviet Union. The doctor is indignant because he has long fought a
futile crusade to establish efficient family planning programs throughout the Soviet Union. He is enraged by the officials in Moscow's
Ministry of Health who until recently refused to disseminate any birth
control information, arguing that such measures would slow down the
nation's birth rate. He is exasperated because until the Gorbachev era,
the prudishness imposed on the Soviet press forbade the use of such

fundamental words as "menstruation" or "prostitution." Such taboos, in Dr. Khomassuridze's words, have maintained "a level of national ignorance relating to all sexual matters equaled only by the most backward countries—Iraq, Iran."

Dr. Khomassuridze had already startled me by stating his estimate of the amount of abortions performed in the Soviet Union—the highest rate of abortions in the world, *between five and eight abortions for every birth.*

And then, still sitting at his desk—two Georgian journalists were also attending the meeting—the doctor suddenly accused leading members of his country's Ministry of Health of being *prestupniki,* "criminals," for having allowed abortions to proliferate by opposing birth control programs. "They should be serving time," he said, "for the harm they've done to women's health!"

My Georgian colleagues looked startled, started taking a few notes. The doctor rose from his desk, walked toward me, and bent over my own notes, making sure that I was spelling the "criminals' " names correctly. "Petrovsky," he enunciated slowly, "Boris Vassilevitch Petrovsky, our former Minister of Health—O—V—S—K—Y—now you've got it right."

He sat down at his desk and repeated: "Criminals, murderers! And they're still in power up in Moscow, continuing to ruin our national health programs . . . they should serve time for ruining the lives of millions of our women!"

Dr. Khomassuridze is a handsome Georgian in his middle forties who cares deeply about women's well-being, about the birth of healthier infants, about the need to curb the population explosion on our planet. And sitting in his office in Tbilisi, still in the presence of several of his compatriots, he went on to tell me how he had broken his government's laws for the sake of Soviet women's health:

"Our state laws demand that we write out a *napravlenie,* an official document, to register every contraceptive device or treatment a woman receives. Well, I decided that this law is harmful in a country as obscurantist as ours. I decided to treat women without this document, anonymously, without even asking their names. We made announcements in the paper to advertise our services, and here we are! No one's punished us yet."

SOVIET WOMEN

Khomassuridze is a man with a passion for statistics on all matters of procreation. And after relating his acts of civil disobedience he went on to give me some even more detailed figures on the absence of contraceptive use in the Soviet Union.

"Guess how many women in this country are using some form of birth control—I'm including pills, condoms, IUD's, rhythm, any method available? Only 18 percent. But of this 18 percent, guess how many use decent contemporary methods, the pill, IUD's? Only 5 percent. That's the lowest in the world, lower than Bhutan or India. And what's that percentage right here in Georgia? Hold your breath . . . only 3 percent.

"When will those idiots in Moscow realize that the damage done to our women by abortion is quite equal to the harm done by narcotic addiction, alcoholism," he continued indignantly. "If women knew the harm done them by abortion they would simply abstain from all sexual life, become like nuns. . . ."

He leaned forward, angrily striking his desk. "Do you really want to know why so many of our doctors oppose birth control? In many areas of the Soviet Union—Georgia is one of them—much shame is still attached to abortion, and our doctors oppose birth control because they make so much money out of *criminal* abortions performed at home . . .

"Bring us our treasures," he curtly commanded one of his interns. Like many lonely crusaders, Khomassuridze has a stern, dictatorial streak. And his assistant, a docile young doctor who addressed his superior with filial deference, immediately presented me with a drawerful of oral contraceptives from East and West Germany, Holland, Hungary, Denmark, Great Britain, Sweden, Norway, Finland.

"Foreign aid," Khomassuridze commented dryly, "charitable gifts from abroad. How could you expect us to make decent medications of this kind in the Soviet Union, when we are so backward that half of our condoms still break upon first use? Ah, *Gospozha* Gray, our government is barely beginning to learn what human needs are."

———

Archil Khomassuridze, a very cosmopolitan, multilingual native of Georgia, won the Komsomol Prize for his doctoral dissertation (it is the highest national honor available to any new Doctor of Science) and was the youngest candidate ever to receive that award. He worked for several years as chief gynecologist at a Moscow hospital before returning to his native Tbilisi, where he had been offered the director- ship of the Zhordania Institute for Human Reproduction, then a nearly defunct clinic using antiquated methods of curing infertility. Since 1983, Khomassuridze has transformed it into one of the most visionary institutions in the U.S.S.R., and the only Soviet medical center that is a full-fledged member of the World Health Organiza- tion.

The original headquarters of the Zhordania Institute, a ram- shackle three-floor structure a few blocks from Tbilisi's main square, left much to be desired. Khomassuridze took a measure that would have been unthinkable before Gorbachev's *perestroika:* He entered into a joint venture with West German scientists to build new facili- ties for his center, for which the Germans will provide all building material and technological equipment; in return, Khomassuridze will offer free treatment to all patients sent him by his German colleagues. He will be repaying his debt, in effect, by man-hours of labor, a com- modity far cheaper in the Soviet Union than in Western Europe.

Khomassuridze's dedication to curing infertility is as passionate as his crusade to lower the nation's appalling abortion rate; he is one of the first scientists in the U.S.S.R. to have experimented with *in vitro* fertilization and artificial insemination. Yet however advanced his techniques, many cultural handicaps still stand in his way. One such obstacle is the widespread machismo of Soviet men, who have tradi- tionally blamed women in any instance of childlessness, overlooking the possibility that men could be at fault.

"Statistics tell us that 60 percent of all infertility is caused by the male partner," Khomassuridze says, "but try to get the average Soviet male to have a sperm count! Easier to teach a bear to thread a needle. Yet another double standard of sexist behavior, our men simply con- tinue to torture their women with guilt feelings for being bar- ren . . ."

National machismo is accrued by the Soviets' deep-rooted puritan-

SOVIET WOMEN

ism, which, according to Khomassuridze, also accounts for phenomenal rates of female frigidity and male impotence. "Do you know that some 70 percent of our women have never had an orgasm? And that over half of the Soviet women polled outrightly state that they detest sexual contact? How can it be otherwise, since parents are embarrassed to tell their young the most basic fundamentals of sexuality, and our school system remains equally silent?" ("In your U.S.A.," he added admiringly, "the rate of female frigidity is only 34 percent.")

Khomassuridze went on to deplore the dearth of basic commodities for female hygiene in his country. There are no sanitary tampons or napkins to be found in the U.S.S.R.; women must resort to wads of cotton, or, on those very frequent occasions when pharmacies run out of cotton, to carefully saved cotton rags. Khomassuridze has begged his "charitable Western friends" for ton loads of Modess and Tampax, and distributes them as prodigally throughout Georgia as he distributes contraceptives.

"It is ridiculous that women should lug huge packages of cotton everywhere, to work, to theater, on trains, and where do they have to throw it but in the toilet; no wonder our Soviet plumbing system is constantly, catastrophically clogged . . . well, perhaps one of the finest results of our *glasnost* will be the manufacture of Tampax."

Yet there are a few incongruities in the attitudes of this dauntless scientist who dedicates his life to the health and happiness of women: Like many contemporary Soviet men, he is engaged in a distressed reevaluation of the emancipation brought women by the 1917 Revolution, and has a deeply conservative view of their social roles. At the end of a four-hour visit, as the traditional feast of tea and Georgian pastries was brought into his office, I asked Dr. Khomassuridze if there were prejudices against women gynecologists in the Soviet Union. This is how he replied:

"Of course there are prejudices, as well there should be! The brainier the woman, the more she tends to prefer men doctors, because our best specialists are clearly men. As you know, over 75 percent of Soviet doctors are women, but they just don't work well. A child gets sick, they take those days off, they take more time off to have babies, they get behind in their research, they're useless to us . . ."

"*Gospozha* Gray," he continued in a lecturing tone, "in every area of nature, in each species of animal and plant life, there is a specific function which is akin to a vocation, a calling. Snakes, say, must move by crawling on the ground, the clematis vine will only grow up a steep wall. And woman's first calling is to educate her family; men will never be able to do it as well as women, never, you need that fine female touch . . . what would be the future of the planet if women ceased to look on family as their first priority? *Kaput!* Here at this clinic, I have officially declared that I don't accept women doctors on my staff. Let them complain, let them feel abused. . . ."

The gallant doctor suddenly looked at me with a certain terror, perhaps aware that such statements are not currently popular in the United States.

"Forgive me, please forgive me, of course there may be some exceptions . . ."

I told him, somewhat stonily, that he had already done a great deal for women.

"Thank you, thank you," he repeated, still trying to pacify me. "I shall continue to refuse employing women, for their own sake."

I was to hear similar prejudices against women doctors throughout the Soviet Union, regardless of class or ethnic backgrounds.

"I gave birth to two children," a journalist in Irkutsk told me, "one with a man doctor and another with a woman, and what a difference! How much more powerful and gentler the man!"

Even the most prominent women's rights activist in Leningrad (she deems herself to be the only one in the city) echoes these prejudices:

"Soviet women doctors can carry the patriarchal mentality more brutally than men," says Olga Lipovskaya, who edits the only feminist magazine in the Soviet Union, *Zhenskoye Chtenie (Women's Reading)*. "They're under great pressure to be even harsher."

The abortion experiences of thirty-five-year-old Olga Lipovskaya are precisely the kind which Dr. Khomassuridze wishes to abolish from Soviet life. Olga is a wiry, beautiful woman who helps to support her family by working twenty-four-hour shifts as a night watchman at a factory; she brings her typewriter to her workplace, where she translates Kate Millett, Juliet Mitchell, and other Western feminists for her newsletter. (She estimates that her publication reaches only a few dozen readers, mostly "progressive-thinking men.")

Married three times, Olga has had two children and seven abortions. She estimates that she will have had about fourteen abortions "before it's all over"; she considers fourteen to be the national average, and knows some women who have had twenty-five. The ignorance of birth control methods in the U.S.S.R. is such, Olga reports, that among her friends the most popular contraceptive formulas are still the following: 1) Douching with the juice of a lemon after intercourse; 2) Jumping off an icebox when your period is three days late. Olga describes her experiences at a Leningrad abortion clinic:

"You stand in line before the door of the operating room, seven or eight of you, waiting to be taken in. The clinic's staff is too busy to do anything but operate, so as each woman who's finished staggers out you take turns getting out of line for a few minutes, just to help her get to the resting room down the hall. Then it's your turn, and you go into a hall splattered with blood where two doctors are aborting seven or eight women at the same time; they're usually very rough and rude, shouting at you about keeping your legs wide open et cetera . . . if you're lucky they give you a little sedative, mostly Valium. Then it's your turn to stagger out to the resting room, where you're not allowed to spend more than two hours because the production line, you see, is always very busy."

"We've been brought up to look on abortion as salubrious, almost 'cleansing,' " Olga adds, "and on birth control devices as harmful and unreliable."

According to the Soviet Ministry of Health, there are between two and three abortions for every birth in the U.S.S.R. (already five or six times more than in the United States). But the ministry's statistics include only legal abortions. Dr. Khomassuridze's more realistic estimate of five to eight abortions for every birth takes into account the large amount of dangerous unregistered operations performed for bribes in private homes (many women choose this alternative to ensure proper anesthesia); it also includes the abortions effected in conservative regions where the procedure is still seen as shameful—Georgia, Armenia, Central Asia.

Khomassuridze's statistics are consistent with United Nations data, which report that among the world's developed nations, Soviets have the second-lowest access to birth control information, surpassed in ignorance only by Rumanians.[2] And my conversations with other honest specialists quite confirmed Khomassuridze's alarmist views of Soviet gynecology. The admirably dedicated Dr. Evgeny Volpin, who directs one of the most esteemed maternity clinics in Moscow, candidly admits to the many flaws and deficiencies in his field of medicine.

Dr. Volpin is a forthright, genial man in his fifties who much admires our medical system. On the main wall of his office, close to the inevitable portrait of Lenin, there hangs a large American poster of a chimpanzee sitting at a desk, dressed in surgeon's smock, with the slogan "The Boss Is Always Right" above his head.

"As you probably know, an IUD can only be used by one out of three women—women with absolutely perfect organs," he told me. "And only a small amount of foreign-made IUD's—extremely scarce —have been available to us in the past three years. As for the diaphragm, it's not popular here because we only manufacture the metal kind, which can do great harm to the cervix."

Unlike Khomassuridze, Volpin is opposed to oral contraceptives because he believes that their side effects are still unclear. ("Why should the woman take the risks, why should she always be the one to suffer?") So while pressuring the Soviet Ministry of Health to manufacture better diaphragms, he is restricted to advising rhythm and the condom (called "galoshes" in the U.S.S.R.). "But unfortunately our condoms are of wretched quality, and the production does not equal

SOVIET WOMEN

the demand . . . all this contributes to the tragic amounts of deaths we've had from illegal abortions, of which one out of five is fatal."

Volpin is also candid about the severe flaws in obstetrical care in his country. Some current data show that over 2.5 percent of Soviet infants do not live beyond their first year, ranking the U.S.S.R. in fiftieth place for infant mortality rate, right alongside Barbados; that one out of five children is born with some kind of birth abnormality, and that an increasing amount of babies suffer from brain damage traceable to birth trauma.[3] Volpin blames this on a dire lack of facilities and specialists: In the whole of Moscow, whose population is close to 9 million, Volpin told me that there are only fifteen maternity clinics and three thousand beds. He admits that even his clinic, which has the lowest infant mortality rate in the capital (half of 1 percent), should double its staff and space to function as he would aspire it to.

"It is our nation's gigantism which makes our medicine so unwieldy," Dr. Volpin sighed. "You suffer from the same problem of bigness but you handle it better—ah, to attain the low infant mortality rate of excellent little Japan, that is our dream, our Utopia . . ." (Japan as a model of technological efficiency, creative labor incentives, ideal human services—features their society is notably deprived of— seems to have become a Utopia for many progressive Soviet citizens.)

But in gynecology as in many other fields, *glasnost* era candor such as Khomassuridze's and Volpin's still alternates with instances of chauvinistic hypocrisy equal to that of the darkest Stalin years.

One such patriot is the head doctor at Maternity Clinic No. 7 in Tashkent, Uzbekistan, a loyal Party *apparatchik* with a chest full of government decorations and a despotic manner, whom I referred to as Dragon Lady. She displayed great pride in her "brand-new modern clinic." Although it had been completed only a year before, handles were already falling off doors, floors and ceilings built at crazily askew angles were cracking, cement shower stalls and bathrooms had the cheerfulness of prison facilities, surgical containers consisted of shabby enamel kitchen pails. Sitting in her office under a larger than usual portrait of Vladimir Ilyich Lenin, Dragon Lady tried to force-feed me the following lies about Soviet gynecology:

"Of course we have IUD spirals, an abundance of them made right here in the Soviet Union; we put the orders in by the tens of thousands, we distribute them to all our pharmacies."

I commented that according to medical sources in New York, Paris, London, Moscow, and Tbilisi, only one woman out of three could tolerate spirals.

"In my clinic *every* single woman can get to use the spiral," she retorted. "If her cervix gets inflamed, we heal it and put the spiral right back in. If it causes cysts, we operate on them, and then back in with the spiral. We can fix *any* contraindication."

I mentioned the dearth of tampons and sanitary napkins that plagues all my Soviet women friends. "But they must be too lazy to go to the pharmacies!" she countered. "Go to any pharmacy; if the tampons are not there today they'll be there tomorrow!"

Unwittingly, Dragon Lady exposed one of the aspects of Soviet gynecology that is most startling to foreign visitors—the practice of several women, anywhere from two to six, simultaneously giving birth in the same operating room. Dr. Volpin had admitted to me that such crowding is due to insufficient facilities and staff, and that one mother giving birth per room, as is the practice in the United States and Western Europe, would be ideal. But Tashkent's Dragon Lady again shrouded the issue with chauvinistic deceit. She assured me that there were no more than two operating tables in each of her clinic's delivery rooms, and that reports of more than two women ever giving birth in the same area were just another example of "anti-Soviet propaganda."

She proceeded to give me a tour of her hospital. "And now," she proudly said, "you will actually see the miracle *happening.*" She triumphantly opened the door to a delivery room: Three women lay there side by side, their stomachs so vertically distended they must have been in the last half-hour of labor. They were attended by only one midwife, who casually strolled between the three stoical, moaning women, screaming at them to push harder. The Dragon Lady swiftly closed the door, her face a study in discomfiture.

An equally curious feature of the Soviet maternity system is that new mothers are forbidden to see their husbands or relatives at any

SOVIET WOMEN

time during their hospital stay. Visiting such institutions, one inevitably passes by a group of young men standing anxiously outside the clinic entrance, waiting for a nurse to lean out of an upstairs window and give them a shout of "A boy!" or "A girl!" My Tashkent acquaintance upheld this custom as one more instance of the Soviet Union's superior hygienic precautions.

"We wouldn't think of letting men into our clinic," she said. "Papa might have a cold, an angina, or wear dirty clothes! It would take too much time to redress him head to toe; our holy duty is to protect the child by maintaining utterly sterile conditions.

"Besides," she added defiantly, "many women do not *want* to see their husbands at such a time; our women are coquettish, they don't have their proper cosmetics here."

"It certainly would be far better for the women's morale, but for the time being our clinics are far too restricted in space and staff to handle visitors," said the ever-candid Dr. Volpin, who like many other progressive doctors has installed a system of video-phones in his clinic: This increasingly popular device enables the young couples to see electronic images of each other while they talk, and gives fathers a first glimpse of their newborn.

As for training programs which enable husbands to assist at their babies' birth, they exist only in one hospital in the Soviet Union, at Maternity Clinic No. 1 in Riga, Latvia. This hospital is also the only one in the nation in which a select number of husbands—those who have completed the "family birthing" training offered expectant fathers—are allowed to visit their wives after their baby is born. The approach is looked upon as strictly experimental: Due to the nation's dire lack of trained specialists, and to its extreme puritanism, the technique might be totally unsuitable to the rest of the U.S.S.R. (Even in Riga, a city whose relatively progressive ethos is rooted in Western Europe's, only some 10 percent of women offered the "family birthing" alternative choose to use it.)

"How could you expect such an advanced method in Siberia or Central Asia, where many maternity hospitals are run by one woman doctor and one nurse," the director of the Latvian clinic remarked to me. "Very few of us have the time, the space, the skill, the energy to use this approach."

One of the greatest ironies of the Soviet Union's backwardness in the field of gynecology is that the technique of "painless childbirth" originated there several decades ago. The Frenchman who introduced it to the West, Dr. Lamaze, had actually learned it in the U.S.S.R. in the early 1950s from two Soviet doctors, Platonov and Velkovskii.[4] The guiding principle of the method is that women can prevent pain by overcoming anxiety and fear, which depends on their retaining total control over the way they give birth. But precisely opposite conditions prevail today in Soviet medicine: women have nothing or little to say about the conduct of their labor. Those who wish to remain conscious may be forcibly injected into deep sleep; those who long for relief may be denied it. And as I visited maternity clinics throughout the U.S.S.R., I kept recalling stories related to me by Soviet women friends about the terrors of their birthing experiences.

One acquaintance of mine in Moscow whose fragile pregnancy needed clinical observation was assigned to a ward filled with women recovering from badly performed abortions (her sister was so shaken by this episode that she never reported for any gynecological examination until the eighth month of her first pregnancy, only to receive crude reprimands from the doctors).

"The doctors keep screaming at you 'Get on with it, get on with it,' " reports my friend Xenia Velembovskaya, mother of a fourteen-year-old daughter. "The treatment is inevitably rough, impersonal, crass, as in a production line; we're treated as if sex and birth are a big crime. There was so much pain that I had nightmares about it for many years afterward—the brutality of our maternity wards are the best contraceptive method we have; very few of us *ever* want to go through it again."

My own visits to Soviet maternity wards confirmed my friends' reports. Apart from a few admirable clinics in Riga and Dr. Volpin's in Moscow, I was appalled by their lack of warmth or personal attention and by their often slovenly conditions: There is a frequent lack of any bathing or shower facilities in the wards; the sheets of nursing mothers' beds, and their shabby, prison-like hospital gowns, are often smeared with blood, the linen obviously unchanged three days after delivery: young mothers report that their infants are coming home with an increasing amount of staphylococcus infections, all traceable to this grim lack of hygiene.[5]

But my most vivid impressions of all concern the melancholy, depressed faces of the young mothers in these forlorn clinics, in which I never saw a sign of women's practical or emotional needs: no personal effect such as a nightgown or robe is allowed, no flower or card or photograph or any other token of home, not one object which might console new mothers for the absence of their loved ones is allowed to taint Soviet maternity wards' supposed "sterility." I seldom saw one smile or heard a happy voice in these institutions. I saw only a glum, resigned stoicism, desolate faces, many women in tears from the inevitable postpartum blues. These wards run by women doctors, devoted to the happiest and most fragile moments of women's lives, only expressed the joylessness and general inefficiency of Soviet life, and a nation's curious lack of concern for its citizens' psychic health.

Even the red-faced Tashkent babies lying tightly swaddled, neck to toe, in their tawdry metal cribs, looked as tragic as they were silent.

Dr. Volpin of Moscow is adamantly opposed to swaddling, which he believes can cause serious damage to the infants' lungs; but he admits that the archaic practice, common to most parts of the Soviet Union, is extremely hard to eradicate. Tashkent's Dragon Lady is still dedicated to the custom. "Swaddling keeps babies quiet," she curtly explained.

Why the phenomenal backwardness on the issue of women's and children's health? I kept asking throughout my trip to the Soviet Union. Why this inability, on the part of such a technologically advanced nation, to develop even a modest system of birth control?

"What do you mean, 'advanced'?" most of my conversants retorted in the fashionably self-deprecating manner of the Gorbachev era. "We're lagging at least twenty years behind you in most every area of technology."

"Don't you realize," they went on to say, "that in the past decades our only slogans were Defending the Nation State, Building Communism, our only priorities were defense and tractors . . . an issue such as personal health was about number 137 on our list of national priorities."

For the decline of standards in Soviet gynecology and obstetrics must be seen in a wider context—the general deterioration of Soviet medicine. It was once filled with heroic achievements (infant mortality rates were cut in half between 1914 and 1925, a historic record); it is now rife with hair-raising tales of neglect. The flaws may be in part due to doctors' low pay: their average earnings of 250 rubles a month are strikingly out of proportion to the 450 rubles earned by a skilled industrial worker.

A computer specialist in Leningrad whose young son has severe asthma reports that she has never been able to consult more than once with the same pediatrician at the "district clinic" to which she is officially assigned, thus denying her very ill child any consistently pursued medical care.

A fifty-two-year-old publishing executive in Siberia told me that she had severe cardiac fibrillations and a blood pressure of 180 over 120; she had never heard of the word "cholesterol," and no doctor had ever instructed her to restrict her intake of animal fats or salt.

Cholesterol measurement and dietary precautions were also lacking from the regime of a thirty-eight-year-old Moscow journalist with a similarly alarming blood pressure; she had merely been prescribed powerful sedative medications, without being informed that driving a car might be dangerous in her lethargic state.

The slipshod care offered these members of the professional elite makes one shudder at the treatment of less-privileged citizens. A popular saying about the Soviet medical system is *lichitsa darom, darom lichitsa,* "free treatment isn't worth a cent." If the 1988 laws permitting private cooperative clinics are not encouraged, one can safely predict that citizens will continue to resort to the time-honored Soviet custom of medical *blat* or illegal payoffs—bribing doctors to make home calls, bribing hospital nurses to obtain such rudimentary comforts as bedpans, clean sheets, towels.

"Do Soviet women engage in *blat* as much as men?" I innocently asked a colleague, the writer Zoya Boguslavskaya, at the beginning of my research.

"How can you ask me such a question," she answered petulantly, "when every child over the age of nine engages in *blat?*"

"It's so much easier to bribe women doctors than men doctors!" a Moscow friend once told me. "What are our favorite bribes, after all? French perfume, Hermès scarves, Swiss chocolates, champagne—how much more natural to give such presents to a lady."

III

The Women's Century

The heroine of one of the most popular works of Soviet fiction of the past decades, Natalya Baranskaya's novella *Nedelya Kak Nedelya* ("A Week Like Any Other")[6] is a young scientist so harassed by the double burden of career and motherhood that she constantly feels guilty of being a failure at both. The most commonly repeated verbs in this text are "run" and "fly."

Like many working mothers, the heroine, Olga, lives over an hour away from work, in a new district of the Moscow periphery where there are as yet no stores; she runs into her laboratory on Monday mornings, often late because of some crisis with her children, interpreting every look or word from her superiors as a reprimand; after work she runs and flies from bus stops to trolley stops to subway stops to sparsely stocked grocery stores, her arms laden with groceries, often stumbling, scraping her knees. Yet this is a privileged life. Olga and her husband are research scientists with advanced university degrees. Olga shares a laboratory—where her job is to test polymer materials— with eight women colleagues who live in states of "constant anxiety, eternal rushing, fear" somewhat akin to hers.

Written in the form of one week's diary entries, "A Week Like Any Other," the angriest woman-centered text published in the U.S.S.R. since 1930, expresses with unsurpassed poignancy the nightmares of Soviet women's daily life: Food shortages; eternal queues; indifferent doctors hastily attending children who constantly get ill from sloppily run nursery schools; a dearth of the most basic household implements or services; passive husbands buried in TV or newspapers who never lift a finger to help out.

At the office, as she fills out a government-issued "Questionnaire for Women" which asks her how many hours she spends on "leisure," Olga sardonically muses: "What nonsense. Lei-sure. Personally, my sport is running." The next question puts our heroine into a state of panic: She must count the days of work she's skipped for reasons of illness—hers, her family's. There are only fourteen days of paid sick leave a year, and she's absented herself for seventy-eight whole days because of the colds her children constantly catch at the day care center. As her colleagues chat sardonically over the questionnaire, Olga asks a subversive question: "What exactly does the concept of 'a real Soviet woman' entail?"

Olga's mornings are a particular nightmare. The children are two and four, her husband helps but grudgingly to get them washed, fed, dressed in the many layers needed in a Moscow winter. "It is five past seven and I am running, of course . . ." Throughout this narrative, one senses that the most precious part of Olga's life, outside of her beloved children, is the daily support of the women in her work collective. They take turns shopping for each other, sacrificing their lunch hour to buy communal kilos of butter, bologna, bread, liters of milk. The pressure of a woman friend's hand across Olga's cheek is the week's only reassurance, its only soothing moment.

In the evenings, if there has been a late meeting at the lab, Olga runs back toward the subway and bus stops, flies across empty lots, runs up the stairs to find her hungry children ruining their appetites by munching bread while her husband remains buried in technical journals. After dinner, while he continues reading, Olga does the dishes, washes and mends her children's and husband's laundry, prepares their clothes for the morning, sweeps the kitchen. In constant terror of the 6 A.M. alarm clock, she is seldom in bed before midnight, and must often get up during the night to soothe a child made sick by the nursery school diet.

Olga's husband, Dima, does take out the garbage.

It has been years since the couple have "been" anywhere together —a film, a ballet, even a café. It is intimated that although they "love" each other and seldom quarrel, their life is so harassed that sexual contact occurs but rarely.

Olga belongs to that new generation of Soviet women who cannot count on *babushkas* to take care of their children; their mothers are too busy with their own careers.

At work Olga is in constant anxiety of being fired.

"Am I that good a mother?" she also worries as she runs homeward from subways to trolley stops. If she forgets to alert her husband about a late conference she finds an angry spouse, children weeping again with tiredness and hunger, or made ill by the supper their father has hastily prepared.

When the longed-for Saturday morning finally comes around, Olga, promising research scientist at a distinguished laboratory, makes five days' worth of soup, dusts, scrubs floors, does the week's heavy laundry, puts up dry fruit compote, grinds meat for hamburgers, sends her children out with their father for their only fresh air of the week, irons, sews, has her weekly shampoo.

Throughout these days Olga has kept reminding herself that she's a luckier woman than most—luckier than her colleague Shura, whose husband is a drunkard; or her colleague Lyusa, who was abandoned by a married man late in her pregnancy. Still, on Saturday night there are harsh words exchanged between the spouses because Dima considers it his privilege to read while Olga continues working. After dinner she breaks down into tears during the children's weekly bath, slaps them unfairly for some small misdemeanor.

"I'm tired, do you understand? Tired!" Olga shouts out. "The undone work keeps growing!" She breaks down and sobs. "My youth is passing . . ."

Her crying fit keeps growing, Dima puts her to bed like a child as their babies howl about them, brings her a cup of tea. But later that night Olga and Dima resume their argument. Why, with two careers, do they have barely enough money to make ends meet . . . half of their salary is spent on food. . . . How to solve their dilemma . . .

Dima's suggestion is similar to many being currently proposed by Soviet husbands: Olga should stop working and stay home to take care of the family—what with all the "sick" days she takes off she earns next to nothing anyhow.

But Olga is appalled by the suggestion: "You want to shut me in here for the whole year! How could we live on your salary!" Dima replies that if he could be freed of "his share of domestic chores" he could earn more.

"All this boring stuff is for me alone," she exclaims, pointing to the kitchen mess, "and the only interesting things are for you!" What about Olga's five years of graduate study, her dissertation, her professional standing? At week's end, the couple are as harassed by the burdens of everyday life, their marriage is more tense than it was at week's beginning.

Olga's nightmarish week is hauntingly close to the plight of women deplored by Lenin in 1919, when he wrote:

"Woman . . . continues to be a *domestic slave,* because *petty housework* crushes, stultifies, and degrades her, chains her to the kitchen and the nursery, and she wastes her labor on barbarously unproductive, petty, nerve-racking, and crushing drudgery."

Olga's plight is surely not what Lenin had in mind for Soviet women when he wrote, in the same essay:

"The real *emancipation of women,* real communism, will begin only where and when an all-out struggle begins . . . against this petty housekeeping."[7] (The italics are Lenin's.)

I met many Olgas during the past year—in Riga, Leningrad, Moscow, Tbilisi, Tashkent, Irkutsk—as I traveled throughout the U.S.S.R. as the guest of a generous Moscow publisher, Progress. Progress assigned one of its editors to be my guide throughout my Soviet journey, the wondrously warm, generous, and cultivated Nonna Ionovna Volenko. Like all Soviet publishers, Progress is under the jurisdiction of a government publishing committee, *Goskomizdat*,[8] which has a branch in all of the U.S.S.R.'s major cities. Thus the local *Goskomizdat* of each region we visited could assign one of its employees to be our local guide; and it made appointments for us with women of various professions—doctors, lawyers, teachers, journalists, psychologists, factory workers—while leaving us free to speak with any other citizen who wished to open her heart to us.

Throughout the weeks of our travels together, as Nonna and I shared hotel rooms, meals, grueling night flights, and a growing friendship, we heard women complain about the double burdens of home and career in a mood of candor, bitterness, and frequent anger made possible only by Gorbachev's *glasnost.* In this nation where over 92 percent of women are fully employed, and comprise 51 percent of the nation's work force, the word we heard most frequently was *peregruzhennost',* "overburdening." It is the same word one sees in all Soviet elevators, warning passengers of the perils of overloading the vehicle with one passenger too much.

Few communal fates are more ironic than that of contemporary Soviet women. For upon the Revolution of 1917, the Bolshevik regime became the first government in history to declare women's emancipation as one of its primary goals, and to inscribe it into its constitution. Laws ensuring equal pay for equal work—akin to our doomed Equal Rights Amendment—were instantly effected. And women's right (if not their obligation) to work became central to Soviet notions of citizenship. According to Engels and Lenin, women's full participation in the labor force, and the communal households that must replace the nuclear family, would put an end to the "open or disguised domestic enslavement" (Friedrich Engels' words) imposed on them since time immemorial. The Soviet founding fathers also predicted that the overthrow of capitalism would automatically effect a radical change of male attitudes that would assure women full equality at home and at the workplace.

Yet after the first fifteen years of Soviet rule, it became evident that the Leninist ideal of freeing women from the fetters of wedlock, diapers, and saucepans was still a distant Utopia; that the government was not able or willing to implement any communalizing of household tasks, or of effecting that "radical reeducation" of the male psyche promised in 1917. In retrospect, it is also evident that the U.S.S.R.'s commitment to women's equal employment has never been ideological; it has been based, rather, on pragmatic, demographic factors—rapid economic growth, labor shortages, and a frequent deficit in the male population.

In a country as phenomenally backward as the Soviet Union, female labor, from the onset of the first Bolshevik government, was considered essential to the speedy industrialization process central to the country's survival. Stalin's Five Year Plan of 1928, and the tragic loss of men's lives caused by succeeding historical events, incited the state to mobilize still vaster amounts of women into the work force: It is now estimated that some 40 million men died in the process of coercive collectivization, in World War II and in Stalin's purges.

The Stalin years also brought a startling reversal of all earlier Bolshevik ideals concerning women and family structure. In the 1930s, the legal abortions and liberal divorce laws originally legislated under Lenin were repealed or severely curtailed. As Stalin's regime realized that rapid industrialization, contrary to original expectations, did need the discipline of family life, there arose a cult of motherhood quite as intense as it had been under the czars. The state evolved a vast hierarchy of rewards glorifying fertility—Motherhood Medals, Order of the Glory of Motherhood, Mother Heroines (ten children or more).

Divorce and abortion laws were liberalized again after Stalin's death. And in the succeeding decades severe social flaws—dire scarcities of food and housing, an enduring tradition of male chauvinism, increasingly ineffectual social services—consistently thwarted the government's appeal for larger families. Thus since the early 1960s, the Soviet leadership has been confronted by a perhaps insolvable dilemma: It needs woman as both producer and reproducer. It is faced with impending labor shortages, a dramatic increase of divorces, and an alarming decline of births in those European parts of Russia where its major industries are clustered (a shortage of 1.7 million industrial workers is forecast for the year 2000).[9] It is thus encouraging more women than ever to work full time; but in order to salvage its future labor force, it is simultaneously demanding an increasing amount of offspring—preferably three per family—from a nation of women so harassed that they are more and more reluctant to bring up more than one child.

Ironically, the government's propaganda for larger families has helped to heighten women's awareness of their second-class citizenship. Citizens such as the archetypal Olga of "A Week Like Any Other" have become increasingly conscious of the paper equality offered them, of their segregation to poorly paid sectors of the economy, and of the sex-role stereotyping that causes their poor promotion records.

For in the past decade the average female worker, although slightly better educated than her male counterpart, earned only two thirds of the average male income—a proportion close to those of the last prerevolutionary years. Nearly half of Soviet women are employed in unskilled manual labor or low-skilled industrial work.[10] They comprise, for instance, 98 percent of the nation's janitors and street cleaners, 90 percent of conveyor belt operators, one third of railroad workers, over two thirds of highway construction crews and of warehouse workers—much of it heavy physical labor that can be extremely harmful to women's reproductive systems.[11] As for that fast-declining population still employed in agriculture, a whopping 85 percent of the mechanized operations are run by men, leaving women to perform a major part of the more arduous manual work.

The higher professions are equally unbalanced: Over 80 percent of school teachers are women, yet they comprise only about one third of school principals. Some 77 percent of doctors are women, but 52 percent of hospital administrators are men, who remain in charge of formulating all national health policy. The inequity is even more striking among engineers and skilled technical workers, 70 percent of whom are women: In those fields, women only constitute 6 percent of work collectives' leadership, from section chief to enterprise manager.[12]

SOVIET WOMEN

This inequity prevails even though the quality of women's work is unanimously admitted to be better than men's. Upon my very first week of researching this book I heard one of the chief editors of my Moscow publishing house state his preference for women employees. "If I have to choose between a man or a woman for a *middle-level* editorial position," he said (he emphasized those two words), "in nine cases out of ten I'll choose the woman. How much more careful, responsible, punctual, neat, conscientious, they are in their work!"

I would repeatedly hear these flattering attributes concerning the working habits of the "Fair Sex"—a phrase still traditional to Soviet men, now used ironically by women to stress their growing discontent.

"Our women work well out of a sense of duty, even if the task bores them," says physicist Ivar Knets, the rector of Riga's Polytechnic Institute, who has spent two years in the United States on exchange fellowships. "Whereas Soviet men have a shorter attention span, keep changing lines of work out of restlessness, will only work decently if they feel the immediate usefulness of their labor."

His fellow Rigan Monika Zile, editor of Latvia's largest women's magazine, believes that the quality of Soviet men's work is too often undermined by their lack of self-esteem.

"In any working situation men need far more compliments than women do," she says. "They must be constantly reassured, constantly thanked for what they're doing. We must evolve some way to boost the morale of our male workers, perhaps on the model of the Japanese managers, who handle morale brilliantly. Somewhat like the Japanese, our women are motivated by their pride in their work rather than by their level of material achievement, which is the way it should be." (Soviets often refer to women workers as "our Japanese" because of the meticulous, self-assured diligence of their work patterns; I have also heard it said that one of the aims of *perestroika* is to motivate men to work as well as women.)

Yet however esteemed their work habits, women remain clustered in positions of lower wages and lesser power because they are viewed as an unstable work force: Due to childbearing and the need to care for their children when they are ill, they have a high rate of absenteeism. In any branch of skilled work, male employers are wary of the loss of research knowledge caused by such absences.

These imbalances of power in a nation founded on the principle of sexual equality cannot be solely attributed to patriarchal attitudes. In analyzing Soviet women's absence from the higher echelons of politics and labor, Western feminists have tended to put too much blame on men's sexist biases. Soviet women are the first to admit that their numerous material hardships, such as the daily stint of standing in long queues for the family's evening meal, rob them of the spiritual and physical energy to strive for positions of greater power. And in the *glasnost* era they often note, with a touch of irony and pride, that in view of the totalitarianism and moral debacle of past Soviet regimes (only recently disclosed to them) their skeptical reticence toward political power may have been prophetic.

"Politics always struck me and my women friends as something deeply unethical, as dirty work," says Olga Lipovskaya, a young Leningrad mother who supports her family by working as a night watchman in a factory. "We've always sensed that personal goals were more important."

"From earliest youth women have far greater distrust than men of political slogans, of all political activities," says Leningrad fashion designer Aleksandra Sokolova. "That's because we've got sharper minds."

Politics seems to be equally distrusted by women of the "working class," as industrial workers are still habitually (and admiringly) designated. I once asked a Moscow factory worker why, in her opinion, women, in any average year, have formed less than 5 percent of the Central Committee.[13] (Only two women, Yekaterina Furtseva, and, as of 1988, Aleksandra Biryukova, have ever been a member of the all-powerful Politburo.)

"Thank God there are so few of us on the Central Committee," she quipped. "Let the guys fight it out up there with their power games, why should we bother with such junk?"

By the early 1980s, at the end of those Brezhnev years now referred to as *Zastoi*, "the Great Stagnancy," the heroic tolerance of

SOVIET WOMEN

Soviet working women was showing signs of wear. They had begun to use the ironic phrase "We have *too much* equality." To many of them, equality had begun to mean the equal right to carry hundred-pound sacks of grain or bricks, weight loads that often infringe on the thirty-pound limit defined by the state for women workers. Meanwhile, many of the social structures and services which enabled their mothers and grandmothers to pursue careers, and which had once made the Soviet Union a showcase welfare state—free medical care, preschool centers, government family benefits, parental help—had degenerated beyond recognition.

The *babushkas* who helped to rear a generation of youngsters in the first Soviet decades have begun to be an extinct species, for the mothers of most young women are themselves hard at work. An increasing amount of young mothers are therefore jeopardizing income and careers to stay home with their children for three years or more in order to keep them out of poorly run government crèches. There have been numerous reports, from such institutions, of corrupt *nyanyas*—day-care workers—who adulterate the little ones' milk with water, and mix bread into their meat rations in order to take the food home; of centers so carelessly run that the youngsters frequently get lice and other skin diseases; of centers so understaffed that their supervisors keep windows open throughout the coldest days, deliberately inducing respiratory infections in order that more children might stay home. For throughout the Soviet Union, the dearth of day care centers is such that some 3 million youngsters are wait-listed for them.

In the past two years, when Gorbachev's *glasnost* began truly to flower, and ravaged the seventy-year-old myth of a Perfect Society, many women have become vociferous in their complaints against such social flaws. My friend Olga Voronina, a philosopher, points to the appalling disparity between Soviet women's arduous schedules and the relative freedom of their men. The average working mother, she notes, spends a staggering forty hours a week on shopping, food preparation, housecleaning, and laundry. The corresponding amount of time spent by men on domestic tasks amounts to less than five hours, most of it devoted to shopping.[14]

"We still apply the old stereotype of the all-capable and resilient [Soviet] woman," historian Anna Pankratova recently wrote in the popular weekly *Moscow News.* "Yes, she *can* do everything, but she *doesn't want to any more.*"[15] "Everything has been proclaimed, but all still has to be obtained," another protester writes in the same newspaper, comparing Soviet women's so-called emancipation to "Atlases putting all their load on the shoulders of caryatids." A sociological tool seldom used before the Gorbachev era—public opinion polling—shows that even though the working mother still enjoys far greater prestige in the eyes of her children and husband, and the term *khozyaika,* "homemaker," remains very derogatory, one out of five Soviet women would willingly give up work if they could so afford.

Karl Marx liked to quote the words of the French Utopian socialist Charles Fourier: "Social progress can be measured accurately according to the social status of the fair sex."[16] Due to their arduous double shift, and to the lack of any national tradition of collective action since 1917, women have little opportunity to lobby for the fulfillment of this particular Marxist ideal. They are also hindered from cohesive action, to this day, by their government's censure of any "feminist" movement that would function outside of Party control (such an activity is still branded as "bourgeois deviation"), and by their curious lack of solidarity.

For in our decade, the deep, loyal friendships for which Russians have been fabled seem to have waned among women. There is a striking lack of trust among females—a result, perhaps, of the scarcity of men that has prevailed since World War II, women's abiding sense of competing for the precious male. Most professional women, even in a society of traditional Moslem roots like Tashkent's, will admit that there are few members of their own sex, beyond their mother or grandmother, on whom they can rely; their most trusted confidants seem to be men, "platonic friends" who are usually members of the same work collective.

"We simply don't have enough energy left to have friendships outside of the workplace, we have no time to pick up the phone and communicate our grief and weariness to a sister soul," a school teacher in Leningrad told me. "In such solitude, with such a heavy professional and domestic work load, how do you expect us to fight for women's rights as you do in Chicago?"

One of the most poignant outcries I heard against Soviet women's

SOVIET WOMEN

"double shift" came from a young mother of two who is a program producer at the government television station in Riga, Latvia. In the company of four of her colleagues and of my traveling companion Nonna Volenko, we had again been discussing Soviet women's central complaint—the overburdening duties of career, housekeeping, and child-rearing summed up by the constantly recurring phrase *trudnosti byta,* "the hardships of everyday life." Who is more lonely *within* marriage, I'd asked her, men or women?

"Women are far, far lonelier," the television executive said with bitterness. "Look here, I come home, I'm exhausted. I feel lonely because I'm so exhausted that I can't and don't want to love any one, I only want to rest, they all just bother me, all my womanly instincts have been drained out of me . . .

"I'm too tired to love!" she exclaimed on the brink of tears.

A vehement chorus of agreement, and of anger toward men, rose from her colleagues. "Of course, when *they* come home they can all rest, they have nothing else to do, or else they pretend to tinker about the house again. . . ." The group went on to agree that "no man we know is capable of washing his own plate."

And yet many women I've talked to prefer to remain exhausted, to continue complaining, and to keep their husbands out of the kitchen, where "it is not their place to be." As nineteenth-century Russian literature evidences, women's suffering as redemptive force is a central theme of Russian culture. And many contemporary women admit that their tradition of heroic self-sacrifice is a form of power play, a way of retaining their aura and their status.

"Of course we're grossly overburdened," a factory worker in Siberia told me. "But we're so used to it we wouldn't give it up for the world. We take such *pride* in surviving it."

IV

Growing Up Powerful

Nonna Volenko and I visited Tashkent's Governmental Day Care Center No. 440 in mid-afternoon, when the children had finished their nap and were beginning another play period. The spacious, sunny space we were taken to was one of a dozen such rooms, each of them assigned to eighteen youngsters of a particular age group, in a two-story building that overlooked a large, cheerful playground. The first detail that impressed me about this *yasli* (the Russian word for crèche or day care center literally means "cribs") was its scrubbed, almost military orderliness: White pillows were puffed up into neat tall triangles on each of the eighteen immaculate beds, toys were aligned like soldiers along one wall.

At a corner table, a *nyanya* in white smock and starched white hat was preparing a snack for the youngsters, who stood about a piano with their music instructor, rehearsing a song about Vladimir Ilyich Lenin. As we walked into the room the children's chief caretaker immediately called her wards to order with a rich array of terms of endearment—"little blossoms," "little paws," "cherries," "little sunshines"—bidding them to gather about her and greet their guests.

These gorgeously healthy, plump-cheeked youngsters, five and six years old, were as ethnically mixed as those of our Hawaii kindergartens. Drawn by its prosperity and superb climate, Russians have been migrating to Uzbekistan for decades and now make up over half of Tashkent's population; and in this classroom flaxen-haired Slavs stood hand in hand with swarthy little Uzbeks, with Tartars whose features were similar to those of youngsters in a Peking kindergarten.

I instantly noticed, as Nonna and I walked into the room, that as the children ran up toward their warden the girls gathered at the very front of the group, the boys hovered in back. They all stared up with intense curiosity, their heads turned toward us as uniformly as their neatly aligned toys and pillows. "Well, my kittens," the caretaker urged them cheerily, "aren't you going to say hello?" "*Zdravstvuyte,*" a chorus arose, girls' voices several decibels louder than the boys'. "And next, let's have some questions," the caretaker needled on. "Aren't you going to ask our guests about the big trip they took to see us?"

A half-dozen girls immediately stepped up to the very head of the group, asking in loud clear tones for our names, how many days it had taken us to drive from our homes to Tashkent. While engaging in the banter, two of them, one a blue-eyed Slav, the other an Uzbek charmer with sleek black braids to below her waist, grabbed objects from a nearby table as presents for us: a paper flower, a toy broom. Other girls followed suit, until the room was a mayhem of their greetings and gift-giving, and the supervisor gently remonstrated that they could draw special presents for us in a few minutes, but mustn't give away school belongings even to the nicest visitors.

During this hospitable demonstration, the nine boys in the group hovered uncertainly at the back of the room, some fiddling with a small toy, others just standing about, their hands behind their backs, craning their necks left and right to see what the other fellows were doing. "Well, has the cat got your tongue, my pigeons?" The caretaker addressed the boys with an edge of reprimand. "How could it be *you* don't have any questions?"

The boys continued gaping at me sideways, eyes averted each time I tried to meet their gaze, nudging each other with awkward grins as the teacher pressed on: "What's the trouble with my little lambs, did you get up on the wrong side of the bed? Come come, one nice little question . . ."

By this time, the girls were all over me, riffling, at my invitation, through my pocketbook and camera equipment, asking to see photos of my own children and pennies from my country. Back home during my sons' youth, throughout my long acquaintance with similar institutions, I had noted that a bunch of ebullient, often unruly boys were usually the first to step forward with questions and demands, while the girls, shier, more prim, tended to stay in the background. Here the situation was quite reversed. However much she urged, the caretaker could not get one word out of the boys, who throughout our hour's visit would hold back, silent, undecided, diffident. This pattern would be more or less repeated among any group of youngsters I gathered with throughout the U.S.S.R. The aggressiveness of Soviet women, I have noticed, begins very early in life, whatever their ethnic background.

Throughout my stays in the Soviet Union I had heard a great deal about the deterioration of government day care centers, which has been exposed with increasing candor by the *glasnost* press. But this center in Tashkent was reserved for the offspring of one particular work collective which helps to subsidize it, a prosperous fashion design workshop directly across the street, and seemed to be a model one. (The quality of care offered by Soviet preschool programs depends vastly on the wealth and status of the professional groups that subsidize them. A friend of mine who as a child attended a *yasli* for the offspring of Central Committee members reports having caviar every morning for breakfast.)

Like most of the nation's preschool groups the center I was visit-

SOVIET WOMEN

ing in Tashkent functions from 7 A.M. to 7 P.M. to accommodate the needs of working mothers. Because of its relatively luxurious facilities and competent staff, many Tashkent mothers who work in other parts of town aspire to send their youngsters here, even if it might entail an hour's extra commute across the city.

As we sat down to tea with the *yasli*'s head supervisor, a group of caretakers, and three of the youngsters' mothers, they explained that outsiders have to register their child at birth to apply to this center, and then go through a complicated and seldom successful exchange system. "If an employee of our collective lives far away she could put her child at a center near her home in exchange for us taking the child of a family who lives near our employee," one mother explained, using that special motion of the hand which in Soviet body language implies the exchange might involve some *blat*—tipping, illegal bribes. "But that takes a lot of string-pulling."

We went on to talk about the caretakers' handling of the children's behavior problems. I was struck by the women's rigidly deterministic views of all children's innate goodness ("There isn't a mean streak in any child! All children are uniformly good, there are only bad caretakers!") I also noted the heavy-handed way in which they attempted to shape the youngsters' view of good and evil: "We read them fairy tales and say, 'This character is evil, mean, cruel, and this one is kind, softhearted. Which one do you like better?' And the children always say that they love the softhearted character best."

I also noticed the women's unanimity on the issue of gender differences, which led to a chorus of praise for girls' conduct and characters, with not one mention of boys': "Little girls are such tender little things, all so soft, so good and tender. That's not just the way we raise them here, cruelty simply doesn't *exist* in little girls."

I then asked the mothers and caretakers what kind of language the children used when they'd realized they'd been naughty. "Oh, they use the Lenin oath," the women answered, "how endearing that is!" I asked more about the "Lenin oath." The women explained that a boy or girl who had misbehaved always said "I promise I won't ever do it again, I give my Lenin oath!"

"It's the holiest of pledges to them, truly sacred," one of the mothers explained further. "Even a five-year-old who wants to swear that he has told the truth raises his hand and says 'Honest as a Leninist!' "

The mother and the day care workers slapped their hands and laughed, praising the dear little paws, the dear little five-year-old blossoms, who had already developed such a high sense of patriotism. I asked them for the words of the Lenin song I had heard the youngsters singing when I first came into the day care center that morning. One of the caretakers—the music instructor—eagerly ran it through for me in a clear, lovely voice while Nonna wrote down the words. Here are excerpts from it:

> In this communal room, no one is ever bored
> For in the most visible place hangs the portrait of Lenin.
> To you, happy children, he opens the wide world
> He looks at us with a big smile, as if about to speak
> Be happy, little ones,
> Grandchildren of the October Revolution.
> Lenin lives eternally!

The women looked very moved to see their foreign guest learning the words of the youngsters' favorite song.

"For them Lenin is still truly alive," one of them said. "That's why he recurs so much in their conversation. For instance, they often say to each other: 'You can fool me, that's one thing, but you can't fool Lenin!' "

"Yes," another mother agreed, "until our children are six or seven, they totally believe that Vladimir Ilyich is alive!"

"So," I asked, "how do the kids take it when they learn that he's really *not* alive?"

The day care workers looked at each other uncertainly. "They must learn about it at home," one said, "we don't know quite for sure how or when it happens."

"It usually happens the first time they see an old film of Lenin's death on television," a mother suggested, "and they see the tears on the faces of workers' attending the funeral."

"The boys take it far harder, it affects them deeply," the chief supervisor admitted. "I had one little boy who came in crying so hard one morning, he'd seen it on the television the night before. 'I've lost my best friend,' he wept, 'I've lost Vladimir Ilyich . . .' That child wasn't himself for several weeks."

Well, I thought, they do get an early training in disappointment.

Throughout my stay in the U.S.S.R., I kept remembering these early glimpses of male passivity and disillusionment, of female power and self-esteem, while talking to the few scholars who are beginning to research patterns of gender differences in Soviet society. Due to the distaste for gender analysis that prevails in any Marxist state, it is an area of psychology which until recently has virtually been untouched in the U.S.S.R.

Olga Voronina, a Moscow philosopher who is one of that even smaller group of scholars who consider themselves "feminists" (she estimates that there are only twenty or so women in Moscow who would accept that label) analyzes the situation this way: Soviet girls are favored by teachers from earliest preschool days because, having stronger role models, they are more obedient than boys and do far better in school.

"Even in such patriarchal organizations as Pioneer groups," she notes, "until the age of fourteen or so the girls were always far more active—I say "were" because the popularity of such Party organizations has much decreased lately. Look at their role models: Mother often alone at home ruling the roost, an all-female cast of teachers, and all around them, women handling the double shift of career and home. The girls absorb this female energy and are more active on every level throughout their school years. But as they reach adolescence they tend consciously to slow down, curb themselves; they think an overly active woman is less appealing. . . . Well, God only knows how aggressive we'd be if we *didn't* curb ourselves a little bit!"

"I know that a majority of public school teachers in the U.S.A. are also women," says my friend Elvira Novikova, another feminist scholar. "But it's a Soviet phenomenon for teachers to favor girls as much as we do—this creates a pattern of anti-social behavior among boys, it leads them to feel that it's not "cool" to get good grades, and it reinforces their resentment of women. A boy's ego is further undermined because he spends most of his time at home with his mother; his father—if he has one—is often too passive or too macho or not sensitive enough to deal with a child's problems and become a proper role model."

"Our young men have gone out into the world with the attitude that they're little boys, still under the wings of their mommies," says Monika Zile, the editor of Latvia's largest woman's magazine. "When they've had to take a responsibility or make a decision, a woman has always stepped in to take over."

Maria Osorina, a Leningrad psychologist, offers more complex historical reasons for what one could call "The Powerful Woman Syndrome" in Russian society. She sees a breaking point in nineteenth century history, the Decembrist Movement of 1825: When this first wave of political dissent was brutally crushed by the Czar, Russia's male intelligentsia lost much of its self-esteem, began to feel marginal and helpless before an immutable authoritarian regime. She also believes that the deepest traditions of Russian culture—the high value of inner emotional life, of the life of the spirit—are far more feminine than those of most other nations.

"Compare our traditional values, for instance, to the very masculine, pragmatic, utilitarian German ethos," she says. "For some eight centuries, we praised and upheld all that was connected with *dukhovnye tsennosty,* spiritual life, and we were taught to disdain most practical aspects of existence. This reverence for values associated with the female principle gave women an immense psychic power, even throughout the feudalism that lasted until the late nineteenth century, even before they were allowed to have schooling and careers. Ironically, this unison between feminine and national values has continued right into postrevolutionary times. Teachers have favored girls because their behavior is more closely modeled on the Soviet system of social values—on communitarian obedience, orderliness, altruism, dutifulness."

Throughout all levels of Soviet society, one is constantly awed by women's keen sense of their greater patience, diligence, optimism, endurance, shrewdness, and self-esteem—a self-esteem apparently heightened by the very arduousness of their everyday duties, their incessant foraging for basic necessities of food and clothing. This sense of female superiority is summed up with eerie precision by the following Russian proverb: "Women can do everything; men can do the rest."

What are some other reasons that make it easier for women than for men to grow into powerful, responsible citizens with superior work habits? In the *glasnost* era, when answering that question most Soviet citizens feel free to put the blame on their nation's history: Throughout centuries of serfdom and seven decades of dictatorship, men have never had a chance to develop their initiative.

"In a culture in which men have never felt masters of their fates, never felt any real worth in their work," Riga editor Monika Zile asks, "how could they develop a sense of responsibility? Women, on the other hand, kept right on ruling over their little domestic kingdoms, and never suffered an equal sense of helplessness. And upon the Revolution, when only some 10 percent of our women were literate, they had to take such huge leaps that somehow they just kept leaping on and on, bypassing the men in many ways, in levels of education, of steadfastness, and particularly of diligence."

Soviet women's remarkable self-assurance (if not their superiority complex) leads to an often derisive view of men which might make the most committed American feminist uncomfortable. I felt it painfully at the discussion I shared in Riga with television producers. They had stated the recurring complaint of *peregruzhennost'*, "overburdening," and one member of the group had cited some striking figures that often recur in women's conversations: Soviet husbands have some forty hours more free time a week than their wives. To women, this adds up to nearly two "stolen days"; due to the extent of their chores, they enjoy one hour less sleep at night than men, and, as some statistics suggest, have only an average of twelve minutes a day to spend on their children's education.

I asked my Riga acquaintances what the average man might be doing with that free time. The group dissolved into raucous laughter.

"He takes out the dog. . . ." one said. (Much giggling.) "He looks at television and occasionally remembers to play with the children," a second one butted in. ("Yes, yes," hoots of derision.) "He mostly takes out the dog," a third one repeated. (More laughter.) "He tinkers with the car . . ." (Further hilarity.) "He tinkers with the car to *pretend* he's doing something . . ." (More approving laughter.)

Analyzing the mysterious force of Russian females, and the relative passivity of Russian men, some of the more thoughtful women put the blame on their own sex. "Russian women have a need to control that verges on the tyrannical, the sadistic," says Elvira Ossipova, a professor of British and American literature at the University of Leningrad, and a very wise observer of national habits. "If our men can't manage to curb the aggressive, sadistic element in their spouses' characters, women will always end up tyrannizing them, like no other women I can think of in history."

After dozens of evenings spent with distraught, henpecked men and with a dismaying abundance of superwomen, I reached the conclusion that the Soviet Union might be as much in need of a men's movement as of a women's movement. I tried out the idea on some of my acquaintances, and found it very well received.

"The principal function of a women's movement in this country would be to quiet our women down, make them more capable of reassuring their men," says psychologist Maria Osorina. "A good feminist movement would make our women more gentle, restore the sexes to that fine balance they had in Pushkin's time . . . look at the Decembrist men—powerful, positive heroes with heroic, strong but gentle wives."

"With emancipation we not only freed ourselves, we created a generation in which too many women tried to be the heads of families," says Riga marriage counselor Anna Livmane, who like many of my Soviet acquaintances has a tendency to quirky metaphors. "Excuse the rudeness, but I shall put it this way: Man should always be the Minister of Exterior Affairs, the woman should be the Minister of Interior Affairs. Now women try too often to be both kinds of minister, and men, who are lazier by nature, withdraw."

Thus one of the central benefits of *perestroika,* most Soviet women would agree, is that by freeing them from some part of their historic double burden it might allow them to step back, relax.

"Much of *perestroika* is about waking up the *lichnost',* the individualism, in our men so that they cease feeling superfluous," says editor Monika Zile. "It is about creating a society of less aggressive females who can at last regain their womanliness."

V

Marriage, Mother, and Divorce

One day in Leningrad, my travel companion Nonna Volenko and I found ourselves in the apartment of an attractive and affable woman, a program editor at the local television station, who lived alone with her twenty-year-old daughter. "My husband couldn't stand my having a career equal to his, my earning a salary larger than his," she said as she served us tea from the old-fashioned samovar that stood on a table of her living room. "My success threatened him terribly. He began forcing me to make a choice between marriage and career, and of course I chose my career; that wasn't a difficult choice at all," she added casually.

On my hostess's living room couch sat her daughter, a determined-looking university student in faded blue jeans. "Mama was right on target," she shrugged. "She's just like my generation. Here's the way our order of priorities go: One—career. Two—a child. As for a man, that's irrelevant. He can go on his way as soon as the child is conceived."

On my left sat the very smart, handsome, cool-mannered young editor, Vadim, who had been assigned by the local *Goskomizdat* to guide us through his city. A few hours earlier, Nonna and I had been quizzing Vadim, who is twenty-seven, about which domestic responsibilities he felt ready to take on when he married. His usual aloofness had melted as he described his love of children, and vaunted his gifts for cooking. "I'm a good chef," he said with pride. "I've watched my mother make *borscht, shchi, kissel, pirozhki,* and I can make them almost as well as she can." I asked him whether his father also had domestic talents. His glacial, reserved manner immediately returned. "I've never met my father," he said curtly.

We were having tea at the television editor's home a few hours after we'd arrived in Leningrad from Riga, and as I sampled my hostess's delicious homemade cake I recalled some of the impressive Latvian women I'd met earlier that week.

There was Dasya, our Riga guide, an athletic twenty-five-year-old woman who lived alone with her engineer mother. As we toured the city's superbly restored medieval landmarks, whose Westernness manifests Latvia's centuries-old links with Germany and Scandinavia, I'd asked Dasya if her father also lived in Riga. "Yes, he does," she'd answered the question as curtly as Vadim. "But I've only seen him a few times in my life."

Upon our first morning in Riga, Dasya had taken us to visit magazine editor Monika Zile, who lives alone with her sixteen-year-old daughter. "My family is a mirror-image of our national matriarchate," Zile had said. "My husband's father was killed in the war, and he and his four siblings grew up with only a mother. My husband and I were divorced after seventeen years of marriage—at some point he became jealous of my achievements. But everything turned out wonderfully because my mother—she also was widowed in the war—lives with me and has helped to bring up my daughter.

"You see," the editor sighed, "thirty, forty years after the war we seem to continue this all-woman tradition through sheer force of habit

. . . I fear that my daughter will follow my example, take me as a model, our matriarchal ways have become chronic, infectious. . . .''

Another Rigan I'd been most impressed with was the head gynecologist at a maternity clinic in Riga which is regarded as the finest in the Soviet Union. Dr. Anita Caune, a seductive divorcée in her early fifties with a beehive of teased blond hair, is also director of the Maternal and Child Health Protection Agency for the entire republic of Latvia. She had given me the following account of her daily morning schedule:

"I live alone with Mama, who is a wonderful eighty-nine years old," Dr. Caune had said. "And the first thing I do when I get up at six is prepare breakfast for Mama, and rearrange the flowers and change their water so that everything will be ready and pretty and cheerful for her when she gets up. All her life she got breakfast for me and my children, so I do that for her . . . then I get to work by seven-thirty, and since I live across the street from the maternity clinic, I give Mama a chance to show her love for me and go home for lunch."

Dr. Caune and her assistant director, Dr. Sarmite Hartmane, an athletic, equally handsome divorcée who was once a slalom ski champion, are pioneers in what Soviets call "family birthing," the psychological preparation of both husband and wife for their baby's delivery. Sitting in the flower-filled office of these archetypal Soviet superwomen—ebullient, brilliant, and intensely feminine—I had teased them about the prevalence of women on their staff: For during my hour's visit of their clinic, I had not seen one male doctor.

"Oh yes, we have a few men doctors," Dr. Caune said, laughing, "a few tall, thin, very handsome men . . . we keep them around as a tonic. Without any men, women don't dress as well, don't behave as nicely."

"So the men are here for decoration?" I asked.

"The men are a tonic," she repeated.

"Like a Finnish sauna?"

"Yes, that's it, they're like a Finnish sauna!" (Hearty laughter from all the women.)

A few moments later, I asked the two glamorous divorcées whether they envied women who have husbands.

SOVIET WOMEN

"A husband, that's, how can I say . . ." Dr. Caune hesitated.

"It's an elective obligation," her colleague Dr. Hartmane suggested.

Approving laughter again about these views of man-as-disposable-commodity. "Absolutely correct, an elective obligation!" Dr. Caune repeated.

Enjoying my pleasant companions at the Leningrad tea party, I also recalled a description given by my friend Elvira, a university professor in her fifties whose mother lives with her, of the only unhappy days of her life: "They're the summer days when Mama is at our little *dacha* out of town and I worry about her so much I can barely work; she's alone there, seventy-nine years old, I call her several times a day to check that she's all right . . ." I recalled, in turn, the many women I knew in Moscow who had divorced because their mothers did not get on with their husbands, and in choosing between the two alternatives, "Mother always comes first."

So on that afternoon in Leningrad I looked at the homey living room in which my hostess and her very independent daughter were graciously pouring tea, its walls hung with travel souvenirs from Poland, Hungary, and India, its mantelpiece and tables filled with photographs of what seemed to be exclusively female ancestors—mothers, grandmothers, great-aunts, with nary a male in sight. Observing this female intimacy, these tokens of indissoluble mother-daughter ties, I thought of those gaily painted wooden *matrioshka* dolls that are a staple of Russian folk art: Breaking apart at the stomach to spill out many identical dolls, parthogenetic females fitting snugly into the next, generation after generation . . . no artifact, I mused that day in Leningrad, is more symbolic of this country's sovereign matriarchies.

In the notebooks in which I documented my months of Soviet research, I listed several dozen basic categories of human experience with which to organize my themes: Friendship, family, childhood, heroism, education, sex, marriage, religion, etc. I realized upon finishing my list that there was one fundamental category missing from my list: Love.

It was not an oversight. Throughout my months in the U.S.S.R., I barely if ever heard one mention of the word *liubov'*—"love" in its heterosexual, romantic sense. It confirmed my suspicion that love in the Soviet Union is a luxury, an accessory, but hardly a prerequisite for marriage or happiness as it is in Western Europe or the United States.

For conversations with Soviet women make it clear that heterosexual love tends to recede in importance before the far deeper bonds of blood kinship, filial responsibility, matriarchal ties; and that they tend to look on marriage as a coolly pragmatic commodity resorted to for a variety of utilitarian reasons: A chance to move to a larger, more attractive city; an improvement in housing conditions; a way of escaping the nightmarish lack of sexual privacy that results from living with parents; and above all, an enhancement in job opportunity and social status. In sum, some form of marriage, past or present, loving or utterly loveless, is a cornerstone of social and professional respectability.

For in the Soviet Union it is just splendid, and utterly normal, to be a single, divorced mother. Outside the circles of the progressive intelligentsia, it is still a considerable stigma to be a spinster, and never to have known the alleged joys of marriage and procreation. When asked why such a great majority of them get married when they could be economically independent, and when marriage is so often a living hell, most Soviet women answer that it is essential to career advancement: The Soviet system penalizes the unmarried sector of womanhood by considering them "morally unstable"; the word *starukha*, "old maid," is a greater pejorative in the U.S.S.R. than in any other developed nation.

For the rigid paternalism that has guided Soviet attitudes to sexual equality has no roots in the central, libertarian principle of Western feminism—women's right to self-determination. It has solely been shaped by instrumental concerns which the state can mold and alter according to its needs. And since the 1960s, the Soviet government's approach to women's social roles has been far narrower and more conservative than in the first decades of its history. The notion that gender differences are immutable, biologically rather than socially cre-

SOVIET WOMEN

ated, and that woman's "natural" role is wifehood and child-rearing—a concept that would have been looked on as subversively bourgeois by the first Bolshevik generation—has become a staple of government propaganda.

This stereotyping of gender differences is one of the many aspects of current Soviet culture that contradict original Marxist theory. For in its efforts to create "the new Soviet person," and in its attempt to combat Western Freudianism, Marxist psychology fiercely attacked the notion of biologically innate traits; it singled out social environment as the central force in the shaping of human behavior, and saw personality as created only through "the process of activity."[17] Accordingly, women in the new Soviet state could easily acquire "masculine" characteristics of "rationality" and "self-control," and men could naturally evolve those traits of "gentleness and nurturing" which current Soviet propaganda assigns exclusively to females (and whose cultivation on the part of husbands would so ease their wives' arduous schedules).

But due to demographers' panic about a dwindling work force, in the past two decades the Soviet regime's former egalitarianism has been replaced by an obsession with gender roles that verges on the neurotic. Parents have been encouraged to scold boys for displaying emotion ("You burst into tears, just like a girl!") and to instill in their daughters a pathological concern for personal appearance and conventional domestic skills.

When questioned about what trait of character she most wishes her daughters to possess for instance, nine times out of ten a contemporary Soviet mother will answer *zhenstvennost'*, "womanliness"—a word made almost nauseating by its repetition. And traveling in the Soviet Union, one is immediately struck by the passionate interest evidenced by the generation under forty-five in traditional domestic rituals—cooking, sewing, embroidery—which their grandmothers never had the time (or the permission) to indulge in.

Outside of a small, growing sector of university students, this new cult of femininity has led to an increasing trend for early marriages. In Soviet hospitals, any woman twenty-five or over giving birth to her first child is referred to as an "aging first-time mother." And however tragic the statistics which state that over a third of Soviet marriages are ending in divorce, the government-bred anxiety to rush into wed-lock is evidenced in a striking new feature of the Soviet press that was unheard of before the *glasnost* era—the "Wanting to Get Acquainted" columns.

Excerpts from just one day's edition of such a column are indicative of the aesthetic, ethnic, and character traits young Soviet women look for in their life partner:

". . . 25-year-old girl of middling height, attractive, responsible . . . would like to meet serious, clean-living, kind young man of 25–30 years of age of Tartar or European origins, no less than 1 meter 76 cent. in height."

". . . 24-year-old woman of Russian origin, 1 meter 52 cent. in height, responsible, cheerful, advanced technological degree, values a sense of humor, would like to meet intelligent, cultivated man of no less than 1 meter 70 cent. of any European origin."

"Attractive, well-built brunette, 1 met. 70 cent., Jewish . . . never yet married, would like to meet kind, intelligent man 29–38 years of age of Jewish or European nationality, capable of deep marital love and maintaining strong family ties."[18]

Perusing many similar announcements throughout the country, it is worth noting Soviet women's strong inclination to ethnic stereotyping. Some vignettes from this very detailed folkloric spectrum: Jewish men are thought of as the most *delovoi*, "actively businesslike, practical," and by far the best providers. Uzbekistan men are thought of as the most skilled sexual partners. Georgian men are known as the nation's cleverest, most diplomatic philanderers, and Russian men as the most awkward at that art. "A Georgian," so goes the anecdote I was to hear countless times, "will have a dozen mistresses and keep them all hidden from his wife, keeping his marriage in a state of sacred harmony. While the Russian will bring his mistress home to the wife, ask the wife to polish the mistress's shoes, torment himself publicly for months about which woman to keep and which to chase out, and finally commit suicide out of indecision."

It is also worth noting the ratio of women and men placing such ads—approximately twenty females to one male.

But these observations have tended to apply to middle-class women of median age, income, status. Attitudes based on class differences differ quite as much in the U.S.S.R. as in any capitalist country. And among the young intellectual elite, a very different picture emerges.

On a crystal-cold winter morning Professor Elvira Novikova—a historian and writer who has become a close friend—took me to visit a branch of her alma mater, the Moscow Lenin State Pedagogical Institute. Founded in 1890, it was the first center of higher learning in Moscow ever to open its doors to women. A highly competitive school, which accepts only one applicant out of thirty, the Vladimir Ilyich Lenin Branch of this institute now graduates many of the young women who will become the next generation of high school and university professors.

The walls of the institute's handsome neoclassical building, pale blue and green in color, filled with Doric colonnades, are still hung with posters of 1942 vintage reminding all onlookers of the Great Patriotic War: Mother and Child clutching each other before a bloodied Nazi bayonet, with the slogan "Warriors of the Red Army, Save Us!" The most famous war image of all, a powerful woman, her head wrapped in a peasant kerchief, her mouth open in a shout of alarm to call out the timeless slogan, "The Motherland calls you!"

For several hours, Elvira and I met with the university's rector, a genial woman of Elvira's stark old-fashioned style, with a messy bun of gray hair and flat, masculine shoes. She had asked eight students to talk to us over tea. These young women were enrolled in vastly different "faculties" of the five-thousand-member university, and were little acquainted with each other.[19]

The first topic of conversation we shared seems to be obsessive to college-age women: The alarmingly growing rate of Soviet divorces, which they link to their mothers' tendency to pressure them too early into marriage.

"My mother and I are absolutely at odds on the issue," said Tatyana, a thoughtful twenty-year-old with long brown hair and an Alice in Wonderland face, whose parents are both factory workers. "All she can think of for me is marriage and kids, whereas my principal goal is to be wise and learned, so we argue a lot. The only support I get is from my grandmother, because of course in the 1930s women never questioned the central role of work and career."

"My grandmother, my parents, my brother, his wife, their child and I all live in the same two-room apartment," said Natasha, a young woman with attentive blue eyes, who is also the child of factory workers. "Seven people in two rooms . . . it's kind of wonderful to all dine together every night, we get a lot of discussion time together! I have the same problem as Tatyana, mother believes that women must start a family early on; my *babushka*'s the one who says it's essential to have both a career and a family."

"My *babushka*'s also the only one who understands why young people want to live together before marriage," Tatyana concurred, "mores were much freer in her time, in the twenties." All the young women nodded in agreement.

"Our mothers' postwar generation passed on this dangerous attitude, the terror that it's a stigma to stay unmarried, that if you wait too long you'll never get a man," said Olga, an aspiring zoologist. "It's a horrible side of our society; when a girl isn't married at nineteen or twenty-one she says, 'I'm an abandoned, useless woman, useless to all.' "

"I'm a very unusual case," said Ira, at twenty-three the oldest of the group. She was a trim blond linguist who had recently married a career army officer. "My mother is Estonian, so my parents are perhaps more geared to the Western tradition, they simply put me out of the house when I finished high school, and I had to get a room of my own . . ."

Ira's fellow students all turned around to stare at her. A room of her own! It was clear that they'd never laid eyes on a peer who'd become independent that early on.

". . . And I'll be grateful to them to the end of my days," Ira continued proudly. "I worked for two years before entering university, and it gave me time to prepare for marriage. My husband and I were twenty-three and twenty-eight when we married, and I think our union is . . . perfect."

"I was married at age eighteen and had my children in the follow-

SOVIET WOMEN

ing four years," said Masha, a smart-looking young matron with the round, pink face of a *matrioshka* doll. "But I couldn't have started university without my husband's help. He's twelve years older than I, a very serious man, and helps out with everything in the house, diapers, cooking. . . ."

This, too, seemed totally unusual. There were gasps of "Oh, you lucky thing!"

"Thirty percent of our divorces are caused by too many persons living in one crowded flat," said the very programmed Ira, a member of the linguistics faculty. "My husband and I were careful to wait two years; we only married when we were settled in a decent apartment, each earning a good salary." *("Molodetz,* [Smart girl]," the rector acclaimed from her desk.)

"I, personally, wish to bring up a child by myself, without a man," said Tatyana. "A man! Who needs a *second* child?" The young women laughed and clapped in approval. The rector again rocked approvingly in her chair. I asked for a show of hands on the issue. Six out of nine young women asserted that if they hadn't found "an adequate husband" by the age of twenty-six or so, they'd have a child "by themselves."

"And I'm going to wait until I've finished my dissertation to have my first child," said provident Ira. "My field is the British contemporary novel. I'm writing my thesis on Graham Greene, and as soon as that's behind me I'll feel ready for pregnancy."

"Tovarishch!" my companion Elvira exclaimed. "Tell us how you go about planning a family that carefully!"

"Very simple," Ira answered forthrightly. "The spiral."

The young women shook their heads with envy. The group compared notes on the immense difficulty of obtaining spirals, or any effective contraceptive, outside of the country's main urban centers— Leningrad, Moscow. Even there, you had to find a particularly privileged doctor—only one out of ten gynecologists has access to them.

Throughout the discussion, at the back of the room there had sat a pretty, silent young woman wearing a gold-embroidered scarf and a large amount of eye makeup and gold jewelry. Her style differed strikingly from her peers' carefully groomed but simple style, and I asked for her point of view on the issues we'd been discussing.

"My father's a military man and my mother hasn't worked for twenty years," she said with a touch of self-consciousness. "She's brought us up and happily busied herself with her sewing and knitting, and I want to be just like her and have a husband and three children."

Heads turned toward this anomaly with looks of annoyance, dismissal. The painted young woman pouted and looked sorry to have spoken out at all. "Look at her, decked out like a strumpet, selling herself like a slave to the marriage market," my friend Elvira whispered to me. "To think that our government spends its precious money educating her, and all she wants to do is stay home with the kids and do needlework," the rector in turn grumbled to Elvira.

I then asked the young women to describe the most ideal life they could forecast for themselves fifteen years from now.

"My first priority is to love my work," Tatyana announced, "to become an outstanding specialist in the field of teaching English. Once that's established, I can support a child."

"I also want *liubimaya rabota,* a beloved work above all else," agreed Olga. "I wish to go to work everyday as if it were a festival."

"In fifteen years I want to have finished my *doctoral* dissertation in contemporary British fiction," energetic Ira announced. "I want to continue with my community work and Komsomol activities. I want my husband, who's now a major, to have become a colonel. I also want him to have finished his advanced degree in political science. And we've agreed that we want two children, so we'll need a slightly larger flat."

"I want a beloved work above all," said Natasha, the girl who lived with six members of her family in a two-room apartment. "I perhaps want a husband and children, but even more important—I want to remain very close to my parents, continue living with them."

"Bravo," the rector applauded again. "What if your husband doesn't like it that way?" I asked. "The marriage will end," Natasha flatly announced.

After the young women had left—we had talked for almost three hours—I stayed and chatted for another long while with Elvira and the rector.

The two educators continued to berate the societal pressures that forced women into early marriages. And then the rector—who has

SOVIET WOMEN

been married for thirty-five years to a man she describes as "a marvelous person, charmingly infantile," made a statement which might well sum up Soviet women's attitudes to life.

"I'll tell you," she said, "I only have a son. But if I had a daughter I'd suggest she go and have a child without a man. Because *the most important duty of a woman, along with her work, is to have children, far beyond the duty of being a wife.*"

"And the *next* most important thing," Elvira added, "is to keep a sense of duty toward your parents."

"Bravo!" the rector of the first Moscow university to allow women into its doors agreed.

The following day I got together quietly with Tatyana, the serious young linguist with aspirations to bring up a child by herself. We talked for several hours over dinner.

She was formidable. She had just read eight novels of Iris Murdoch's in a row. She had read Bulgakov's *Master and Margarita* a half-dozen times as a teenager, shortly after it had been taken off the government's taboo list. She knew her Stalinist history to perfection. "Among other things, he surrounded himself—excuse me—with ass-kissers," she commented, obviously relishing her command of our slang.

Most young men she'd met in her generation, Tatyana said, are "immature and terribly lacking in respect for women." Apart from books, her favorite distraction is ballroom dancing—waltz, tango. But her male peers disdain such music and only like hard metal rock, which she detests. So she goes to ballroom dancing clubs with groups of women friends, and they dance together, "as our grandmothers did in wartime."

I asked Tatyana how she proposed to support her child. "I'll wait until a few years after I've finished my dissertation," she said, "because after that I'll be receiving three hundred and fifty, four hundred rubles a month, and I can save up from my salary. So after the child is born I'll stay home with him, her, for two or three years giving English lessons and making homemade sweaters—a child needs to be with its mother for at least that amount of time; I can get a good forty-five rubles for a good homemade sweater, and my *babushka* taught me to knit so well I can easily turn out three or four a month. . . ."

Her three closest woman friends, Tatyana said, all planned to raise a child in approximately the same circumstances. And when one of them went out to attend classes or to shop, they would take turns minding each other's babies.

I asked Tatyana: What kind of role, in her view and that of her friends, does a child play in a woman's life?

"A child is . . ." (She thought a little.) "A child is a woman's best friend."

Mother and a cherished vocation as the first loves of a woman's life. The child as the indispensible friend. That seemed to be a prevailing view among the future educators of the nation's youth.

VI

Portraits

Sofiko

Tbilisi, the capital of Soviet Georgia, is an opulent city in the Caucasian Mountains whose citizens are fiercely proud of their ancient culture, of the beauty and riches of their region, of their sumptuous food and wine, of their meticulously preserved local customs. An independent kingdom that was Christianized in the third century, six centuries before the conversion of Kievan Rus, Georgia did not become part of the Russian Empire until 1801, when its king sought the Czar's protection against Turkish and Persian invaders. The Georgian dialect, a venerable idiom with affinities to Tibetan and Turkish, is not related to Slavic or Indo-European languages; it evolved one of the world's earliest written alphabets, and remains, alongside Russian, the official language of the republic. Even Georgia's most educated patriots, such as Soviet Foreign Minister Edvard Shevardnadze, continue to speak Russian, as Joseph Stalin did, with a thick, rustic accent.

The citizens of this sunny, hedonistic province, whose splendor has been commemorated for centuries by scores of Russian poets, enjoy flaunting their privileges with the following fable about the creation of the world: While people from all future nations came to God in turn to ask for their terrain, the Georgians stayed at the dinner table, eating and drinking. "Where the heck were you?" God said as the Georgians finally appeared, "there's no more land left for you!" "We were drinking toasts to your health," the Georgians answered, "come join us!" And God had such a good time at the Georgians' table that He gave them all the land He was reserving for Himself.

In this wealthiest of Soviet republics, markets and dinner tables are filled year-round with bounties of wine and lavish produce direly lacking in the nation's northern cities. Tbilisi's steep residential streets, edged with balconied houses and the remains of many early medieval churches, perch on mountain slopes glowing with lush vegetation—vineyards, jasmine, bougainvillea, olive and eucalyptus groves. The city's spacious central thoroughfares, lined with tall sycamore trees and dotted with sidewalk cafés, have an aura of Mediterranean languor and *bon vivant* ease. Thousands promenade there at night, the women haughtily beautiful and fastidiously adorned, the dandyish, strutting men emanating an old-fashioned macho gallantry. On such an avenue—Rustaveli Boulevard—a plaque on the walls of the former ecclesiastical seminary (now a museum of Georgian folklore) still records the fact that Joseph Stalin studied there from 1894 to 1898. Dominating Tbilisi from the mountainside is an immense aluminum statue of *Deda-kalaki,* "Mother of the Town" or patron saint, who stands on the mountainside holding a sword in one hand and a wine cup in the other, in symbolic greeting to enemy and friend.

On a spring afternoon in Tbilisi I went to visit Georgian actress Sofiko Chiaureli, a tall, statuesque blond woman in her fifties who is one of the Soviet Union's most beloved film stars. She received me at the home in which she grew up with her parents and grandparents, a spacious two-floor house filled with superb turn-of-the-century oak fur-

SOVIET WOMEN

niture. Although it was mid-afternoon, the dining-room table was amply spread, in the prodigal Georgian manner, with *zakuski*, with an abundance of sumptuous fruits and vegetables, with local sweets and much red wine. A housekeeper who has been with the family for two decades scurried about the table constantly refilling our glasses and teacups. (Domestic servants, a well-paid and growing vocation, seem to abound among high-ranking Soviet intelligentsia; some skilled maids and housekeepers are paid four hundred and fifty rubles a month, twice the average national wage; their presence is usually explained away by hosts with the phrase "she is absolutely a member of the family.")

A notably outspoken person with a curious blend of conservative and progressive ideas, Sofiko began our visit on a note of ethnic pride by stating that "Georgia is the happiest of Soviet republics because it's the most matriarchal."

"You see her there on the mountain," she said, pointing out of her window toward the immense maternal statue of *Deda-kalaki,* which dominates the Georgian capital. "The guardian spirit of our nation is not a man, it's a woman, she's the strength and symbol of Georgia . . ."

Two minutes into the conversation my hostess abruptly abandoned these civilities of welcome, and forthrightly asked me how Americans felt about Joseph Stalin. It is an issue I have taught myself never to approach in Georgia. I stammered evasively about our growing knowledge of the leader's crimes. And then, having just driven down one of Tbilisi's main drags, Stalin Boulevard, I quickly asked Sofiko, in turn, whether she thought it right that most towns in Georgia still have streets named after Stalin.

"And how!" she burst out. "There should be triple the amount of streets named after him, and museums to him in every town, and busts of him in every town hall! There was evil in his genius, like in Mussolini's, but he was a genius all the same. . . . Stalin was the true founder of the Soviet Union, not Lenin, and two decades later Stalin is the one who won the war for the Allies! He did much evil but you can't deny him all his great actions. When we tear away at Stalin we're tearing away at our own foundations . . ."

She went on to tell me of the state of shock and grief she had been in, like many of her peers, upon the news of the leader's death: "I thought the sun would never rise again, that it was not worth living on this planet—such was my trust."

Sofiko then opened a cupboard and brought out a photograph of Stalin taken by her father, a close friend of the dictator's who was jailed in the 1950s during Khrushchev's anti-Stalinist purges. Her father had come out of his three-year prison term, my hostess boasted, with even more love and trust in Stalin than he'd had before.

The photograph, she said, had never been made public. It was a candid snapshot, enlarged to two feet square, showing the leader head on, thumbing his nose derisively toward the photographer.

"A man of pure magnetism, of pure strength!" Sofiko exclaimed, holding the photo aloft over her dining room table. "I ask you, which is worse, the blind trust in Stalin which men of my father's generation lived and died with, or the cynicism of my peers and our children's outright nihilism? Since Brezhnev I've been unable to trust in anything or anyone, for years I haven't believed a word of what *Pravda* says. . . ."

But then Sofiko went on to blast her country's record in the Afghanistan war. "If I'd had a son in that outrageous war I'd have set fire to myself, led demonstrations of hundreds of thousands in protest against it, Afghanistan was far worse than your Vietnam, our government tells us we lost thirty thousand boys, but how do we know it wasn't a hundred thousand?"

Yet Sofiko wouldn't allow me to leave her house without reiterating her displeasure at any outsiders' criticism of Iosif Vissarionovich Stalin.

"No republic suffered more from Stalin than Georgia," she asserted, "he killed our entire intelligentsia. But we must always take the family as a model, only relatives have the right to scold their parents or their children. As soon as someone else begins to scold your father, you must start defending him, or else all moral values degenerate. Do you wonder why my sons' friends doubt *perestroika?* How can they not, when successive generations have only been fed lies, and the very rug is being pulled out from under them by the destruction of Stalin?"

This was one of the numerous conversations which led me to cease expecting any consistency or rationality in my Soviet acquaintances' views. It was also a splendid example of the pluralism of opinions which Gorbachev, so far, has allowed citizens to express. For as soon as I had walked out of Sofiko's front door my Tbilisi guide, twenty-four-year-old Kakha, pulled me aside to set the record straight about *his* peers' view of Stalin.

"My generation looks on Stalin as Satan," he said to me in a very angry voice. "Stalin is the devil who's responsible for all our sorrows and failures, we don't even look on him as Georgian, we believe that all the street signs with his name should be torn down, throughout our republic, Stalin is our nightmare, our horror, our shame. . . ."

Portraits, Cont.

Irina's Family

I often enjoy Sunday dinner at the Moscow home of Irina Velembovskaya, a sixty-six-year-old writer and former industrial worker. Her father suffered twenty years of exile in Siberia under Stalin's purges, and she herself spent two decades working in mattress factories in the Urals.

Irina is a hefty, genial woman who retains the traits I treasured in my great-grandmother, my great-aunt, the Russian women whom I most loved during my childhood: Prodigal generosity, angelic selfless-ness, a sly wit, a boundless gift for nurturing and domesticity. Not-withstanding her literary reputation and her outspokenly progressive political views, Irina still leads the frugal, insular life characteristic of the Soviet working class: She has never been outside of the U.S.S.R.; I am the third American she has ever talked to; when I take her to dinner at one of Moscow's new cooperative cafés, she informs me that it is only the third time in her sixty-six years that she has been in a restaurant.

Irina was separated from her husband before her only child was born. She now shares her Moscow flat with her forty-year-old daugh-ter, Xenia, a pretty redhead who works as a magazine editor; her very bright fourteen-year-old granddaughter Iulia; and her outgoing son-in-law, Sasha Vassin, a computer programmer who has founded a cooperative (named *Uelkom)* which will offer foreigners Bed and Breakfast accommodations with Moscow families. The decor of their apartment —dark, intimate, snugly curtained and upholstered, filled with wondrously kitschy pictures of maidens in deep prayer, of dancing, sleeping, or stalking bears, of nineteenth-century couples walking dreamily through green woods—reminds me as few interiors do of my own Russian childhood in Paris.

Unlike Americans, Soviets are notably reticent about their private lives or emotional problems but announce their salaries soon upon acquaintance, almost as a way of introduction. So upon first meeting them I instantly learned that each adult in the Velembovskaya-Vassin clan earns between 250 and 450 rubles a month, a good cut above the average national wage of 200 rubles, or 320 dollars. They are able to share a five-room flat in the heart of Moscow for which they pay only 45 rubles. Xenia points out that it is a surreally small sum compared with the price of a pair of poorly made Russian shoes, 60 rubles, or decent, foreign-made black-market shoes, 150 rubles.

Irina and Xenia are both superb cooks who excel in the most traditional Russian dishes, *pelemeni, kulebiaka, okroshka.* Throughout the produce-starved winter, their table, like those of many Moscow families, is enriched with edibles—tomatoes, apricots, mushrooms, beans—preserved or dried during the summer at their tiny one-room *dacha* a few miles outside of the capital.

During the course of one particular dinner, some tension had arisen between Xenia and her husband—a rare event in this unusually harmonious family—when Xenia had launched into one of those diatribes against marriage which have become very fashionable among the Russian intelligentsia.

"How I envy those girls who're *choosing* to have a child all on their own, without getting married," said Xenia. "They just can't *find* a handsome, gentlemanly man who earns decent money. And women are so much better educated! They finish university, read Tsvetaeva and Akhmatova, go to theater and gallery exhibits, while the men of their milieu have barely finished high school and come home from the factory to collapse on the divan and watch television . . ."

"A vast exaggeration, as usual," Sasha retorted.

SOVIET WOMEN

"Don't interrupt," Xenia snapped back. "Any young woman in her right mind is better off living alone with her child than sitting home with a man who constrains her by never wanting to go out anywhere, and doesn't lift a finger at home, and creates scandals with his drinking. . . . Why should any woman be stuck with *two* children?"

Such outbursts against marriage had become familiar to me, and I changed the subject.

"Irina," I turned to Xenia's mother, "who were the major role models for your generation, when you were growing up in the 1930s?"

"Stalin, Voroshilov, Molotov, all the ghastly guys who were in power then," she replied in her pesky voice. "I hate to admit, those were our heroes. We were all modeling ourselves on men in those days, I can't think of one woman in the public eye we admired. And as Pioneers the ideal imposed on us by Stalin was Pavlik Morozov, a little idiot criminal who squealed on his father and had him put to death on some trumped-up charges in return for a cash award from the secret police . . . in every town there were parks, schools, swimming pools, skating rinks named after Morozov. To think that up to two years ago they were still trying to cram that Morozov garbage down my own granddaughter's throat . . ."

I asked Xenia who her generation's role models had been.

"We may have been the first to take on women role models," she answered thoughtfully, "but what kind of women? Very masculine ones. In the late fifties we admired women truck drivers, tractor drivers, women astronauts. Other friends of mine wanted to go out to Siberia and be biologists, heroic scientists, that was still the great romantic ideal then, to do man's work, really masculine work. . . .

"How things have changed!" she added. "We were so enthusiastic about joining Party youth groups in those days . . . now there are a lot of hooligans in my daughter's Pioneer group, many kids look on the Pioneers and Komsomol as a bore, and among my friends the Party can't find a soul to recruit. My generation has dumped the patriotism and the Siberian ideals, we just want to have more time at home to rest up from work."

"But now that Mikhail Sergeevich is rebuilding everything on new foundations," Irina loyally suggested, "we might *again* have good Pioneer and Komsomol organizations."

I asked Irina's fourteen-year-old granddaughter, Iulia, a schoolgirl with humorous, observing eyes, who some of her role models might be.

"How could I have any role models or any ideals?" she answered wryly. "All was so complicated for me, at school they taught me one thing and then I'd come home and Grandma would tell me that they'd taught me a lot of garbage, I kept wondering who was right, school or home . . ."

VII

Masters and Johnson in Leningrad

Dr. Lev Shcheglov is a frail, genial Soviet Jew in his middle forties with a strong resemblance to Franz Kafka. One of a half-dozen sexologists practicing in Leningrad, he is as overworked a man as one can find in that city.

Lev, who has a doctorate in psychology, invited Nonna and me for Sunday dinner in his three-room flat in the northern suburbs of town. And after offering us pairs of *tapochki,* the soft carpet slippers into which it is customary to change when entering a private house in the Soviet Union, he ushered us into his living-room-dining-room-study. It is a busy, warmly upholstered space lined with books and hung with many photographs of writers who have not always been in favor with

Soviet leaders—Mandelstam, Pasternak—and of some patriarchs of twentieth-century psychiatry—Freud, Jung, Carl Rogers.

"On the issue of sexual education," so Lev began his conversation with us, "one must immediately stress that the Soviet Union is among the most backward countries in the world, somewhere on the level of Bhutan, Afghanistan. We suffer from an obscurantism in all sexual matters which has its roots in the Church-imbued puritanism of the prerevolutionary years, and was further abetted by fifty years of socialist puritanism and government-imposed silence. So what my colleagues and I are trying to do in this city—deal with an adult population of several million, half of whom we estimate to be frigid or impotent—is no more than a pathetic Band-Aid . . .

"You may have heard boasts about a new compulsory high school program called Psychology of Family Life," Lev added with a caustic smile. "It's worthless. Guess what it teaches these kids who've never been told about their most basic bodily functions: how to set a pretty table, how to run a household or keep your manners during a family argument. . . . Besides, such courses are taught by any teacher who can be pressured into taking on an extra credit—grammarians, geographers.

"One of the most appalling aspects of our culture," Lev Shcheglov continued, "is the shame we cast on sexual organs. Take a four-year-old boy at nursery school who takes out his pecker to show the little girl during play period—an absolutely normal, if not essential kind of game for that age group. You should hear the shouting and scolding he'll get! His parents and teachers teach him from the crib that his penis is a criminal object. And when children are brought up with the attitude that sex is a secret dirty lousy thing, and I'm called out to their schools in the spirit of *glasnost* to provide them with the blandest Western sex manuals, it makes them excited in a negative way, gives them a false titillation. They're not ready because they haven't had the properly gradual enlightenment; the generation that's now sixteen may already be totally lost to us . . ."

Lev took a tattered, heavily penciled book from one of his shelves, Masters and Johnson's *Human Sexual Response.* "When our citizens reach maturity," he said, "it's the women, as usual, who suffer the most. The few sexual techniques Russians know about are totally orientated to *men*'s pleasure. Man at the center, woman as a mere tool of his satisfaction . . . so our single most urgent problem is to cure women's frigidity. There are two kinds, of course. There's functional anorgasmia—women who have some kind of biological malfunction. And then there are the perfectly sexed females who for some emotional reason *repress* orgasm."

Soviets seem to have an innate passion for statistics, and I asked Lev whether he had relative figures for the two kinds of frigidity.

"We estimate," he readily answered, "that over half of the frigid women we treat in Leningrad suffer from the latter disease—let's call it Slavic cultural anorgasmia. They repress orgasm because they've been brought up to believe that sexual pleasure is *ne prilichno*, not proper. Soviet women may well have the highest rate of culturally repressed orgasm in the world.

"Look," he continued, "what kind of orgasms do you expect in a society which, on top of all the shame we've loaded on sex, lived for decades in communal apartments? I have one couple for whom I've found no solutions; the mother-in-law still sleeps behind a screen in the same room, the young wife can't allow herself to make one moan, one cry. . . . How, how to make love that way . . . the mother-in-law lying there hearing every creak of the bedding . . ."

(As Lev talked I thought back to a psychologist and family counselor in Riga, Latvia, who was so imbued with the nation's puritanism that she said *izviniti grubost'*, "excuse my rudeness," whenever she spoke the phrase "sexual relations." I also kept recalling the words of my Georgian guide, twenty-four-year-old Kakha, who had been as explicit as Lev on the issue of the Soviets' sexual frustrations. "We have no literature, no courses, nothing," Kakha had told me, "even men of my generation tend to remain virgins until the age of twenty-two, twenty-three, and then we go in groups to prostitutes, a great risk seeing they're so stigmatized . . . But imagine the nightmare of remaining a virgin till you're twenty-three! You can't think of anything else, not of your work, or your studies, or your future, this is physiology, how can you trust the world when this basic urge is so denied . . . and how about the nightmare of early marriage, when we have no notion of what each others' bodies are about? Oh, we are primitives, primitives!")

Comforting smells of *shchav* and *gefiltefish* were coming out of the kitchen where Lev's wife, Zina, was making lunch. Lev perched on a chair, leprechaun-like, casually continuing to relate Leningrad's sexual problems.

"And here's another tragedy: Even though it's the women who suffer the most, the great majority of them continue to sit quietly at home, hiding everything in the dark. Even the most intellectually advanced women—lawyers, engineers, jurists—are ashamed to come to a consultation; they worry that 'Oh, my God, someone will see me there . . .' So all we get as women patients are a tiny bunch of singers, jet-setters, actresses, and 90 percent of our patients are men."

My vocabulary of Russian sexologese expanding at lightning speed, I asked Lev, with Nonna's help, whether his male patients tended to suffer from the inability to have an erection, or from orgasmic dysfunctions.

"Lack of erection is the big problem, but at least I may have solved *that* issue," Lev answered. He began drawing something for us on his note pad. "See, I've invented an erector, a device which allows impotent men to enjoy some sexual life, however artificial . . . Let's say it's like a little crutch."

Nonna and I peered eagerly over Lev's drawing to inspect his wondrous invention. It looked more like a wishbone.

"The main thing," he continued, "is that it will allow *women* to have increased pleasure. And after all, men are overly obsessed with erection, sex is a complex of emotions, tenderness to which male erection is only auxiliary . . . but my erector will be popular, my colleagues and I are having them made in East Germany; soon they will reach our pharmacies, we're impatiently waiting for them."

Lev's wife, Zina, a quiet, serene woman who up to now had remained in the kitchen, called us to sit down to lunch. As Nonna and I sat down at the table I marveled at the generosity of a dinner such as the one foraged by the Shcheglovs, a meal that only the most resourceful citizen could have conjured in produce-starved northern Russia under Gorbachev's Dry Law, which has vastly curtailed the sale of alcoholic beverages. There was vodka, champagne, a remarkable '66-vintage Tokay wine, matzoh balls floating in delicate chicken broth, jellied *kreplach*, beef cutlets with roast potatoes. Could it really be, our hosts asked me as we began lunch, that young Americans move away from home as soon as they finish university? Such independence would be impossible in the Soviet Union. These Jewish intellectuals with ultraprogressive views went on to express great amazement that at the age of twenty-seven and twenty-eight my sons were not yet married, and seemed chagrined to hear that many young Americans of that generation wait until their mid-thirties to start a family. As the meal progressed, while pouring wine, urging us to eat more, Lev continued to describe his clinical practice.

"I've come to prefer couple and group therapy over all others, with Masters and Johnson as the principal text," he said. "Ten people or so at a time is ideal—in a country where there's been centuries of taboo on any mention of sex, group therapy makes patients see that they're not alone in their problems."

I expressed surprise that Lev had ever gotten a group of ten citizens together, given the nation's prudishness.

"Ten at a time is ideally suited to our communal spirit," Lev said. "Once I get them there they could go on round the clock."

How did it work with just one couple at a time? I asked.

"Oh, also superb!" Lev exclaimed. "Let's say I have a guy who's troubled because he's shacked up with one of these newly liberated women, and she's furious because he can't manage to bring her to orgasm. When I check him out by himself I see that his potency is perfect, his prelude is fine, he knows his erogenous zones—a rarity in our culture. I tell him: 'I must have the lady in so we can also hear from her.' He starts whining, 'No no, teach me to give her pleasure without knowing I came here.' I insist on seeing her and when they appear together I realize that he goes through his preludes in a clumsy, formal way—he's read something somewhere but he hasn't followed the details his woman has gently suggested—in other words he's still acting like a typically sexist Slavic oaf.

"But lo and behold! One visit together and they phone the next morning overjoyed. 'Oh, thank you, Doctor, thank you, we got it right for the first time . . .'

"You see," Lev added, "it has to do with our people's love for authority, officialdom; that, *Gospozha* Gray, is truly the worst deformation of Soviet character. Only when a specialist in *white robes* tells a couple something and they hear it together, in an official office with a doctor's name on the door, only then do they begin to listen. I say to the man 'do it to her here, and there,' and the woman says to her man 'you see, I told you so,' and they both listen and from then on everything begins to be just splendid."

But at the end of our visit this charming scientist fighting for women's right to orgasm gave me the same kind of surprise as the gallant Dr. Khomassuridze: Lev blamed "the excesses of women's liberation" as a major cause for the increase of male impotence.

"There may be many other factors of course—the ozone layer, the chemistry of our diet, the increasing noise and hurriedness of our life, but above all it comes from overly emancipated women—the kind of powerful gal who gets a man in bed, and if he doesn't immediately perform—hop, that's it, out of the house, tossed out on his ear . . ."

I commented that in the United States, such disharmonies had been blamed on the women's movement. But since there wasn't an inkling of such a movement in the Soviet Union, how did he account for this female bullying?

Lev shrugged his shoulders. Perhaps he too was perplexed. "All I can say is that I'm finding increasing male impotence among those couples in which women dominate, women with the richer technological arsenal. The powerful women who say, 'I want this, I want that, do it this way'—men deeply fear them. They're afraid of still another oppressor."

VIII

Maya

It was evident from the moment I walked into their living room that Maya and Yuri Krassin's marriage was not doing well.

Maya and Yuri live in the periphery of Leningrad, in one of those vast complexes of already disintegrating housing units, 1970s vintage, that express the bleakness of even the more privileged Soviet lives. The couple's careers—Yuri is a computer engineer, Maya a journalist with aspirations of writing fiction—afford them living quarters which by Soviet standards can be called spacious. Upon arriving at their flat, in which they have lived for four years, one enters a corridor that gives onto a kitchen, a modest room that serves as Yuri's study, and two small bedrooms. Straight ahead, there is a fairly commodious living-and-dining area some forty feet square.

I had been invited to the Krassins' at 6 P.M. for a light Sunday supper. I was struck, upon entering their living room, that this space could not be called a home, that there was no love in it, that its bleakness could come only from a woman's total dearth of caring. The room was furnished with one ancient couch in front of which stood a low, dilapidated coffee table. There was not a chair or armchair in it, no pictures on the wall, no furnishings of any kind, in fact, save for an expensive stereo set of German make placed directly upon the dusty, uncarpeted floor. It occurred to me that this was a new breed of Russian woman I was meeting in Maya, that throughout my several stays in the Soviet Union I had not yet been in one home which so radically lacked the traditional Slavic sense of *uyutnost'*.

For there was none of that traditional gift in Yuri and Maya's bleak flat. All decoration was reserved for Maya, a trim woman with carefully coiffed dark hair and a pert, expertly made-up face, who wore, that evening, a turquoise silk dress and quite a bit of gold costume jewelry. As she moved about her bare uncarpeted rooms, her very high heels made a nervy clickety-clack sound which seemed to disturb Yuri—but then, Yuri seemed disturbed by most anything his wife did or said that evening. He is a solidly built man in his early thirties with scholarly spectacles, a reddish beard, and long, thinning hair. Upon greeting us, he had brought in some chairs from the kitchen for us to sit on. And then he had gruffly plunked himself down on one of them, his torso bent tensely forward, his sleeves rolled up above powerful forearms, which were strewn with faint lacerations, as if he'd fallen into a patch of thorny bushes. His blue eyes expressed little else than anger, impatience, and a piteous vulnerability.

Maya, who immediately struck me as a very voluble person, began the conversation with a statement that citizens of earlier Soviet regimes would have found shocking: She was fed up with being a working woman. She wished just to sit home and write. Maya enjoyed working only when the work was *fulfilling*, when it was a *beloved*, freely chosen work. And she immediately launched into a paean to American life: How wonderful, she said to me, that your women can work only *when they choose*, that they are not *forced* to work as women are in the Soviet Union—that was her impression of our system. Constantly interrupting my attempts to explain that millions of

SOVIET WOMEN

women in the United States have to work out of necessity, she went on to lavish praise on that particular aspect of the American way.

I asked Maya what kind of attitude—envy or disdain—was felt by members of her generation toward Soviet women who were not employed full time. Maya's pace thereupon slowed a bit. She couldn't think of *any* woman who was not employed full time . . . except of course the ones who stayed home to take care of their babies, that was the custom of the country, partly paid leave until the child is one year old . . . but no, she had no friends who'd ever stayed home except to take care of a small child . . . as for attitude . . . how did she feel about unemployed women? Envy, of course! And so did all her friends! Who could not envy a woman who didn't have to break her back "for the sole sake of keeping a family fed?"

Throughout this tirade against one of the most central values of the 1917 Revolution—full employment, the universal right to work regardless of gender—Yuri had stayed hunched in his chair, his nails digging nervously into his squat, powerful hands.

"I saw an American movie recently about a couple in which the wife earns the family income and the husband stays home to take care of the family," he said in his low, rugged voice. "It looked like an interesting option."

Maya waved disdainfully toward her spouse, as if he had uttered a total idiocy. "How can there be anything good about such a reversal of roles—the woman becoming a man and the man becoming a woman? Nature made us different, and for good reasons." She turned toward her husband and curtly said, "Do go and put the tea kettle on, won't you?"

Yuri shuffled out of the room, his body angry and coiled, as Maya continued: "Not long ago a friend of mine, a very brilliant man, asked me a question which I thought over for a long, long time. 'What is most lacking to Soviet women?' he asked. I thought about this a lot, because writing novels, of course, is a way for us to answer such questions . . ."

Yuri returned to his chair in time to hear Maya speak the following words: ". . . so after thinking a lot, I decided that what Soviet women lack most of all is a pleasant little dependence, a voluntary dependence, on some beloved man who is stronger and wiser than they are . . ."

Yuri hunched forward even more angrily on his chair, his eyes on the floor. I stared at the scars on his arms. There was blood in the air, the heat of a day-long argument still glowed in the room.

". . . Yes," Maya continued, "Soviet women miss not being able to depend on a beloved man. You know, in this country it was always thought that man speaks with God directly, and woman only speaks with God through her man. And if the men could come a little closer to God, there would be more happy Soviet women. But above all, in Soviet society, there are many women who don't have a good strong man next to them, a man through whom they could come closer to God. For that she would need a man who is a leader, and she can't find him . . ."

Yuri sprung up, his body straightening up like a jack-in-the-box. "And what would happen then?" he cried out angrily. "What would happen . . ."

"Don't interrupt me," Maya snapped. "The smarter the woman, the harder to find a man who's higher, wiser, stronger than she is, and we can't find such . . ."

This time I was impelled to interrupt her. "Why can't we love men who're our equals?" I asked. "What in heck would be wrong with that?"

"Because the man must always remain the intellectual leader," she answered me with a coquettish smile. "He must remain smarter. If his wife is on the same level as he, then she will feel sorry for him, and pity is a motherly emotion, merely what we feel for a wounded child. . . ."

"So that's the way you're putting it!" Yuri returned to the fray. "As those reactionary princes said in Turgenev's novels, the more education a woman has, the less chances she has of being happy?"

But Maya didn't want to let go of her education, about which she had already boasted much to me. She simply wanted her spouse to earn more money than she did (a curiously conservative desire, I thought, in most of today's cultures).

"It appears to me," she answered him, quite cordially this time, "that when men and women started being equal in our society, that's when the disharmony, the unbalance began. All I'm saying is that a man should always remain a *tiny, tiny* bit ahead of his woman."

It was such an adorable Russian term she'd used for "tiny," *"chut' chut',"* the word used for phrases such as "I only want the weeniest drop of cream in my coffee."

"That's a very delicate culinary balance you're asking for," I butted in, "a very complex recipe. That's like asking life to be a perfect soufflé."

"But your husband is an artist," Maya suggested daintily. "Perhaps when both spouses are engaged in creative work you can't compare their levels, you can't say who's better or stronger . . ."

"And science?" Yuri demanded, his furious bushy head turned straight toward his wife's this time. "Isn't science creative work?"

"Well, inventors are creative," Maya said diffidently. "That's something else."

"And where do you draw the line between invention and creative interpretation?" he demanded again.

"Yuri," she said crisply, "can you bring the things in for tea? The kettle's boiling."

Yuri trundled out of the room again. He came back with a tray laden with egg salad, radishes, and sliced cucumbers, a cake, and set it on the coffee table in front of us. It was the first time I'd seen a Soviet man bring food in from the kitchen. As Maya fussed over the remarkably dry, flavorless cake, announcing with pride that it was "the first time all year" she'd baked one, she asked me the age of my children, bade her husband bring a photograph of their ten-year-old son, who was at Pioneer Camp that day, and asked to see photographs of my own family.

A brief calm hung over the frugal, satisfying snack as Maya talked about her career. She detested her job at the newspaper, where she was assigned to the "Youth Page" and made to write reports on such dreary subjects as Komsomol activities. She had an awful schedule, 9 A.M. to 6 P.M., and then the hours of commuting and standing in line for groceries, she was seldom home before 8 P.M. . . . the only interesting part of her life was the fiction she wrote at home in her spare time. She had sold one story entitled "French Silk Stockings" to a Leningrad literary journal. She was hard at work on two others, called

"The Countess" and "The Passionate Flame." Ah, if she could only sit home and "express herself" through writing all day long, she would be happy to work sixteen, eighteen hours a day . . .

I suddenly realized I'd already known many prototypes of Maya: The frustrated women I'd met at writing workshops at Berkeley, Indiana, Duke University, since the 1960s, when our own cult of self-expression boomed. . . . I sprung out of my reverie on American cults of self to hear my hosts engaged in still another angry argument.

"Why always load the blame on men for your unhappiness?" Yuri was saying. "The way it's turning out, the more I earn the more I'm going to be esteemed, the more I help out at home the less you respect me. That's precisely what you're saying, aren't you?"

Yuri's gambit didn't work. Maya had a great talent for changing the issue whenever her true intentions were in danger of being disclosed.

"But *perestroika* is offering us so many new possibilities!" she said, turning to me with another ravishing smile. "Our friend Misha, for instance, has started a cooperative for designing wallpaper and upholstery fabric; he's made such a pile he's expanding into all areas of interior decorating. And Vadim, our neighbor down the block, has started a poodle-breeding cooperative, he's making money hand over fist. So there are all these new possibilities, these guys are using their initiative, supporting their families better . . ."

(I was beginning to read Maya's subtext: "Yuri, you lazy lout, why don't *you* get your fat ass off your computer chair and make some extra money?")

". . . Earlier a man wasn't allowed to use his initiative in such ways," Maya continued; "he'd have to compromise himself working *na levo*, illegally. Now he can make a lot of money in total honesty . . ."

"It's a contradiction of socialism," Yuri muttered.

"Nothing bad in *that*," Maya said firmly. "Cooperatives are the only way of improving our society."

Well, that was as good a moment as any to ask Maya the question I'd been posing throughout a half-dozen Soviet cities. What would be the main impact of *perestroika* on the lives of women? Maya was ready to go to town on that.

SOVIET WOMEN

"It'll offer husbands the possibility to earn more money, to free women to work as much as they *want,* not as much as they *must.* Oh, how we need that! Most of my women friends leave the house at seven-thirty, as I do, and don't get home until eight. They don't have the time to see their mothers, their children . . ."

"You see," Maya added, lighting a cigarette with a serious air, "up to now self-sacrifice has been the central motive of Russian women, that is, after all, the central theme of our literature; but at last we're fed up with being martyrs and heroines, we want fairness, justice . . ."

"And what about the husband," Yuri butted in, "what about us? Men also come home from work after having struggled all day . . ."

"The way Turgenev saw it . . ." Maya tried to interrupt.

"What you're saying," Yuri cut her off, "is that a woman is solely made happy by her husband's money. Well, I recently saw a film in which there's a woman whose husband has such a good job that she can stay home with nothing to do. And guess what happens? She runs off with a *sportsman* and begins to steal French perfume from shops. Out of egoism and boredom, sheer boredom. Without work a woman simply doesn't know what to do with herself . . ."

Now I was reading Yuri's subtext: Leisure, craving for decadent Western goods—demise of the socialist dream—woman's demonic energies becoming uncontrollable when not channeled into the work collective—a threat to the well-being of the state . . . It was Maya's turn to grow livid. She lightly slapped her husband's arm with a paper napkin.

"Foul play!" she raged. "Just because I've written a story called "French Silk Stockings!" All I'm saying is that a woman has to have a choice. She can only retain her spiritual center when she makes a decision from within, whereas when she's *forced* into work she becomes capable of doing anything . . ."

"It all leads to egoism," Yuri repeated. "I want this, I want that, this one has this trip and that dress I don't have, I want it too . . ."

I looked down at the coffee table and stared at the photograph of the Krassins' son, so earnest and smiling in his blue-and-red Pioneer uniform. Another victim of the divorce-plagued Soviet family? Maya had forgetfully set glasses and cups all over the photo. Yuri stood up, removed it from the table, wiped it clean, carefully placed it back into the bookcase.

Noticing her negligence, Maya went to the bookshelf and handed me two of her short stories, "The Countess," "French Silk Stockings."

"Interesting titles," I said. "But listen, why can't you share things more evenly? Vacations, for instance. If a woman earns as much as a man, why not take turns? One year he chooses the vacation, another year she chooses, she can even go on her vacation *without* her man."

"You should go into marriage counseling," Yuri said, with a touch of gratitude.

"Remember how it was in the good old days," Maya continued dreamily. "The men worked and brought home the money, the women took care of the house. Two basic functions. Women don't *want* to do men's work . . ."

"Don't you have women supporting families in the United States?" Yuri turned to me with his blue, wounded eyes.

"Yes," I said, "mostly in black families. Russian society is very similar to that of our blacks . . ."

"We are like *blacks!*" husband and wife said loudly in unison.

". . . Very strong women holding many families together," I continued. "Whereas in our white households, husbands and fathers often have far stronger roles."

Yuri seemed impelled to return to economics. "Well, it turns out that the most important thing for our women is money, material goods. We're not satisfied any more living in communal apartments, we all want cars. . . ."

The evening would have ended like most social gatherings I'd attended in the Soviet Union. At some moment, the wife inevitably says, as Maya did that night: "Women here have a double life, a double shift, they're equally exhausted by work and home, it's very sad, there has to be a way of freeing our time . . ." But Yuri offered an unusual finale.

He went to his study and returned with a manuscript in hand, announcing: "My wife keeps saying that she's a writer, but I'm a writer, too."

"Yuri, you'd better not read anything," Maya giggled nervously.

But Yuri sat down and read his story, which consisted of a telephone conversation between two men. "Victor," it began, "how are things today?" "Not bad, old pal, I stood in line an hour for two quarts of milk, and another hour for a piece of chicken." "Well, the old girl should be very pleased with you, what are you cooking for dinner tonight?" "I thought I'd try a cutlet Kiev with a cucumber garnish on the side . . ."

"Two writers in one house are just too much," Maya interrupted after the first paragraph. "Yuri! Please don't try to be a writer . . ."

Yuri curtly said good-bye, put on a parka, and went (or pretended he was going) to a meeting of his work collective.

I asked Maya which bus I should take to get back to my hotel at the other end of town.

Maya helped me with my coat. As I was leaving her apartment she showed me a little white hamster scrambling about a cage in her kitchen. It stared at us with angry yellow eyes and raged against the glass walls of the cage, thumping its paws at the translucent windows of its prison.

"I look at him and think: 'Soviet women!' " Maya said.

She wanted to walk me to the bus stop. As we went down the dusty, fish-smelling stairs crowded with half-broken sleds and discarded tires, to the grim playground dotted with rickety swings and slides, Maya continued talking about the hamster: Her son had wanted the hamster so badly, it was in a certain month when they didn't have the money for such a luxury; his grandmother bought it for him. Maya was so moved by her mother's generosity that she'd sat down on the kitchen stool and cried, staring at the beautiful little white animal.

"And my son is a man of the future!" she exclaimed. "He has initiative! The hamsters had babies, his classmates all admired them and wanted one, so he sold the babies to his classmates for thirty kopecks apiece and made three rubles in a week! At the age of ten! A true *perestroika* capitalist, right?"

IX

Elvira and her Foremothers

She came toward me the first time we met with her hand held out, welcoming me in her very forthright voice: *"Kak ty, grazhdanka!* How are you, citizen!" Both the word "citizen" and the informal *ty,* "thou," popular in the nation's first decades, went out of fashion well over twenty years ago as terms of public greeting. And Elvira may have feared that they struck her foreign visitor as archaic. So she clutched my hand with both her hands, her eyes smiling eagerly beneath a cap of short, mannish hair, from behind very thick bifocal glasses. "Don't mind the *ty* . . . it's more in the feminist manner, don't you think?"

I, however, had been instantly charmed by Elvira's old-fashioned salute. I had also detected a self-consciousness in the way she said

SOVIET WOMEN

feministka which let me know that she felt quite lonely in that conviction. So I went out of my way to reassure her that her greeting was most gracious and adequate, both in the 1920s and now. And in the succeeding months Elvira Novikova—a historian and professor who is one of a tiny handful of avowed "feminists" in the Soviet Union—became one of my closest friends in Moscow.

Elvira is a sturdily built woman in her late forties with a deliberately drab way of dress, a round, unadorned face, and an expansive, perpetually cheerful manner. Her mother, the daughter of an illiterate peasant woman, graduated university as a railroad engineer; her father was one of the some 20 million Soviet men who died in World War II. Like a third of women in the postwar years, mother and daughter fended for themselves.

Two decades ago, although she had never yet been outside of the Soviet Union, Elvira decided to do her graduate dissertation at Moscow's Pedagogical Institute on the growth of the American feminist movement. The year was 1968. And seeing that not one text of Western feminism had been translated into Russian (Virginia Woolf's *A Room of One's Own*, Simone de Beauvoir's *The Second Sex*, Betty Friedan's *The Feminine Mystique*, remain untranslated to this day) the topic was dismissed as ridiculous by her faculty.

Elvira, who had read these texts in English editions clandestinely acquired from abroad, stubbornly fought on for three years for the right to pursue her theme, arguing that it was an intrinsic part of American social history. A sympathetic woman professor finally persuaded her colleagues to agree to the topic. And Elvira became the second scholar in the Soviet Union ever to dedicate a dissertation to American women—(a sociologist had previously written on the economics of female and children's labor in the United States).

Since then, Elvira has visited the United States several times as a member of Soviet delegations and is eloquent on the difference between the lives of American and Soviet women. "I'm impressed and envious of the way American men understand our problems, go shopping, and look after the kids. And I so envy the way women's studies have become an integral part of your academic and intellectual structure. American feminism is the first movement of its kind to gain universal relevance by embracing the masses."

The phrase "embrace the masses" is crucial to Elvira. For however unpopular her feminist ideas may be in the Soviet Union, she remains a passionate Marxist-Leninist. I know few women of her generation who strive harder to recapture the energy, the militancy, the very diction of the first revolutionary years. She constantly lobbies for working mothers' shorter work hours, writes articles protesting the employment of women in dangerous unskilled work, attacks "patriar-chal attitudes" on television panels. Throughout her debates, she holds up Lenin as a committed feminist whose original vision was distorted by Stalin, and whose integrity is only now being restored by Gorbachev's *perestroika.* "Lenin was a true democrat who said 'every housemaid should be able to rule the country.' "

Elvira has been married for twenty years to an engineer, and has an eighteen-year-old son. Her mother has lived with her since her retirement, and has made possible Elvira's prolific writing and teaching career by bringing up her son, shopping, cooking, and generally running the household. Although she is devoted to her family, Elvira is one of the many Soviet women I know who candidly admits that she married out of peer pressure, that she felt forced into it by her society's "idiotic prejudices against old maids." And she is one of the few Soviet women I've met who still looks on her women friends as the most trusted confidantes.

"I just don't *like* most men," she once said to me casually over lunch. "I neither trust them nor feel comfortable with them. I bet you many women walk down the street every day and think 'What in hell do I need a man for?' "

"Compassion, understanding," I suggested.

"Come on, you get that better from your women friends," she answered.

"What about biological needs?" I asked.

"A German feminist once said to me, 'When I want milk, I don't buy a cow,' " Elvira retorted with a grin.

"I'll quote you Chekhov," she said another day. " 'If you're afraid of solitude, don't marry.' The shameful way our media still push the spiel about marriage being the only honorable state! They've taken two basic images of women in our folklore—the Cinderella sweetie pie who sacrifices her life to family, and *Baba Yaga,* the wise independent

SOVIET WOMEN

witch who lives alone in the forest and is doomed to solitude. They ask us, 'Who do you want to be, Snow White or *Baba Yaga?*' The honey who must run around bringing man his slippers . . . that's the woman they're all pressing us to be, even after seventy years of our being fully employed in the work force!

"You see," she continued, "in this Amazonic experiment we've had here since the war, very few women got used to their independence; the majority deplored it and transferred their fear of being alone onto their daughters. So we're still stuck with the great value of the male, who became so precious when there was such a dearth of them. If you have a phallus you're priceless, so men become like . . . like clothes."

(Throughout my conversations with Soviet women, I kept being struck by the way men were being compared with inanimate, disposable commodities—saunas, tonics, clothes.)

On still another day, Elvira tells me that the mutual task for all feminists, these days, is clearly to analyze and acknowledge the deep differences between the sexes.

"We must own up to our great differences and stop fearing them," she says. "To differ doesn't mean to stand lower . . . I see woman as the safeguarder of society, responsible for preserving all the stable traits of humankind. Whereas the man is responsible for the changes, experiments, mutations. We have figures to prove that the average female population is more balanced and sane than the male, and has fewer birth defects. The abnormalities—both geniuses and idiots, even retarded persons, mongoloids—occur far more frequently among males . . ."

Elvira searches for a metaphor. "I'll tell you what: Women are like Scandinavia, where everyone is economically and socially in the middle. Whereas men are like the U.S.A., where you have Rockefellers and beggars!"

She gives me her wide, joyous smile. She is very pleased with that metaphor. We are walking down Gorky Street in a blazingly cold winter snow squall, Elvira's arm firmly linked through mine. During a stretch of this stay in Moscow Elvira has taken charge of me, become sister and provider, made sure that I'm warmly enough dressed, that my every hour, every meal, is accounted for. Each morning she brings me some new little present—a painted box with a design of forget-me-nots, a crocheted doily of her own handiwork ("It is healthy for feminists to do embroidery," she asserts. "It calms the nerves.").

On this snowy day I can barely cross the street without Elvira admonishing me to take care, not slip, retie my scarf to stay warm, grasp her hand more tightly; in her custody I feel like some figure in a Chagall painting, floating high and safe above the icy pavements. As we wait for the bus I loosen my arm from hers to adjust my hat, and then link my arm through hers. "No, no," she objects, firmly reversing the motion, linking *her* arm through mine, "when you're in Moscow you're in *my* control, I must hold *your* arm to stay fully in charge of you."

As we sit on the bus Elvira talks about her fervent, unshakable hopes for *perestroika.* "You see, our nation is like a bear. The bear sleeps very soundly, more soundly and longer than any other creature, and you have to shake him more powerfully than any other animal on earth to wake him. But when you finally manage to wake him he's got more energy than any one else in the forest . . . that's us, *tovarishch!*"

That night when I return to my hotel room I turn on the television and who's on the set but Elvira, sparring on a panel with moderator Vladimir Posner, the Soviets' Tom Brokaw.

"Soviet women are *not* neglecting their domestic duties," she's saying at her machine-gun speed, her large round eyes shining like headlights through her spectacles. "We're equally oriented toward family and career and that's our tragedy, we want to write our theses but we also feel we should be making *pirozhki.* Most of us end up compromising one or the other, or both . . . We've been brainwashed with the notion that our state has done everything for us to reconcile the two roles, but the state hasn't begun to provide for us . . ."

"We're running out of time . . ." Posner attempts.

"Tovarishch!" she cuts him off. "The only true concept of equality

is the ability to choose. I don't denounce women who find their greatest happiness in the family, but I refuse to have any model of value
projected onto the whole society, which is the way our patriarchal
order is forcing us into marriage. . . ."

I had met Elvira at the very beginning of a five-week trip throughout the Soviet Union. During my travels I went on to look for more
women equally dedicated to fighting for women's causes, and barely
found two others. I dedicate these pages to Elvira because she is so
unique; and because she belongs to a tradition of the Russian past
which has drawn me since childhood and now tends to be forgotten or
suppressed—those women activists of the late nineteenth century who
participated in a social revolution in greater numbers, and with more
selfless ardor, than any other group of women in history.

Elvira is a spiritual descendant of Olga Lyubatovich, who like
several thousands of her compatriots went to study medicine in Zu-
rich in 1871, when not one Russian university admitted women students. She lived in the St. Petersburg underground for years after
serving exile in Siberia, and believed that "It is a sin for revolutionaries to start a family . . . men and women must stand alone, like
soldiers under a hail of bullets."[20]

Elvira is an heir of Elizaveta Kovalevskaya, founder of the Union
of Russian Workers, who a century ago dedicated herself to springing
political prisoners from jail, and during her own prison terms repeatedly went on hunger strikes to demand the replacement of unjust
prison wardens. Elvira might be of the same steel as Sofya Perovskaya,
a participant in the murder of Czar Alexander II, who lived in male
garb for years to escape police attention, and became the first woman
in Russian history to be executed for a political crime.

These were citizens whose revolutionary zeal and guilt were fueled
by serfdom, an institution almost unique in nineteenth-century Western Christendom. Daughters of the privileged landed gentry, they had
left homes and families by the thousands to pioneer two causes which

many Russian liberals saw as indissolubly linked—the liberation of the serfs and the emancipation of women. Making parallels between the subjection of peasants to owners, and that of women to their fathers and husbands, they sought to "go to the people" in factories, printing plants, and distant country schools to help unite them for revolution.

How omitted these women are in contemporary Soviet history books! These daughters of Russia's most privileged classes were the largest group of women revolutionaries in human memory. Between 1860 and 1890, women accounted for nearly one fifth of all citizens arrested in Russia for political activity; they made up one third of the governing board of its most militant underground group, *Narodnaya Volya,* "People's Will."[21]

Living in a country where only some six thousand girls received any official schooling, where women could not even travel from town to town without a parent's or a husband's permission, these nineteenth-century radicals were much influenced by religious values which the Russian Orthodox Church had particularly instilled into its women: The merit of self-sacrifice and redemptive suffering.

They tended to live in austere chastity, rebelling against that cult of the family and of motherhood which was enshrined in czarism, making their closest bonds with sister revolutionaries, retaining strong ties with their mothers, who often shared their sympathies. Satirized in some of Turgenev's novels as shorn-haired, chain-smoking *feministki,* they were the earliest prototype of the devoted martyr-heroine who eventually became the Soviet state's female ideal.

Looking at my contemporary Elvira Novikova, admiring her joyfully combative manner, I also thought of Vera Zasulich, who became a heroine at home and abroad when she shot the military governor of St. Petersburg because he'd ordered a prisoner to be brutally beaten for a breach of etiquette (the prisoner had failed to remove his cap in an official's presence). I thought back to Vera Figner, the militant who spent two decades in prison for having made the explosives used in the assassination of Czar Alexander II.

Vera Figner's prison term ended in 1905, upon the revolution led by Father Gapon, when the former alliance between political reform and women's rights had all but disappeared. That is an issue which

SOVIET WOMEN

Elvira Novikova and I spent much time discussing: The way in which women's causes had been constantly co-opted, since the beginning of the century, by Russia's male power structure.

For despite Vera Figner's efforts, in the decades that preceded 1917 the numerous attempts to form groups modeled on Western women's leagues such as Elizabeth Cady Stanton's or Susan B. Anthony's were equally doomed by the Czar, who was suspicious of any foreign influence, and by the male leadership of the insurgent movement. In an autocracy where even universal suffrage was not yet established, any separatist effort not dedicated to the liberation of the entire society was considered suspect by revolutionary groups, and stigmatized as "bourgeois deviationism." Cut off from the mainstream of Western feminism, hampered at home by government bans, the few hundred women who composed a native suffragette movement were never able to send more than a handful of delegates to the women's congresses that had begun to proliferate in the West.[22]

After the overthrow of the Czar in 1917 and the meeting of the First Constituent Assembly (in which the issue of women's rights was never even raised) it was the valiant former convict Vera Figner who led the first mass demonstration to demand the vote for women. Accompanied by two brass bands playing the "Marseillaise," forty thousand female citizens marched with her in the newly renamed capital of Petrograd, emulating the great Western suffragette marches that had been the envy of Russian militants. One wishes that all demonstrations could bear such swift results: Women were given the vote in the next meeting of the Assembly.

But the founding of a Marxist state, and its inevitable suspicion of any gender-oriented movement, brought obstacles to the growth of a feminist consciousness which confront Elvira and her colleagues to this day. Despite the fact that the radically liberated women of the late nineteenth century participated in Russian socialism's principal goal—the overthrow of czarism—the word *"feministka"* has only had the most odious connotations. It has been associated with rebellion, female independence, the very facets of female energy which the Soviet state has wished to suppress in its female citizenry, and has rechanneled into its own neo-czarist cult of family and motherhood.

The career of Aleksandra Kollontai, the stateswoman and author whom my friend Elvira may admire more than any other woman figure in Russian history, is a prime example of the obstacles that have constantly defeated any attempts at a Soviet women's movement. A dedicated follower of Lenin from her early youth, and an equally ardent activist for women's rights, Kollontai was the first woman elected to the Communist Party's Central Committee, and was appointed Commissar of Public Welfare in the first Bolshevik regime. As a leader in the *Zhenotdel*—the government commission on women's rights that was later dissolved under Stalin—Kollontai was responsible for much of the welfare legislation written for the young Soviet state: Liberalizing of divorce laws and of abortion, founding of free government-run day care centers.

But Kollontai was also an advocate of free love and an outspoken rebel against "the old bondage of the family."[23] Working in the early 1920s—the only publicly libertine years of Soviet culture, when progressive theater, film, and morals were tolerated as they never would be again—the female ideal she upheld was that of the single woman who solely dedicates herself to the emancipation of her sex and the liberation of society. Often controversial because of her numerous lovers (the most notorious of whom was a flamboyant sailor twenty-two years her junior) Kollontai believed that contemporary women must cease to have any emotional dependence on men, that changing sexual partners should be no more important than "drinking a glass of water."[24]

It is in great part on those grounds—her alleged subversion of male authority, her concentration on issues which she considered unique to women—that the first Soviet feminist nearly met her doom. Accusing her of "bourgeois feminist deviationism" and of neglecting her government duties, the conservative factions of the Communist Party Central Committee demanded the death penalty for Kollontai, and she escaped execution only through Lenin's intervention. Kollontai's subsequent appointment to the Ministry of Foreign Affairs

SOVIET WOMEN

was the Bolshevik government's way of preventing her subversive views from polluting the fabric of the new society. By shipping her abroad as the Soviet Union's first woman ambassador, (she would spend two decades as envoy to Norway, Mexico, and Sweden) the new regime kept her safely at bay for most of her life.

In December of 1979, twenty-five years after Kollontai's death, a group of Leningrad women issued a *samizdat* publication entitled *Almanach: Woman and Russia.*[25] It was the first "feminist" text to be issued in the Soviet Union since the early 1920s. The volume's half-dozen contributors tackled no issue more abrasive than the flaws of Soviet gynecology, the pitiful state of the country's day care centers, the scarcity of consumer goods under Brezhnev's rule, the U.S.S.R.'s patriarchal views of marriage, and the general overburdening of its women, problems that today are vociferously aired by citizens such as Elvira Novikova and Olga Voronina in the *glasnost* press. *Almanach* also included a gentle literary essay mildly alluding to the sexual leanings of the great poet Marina Tsvetaeva, whose bisexuality is implied in her verses.

Notwithstanding the blandness of these grievances and allusions, and the fact that only *ten* typewritten copies of the *Almanach* were issued for circulation (until recently Soviet law prohibited private use of any kind of photocopying processes), the authors of *Almanach* were subjected to intensive harassment by the KGB. And a few months after its publication, in the spring of 1980, four of the volume's co-authors—Tatyana Goricheva, Julia Voznesenskaya, Natalya Malakhovskaya, and Tatyana Mamonova—were expelled from the U.S.S.R. The first three settled in Munich. Mamonova went on to a modest lecturing and teaching career in the United States. Their exile has been made particularly difficult by the fact that both in Europe and the United States, the attitudes of most *émigré* and dissident Soviets toward women and toward any form of sexual liberation are often as puritanical and archaic as those of the Soviet government.

The brutal repression of this budding women's rights movement calls for a mention of Soviet attitudes toward homosexuality: By fore-going any punitive measures against homoerotic behavior at the time of the 1917 Revolution the Soviet Union's legal system became one of the first to offer homosexuals equal rights. Some of that era's most prominent writers—Zinaida Gippius, Sofya Parnok, Dmitry Merezhkovsky among them—wrote openly about lesbianism and homoerotic love, and even advocated gay communes. This license was revoked in the early 1930s, under the rigid neo-czarist puritanism reimposed by Stalin; male homosexuality was then classified as a crime punished by five to eight years in jail, a statute which remains enforced to this day. The severity of the law was highly publicized in the 1970s when one of the Soviet Union's leading film directors, Sergey Paradzhanov, was sentenced to five years behind bars for "deviant" behavior.

Since Stalin, official attitudes toward lesbianism have been equally reactionary, but more naive: Although in recent years a growing number of women of the Moscow and Leningrad intelligentsia, disaffected by the passivity and irresponsibility of Soviet males, have formed lesbian ménages; and although one hears it said that a dearth of men has driven many lonely single women to this alternative for decades, Soviet law does not acknowledge the existence of female homosexuality. An anecdote is often told in the U.S.S.R. about a community of women factory workers in the industrial town of Ivanov, whose work force was almost exclusively female: Realizing that this isolated band of women were turning to each other for physical consolation, the government could think of no other alternative than to set up a new army garrison there, and dispatch a large regiment of male soldiers to keep the women company. A darker account of government solutions to the lesbian problem is recounted by *Almanach* editor Tatyana Mamonova, who reports in her publication that women who have overtly expressed their homosexuality have been forcibly sent to psychiatric hospitals.

Such archaic prejudice, and the brutal repression and exiling of the *Almanach* group, illustrates the Soviet government's continuing taboo on any women's movement (or any search for an alternative way of life) that operates outside of strict Party control; it also evidences its resistance to all forms of gender analysis, which might subvert the

SOVIET WOMEN

class analysis prescribed by Marxist theory. Although Gorbachev's *glasnost* now allows a few scholars like Elvira Novikova and Olga Voronina to publish their feminist writings, public hostility to the "bourgeois deviationism" once championed by Kollontai continues unchanged into our time. During the months I spent in the Soviet Union in the past years, I simply banned the word *feministka* from my vocabulary to avoid any arguments. I had been forewarned by a group of Soviet writers I met with in New York shortly before I began my research, at which the following exchange took place:

"Is there the beginning of a feminist consciousness in your literature?" an American editor asked of a Soviet woman poet, known for her progressive views, during the lunch meeting.

"There is no such thing as a feminist consciousness," the poet Yunna Morits curtly replied. "Our problems are in no way different from men's. I refuse all associations with such silliness as your women's movement."

"Who can talk seriously about women's problems?" shrugged a Soviet male writer traveling with the same group.

"Feministka is a strictly pejorative term in our country," said Leningrad novelist Daniil Granin, another noted progressive and an outspoken champion of all liberal causes. "Doesn't the very definition of 'feminist' mean a woman who absolutely hates all men?"

This hostile misreading of the Western women's movement, even on the part of the most enlightened Soviet intelligentsia, is in part caused by their decades of cultural isolation. What with their extraordinary balancing acts of work and family, their awesome self-assurance, many Soviet women speak and act like our most emancipated feminists. But they have never had access to our basic feminist texts, and have only caught echoes of the outdated radical voices of the 1960s "movement." Thus they still think of American feminists as "man-hating separationists," totally unaware that for the past decade we have concentrated on acknowledging the deep differences between the sexes, and on reconciling family life with our newly won careers.

But far beyond that: American women are still fighting for the Equal-Pay-for-Equal-Work legislation which Soviet women were offered by the first Bolshevik regime. American women are still struggling for the freedom *to,* whereas Soviet women are now struggling for the freedom *from*. We have been stuck at home for the past two hundred years, and are still striving for the right to work in coal mines, fire-fighting units, police brigades. Whereas Soviet women are battling to be freed from such labor, and from the many other arduous ones they've been stranded in for seven decades—building the nation's highways and railroad beds, unloading its freight cars, operating its cranes.

So we are traveling in precisely opposite directions. Given the hardships of Soviet women's double burden, given our enormous freedom to organize into collective action, might our emancipation be more genuine than that of our Soviet sisters'?

X

Portraits, Cont.

Dissenters

Tamara, Lyuda, and Natalya are friends. I met Lyuda and Natalya at Tamara's flat in the northeast suburbs of Moscow, in a bleak housing compound reachable from the center of town by three changes of subways and a long bus ride.

Tamara is married to Aleksandr (Sasha) Kalugin, a painter who had the first show of his works in Albuquerque, New Mexico, and has since exhibited in France, West Germany, and in unofficial shows in the U.S.S.R. Tamara is also an editor of *Express-Chronicle*, one of many unauthorized publications that report news which the official Soviet press does not judge fit to print—strikes, demonstrations, jail-

ings, religious events. During the Brezhnev regime Kalugin was arrested several times for his unorthodox views, and served three sentences of forced treatment in psychiatric hospitals.

But Tamara and Sasha remain undaunted. Among the news items
covered in a few typical editions of the weekly *Express-Chronicle:* an
anti-nuclear leafleting campaign in Omsk, jailings of Hare Krishnas in
Leningrad, a demonstration of nurses protesting unsanitary conditions
at their hospital in Gorky, a meeting of Social Democrats in Novosi-
birsk, reports on the health of various political and religious dissidents
already serving time in prison.[26]

The compiling of *Express-Chronicle* is made possible by some
twenty Soviet citizens who call Moscow every Saturday from various
parts of the nation, giving news of equally undocumented incidents.
The Kalugins often provide dinner and overnight stays for members of
the group in their three-room apartment. Since public photocopying
machines are seldom available to Soviet citizens, Tamara, Sasha, and
their friends have often stayed up much of the night making typewritten copies of the paper—ten carbon copies per typewritten set—
which their out-of-town collaborators have distributed in their respective provinces.

At about midnight, Moscow time, when the contents of that
week's *Express-Chronicle* have been assembled, Soviet emigrés begin
to phone the Kalugins from London, Paris, Berlin, and other Western
cities. Members of the publishing collective in Moscow take turns
dictating that week's text to their European callers; by the following
Tuesday some ten thousand copies of *Express-Chronicle* are in circulation abroad, and passages of it are frequently read on "The Voice of
America" program.

Recently, a member of the Kalugins' circle found access to a copy-
ing machine somewhere in the Soviet Union, and several thousand
copies of *Express-Chronicle* now circulate weekly in the U.S.S.R. The
paper is subsidized by donations from subscribers throughout the
world, and by contributions such as Sasha's: He has often brought his
canvases on Sundays to Izmailovo Park (long a center for the showing
and sale of unofficial art) and stood over them with a large poster that
says "All proceeds go to support *Express-Chronicle.*" Although frequently scolded by passersby, he has never once been censured.

SOVIET WOMEN

Sasha is a slender, bearded man with an accentuated stutter and a dark sense of humor. Tamara is one-fourth Jewish and one-half Armenian, a pixie of a woman with short, boyish hair. She used to work as a librarian, but her work collective did not provide the benefits of its own day care center. So like most of her woman friends Tamara has sacrificed her career to stay home with her children because she considers state-run *yasli* "indoctrinating of government propaganda" and "foully run and disease-ridden." Her son, now twelve, caught an intestinal infection in his first month of kindergarten and still suffers from chronic illness.

On one particular Friday afternoon at the Kalugins' house, a crowd has assembled at the table for talk and tea. One corner of the living-dining-room area—an impoverished yet cozy room furnished with a few chairs and rickety tables and many pieces of bright paisley cloth—is decorated with scores of icons; the Kalugins rescued them from refuse heaps in the 1970s, when many churches were still being destroyed. To Tamara and Sasha, Russian icon painting and the work of Jackson Pollock, which has recently been shown in the U.S.S.R. in exhibits of American art, are most communicative of that "striving toward freedom and toward God" which they believe central to the best art. The walls of the Kalugins' flat are also hung with Sasha's own paintings and prints, surreal landscapes and acerbic portraits which blend the influences of Chagall, De Chirico, George Grosz, and medieval Russian icons.

Seated at the Kalugins' table are Lyalya, an ebullient, disheveled woman in her fifties who has no specific political ideology beyond the fact that she "hates the Soviet way of government;" trained as an agronomist, she left her job to stay home with her grandson in order to keep him out of day care centers. Alongside her are two other *Express-Chronicle* collaborators: Lyuda, a pretty young mother in her mid-twenties who has sacrificed her career as an economist to take care of her two youngsters—she took her daughter out of a government-run day care center after one month, when she found the child's hair full of lice; and Natalya, who left her job teaching history at a museum school to stay home with her four daughters.

We are soon joined by Slava, a quiet, thoughtful eighteen-year-old conscientious objector who has just been called to the Army. The company discusses his narrow field of options: he can either spend time in jail, serve a sentence in psychiatric hospital, or emigrate— there are no other choices, in the U.S.S.R., for conscientious objectors. "If you go to jail you can hang out with superb women policemen," Sasha Kalugin teases, "all our policewomen seem to get jobs in prisons. Ah, the beauties I met in jail, beehive hairdos, such asses, such boobs . . ."

Enters Oleg, a young jazz guitarist who also helps out with *Express-Chronicle*. Several years ago he emigrated to the United States, but after six months he felt lonely there and returned to live in Moscow. He has brought a bottle of champagne. Glasses are poured all around. Slava's dilemma is temporarily overlooked as the women give me an overview of the meager child support programs offered by the Soviet government.

"First, there are the one-time grants given at the child's birth— they invented them in 1980, to boost our glorious Motherland's birth rate and expand its work force," says Natalya, who is a considerable expert on the issue. "Fifty rubles for the first child; one hundred for the second, seventy-five for the third, eighty-five for the fourth. Then, if you're employed, there's the thirty-five rubles a month of so-called paid maternity leave you get for the first year you stay home with the child—however high or low your salary, thirty-five is all you'll get." (Thirty-five rubles is fifty-six dollars.)

"And don't forget our government's largesse toward parents whose individual wages are less than seventy rubles a month," Lyalya says. "Twelve rubles a month for each child until the child is eight years old, enough to keep him fed for three days."

"I don't know who should be more ashamed, the government doling out such peanuts, or the family receiving them," Lyuda quips.

"And they're pressuring us to have three kids apiece!" Lyalya cackles.

"The lowest child support payments in the developed countries," Natalya says with authority.

At five-thirty I go to the Kalugins' kitchen to phone for a taxi and see a huge pile of *blini* and a casserole of chicken and potatoes warming on the stove. It is clear that most guests who drop in on Tamara at this time of day will stay on for supper, and perhaps far into the night.

SOVIET WOMEN

As I put on my coat Tamara expresses chagrin that I always hurry, that I am not staying for supper. "But I came at three o'clock, that's not even tea time!" I protest. "In this country you know perfectly well it's bad manners not to stay for dinner," she says.

Tamara stares at her stove, and tells me she is trying to decide what she will cook for the thirty co-workers who are coming to her the following night, Saturday, to compile the next issue of *Express-Chronicle.*

"I've already made a large pot of *borscht,*" she says, "I'm trying to decide what I'm going to give as a second course."

"At such gatherings in the 1960s in the U.S.A.," I suggest, "we used to mostly put out a lot of cold meat and cheeses and breads."

"You Americans don't understand," Tamara says; "the kind of people who come to us on Saturdays may not have had a decent meal for the entire week, one *must* give a second hot course."

I keep being overwhelmed by the decorum that accompanies the proverbial Russian largesse, even in the direst circumstances.

Some years ago, Tamara and Sasha applied for emigration papers for the United States. Their first application was not accepted; they still hope to obtain the proper documents in the future.

Early one morning a few days later, on the way to visit Tamara's friend Lyuda in the vicinity of Pushkin Street, I stop at some food stores to look at the availability and prices of basic staples. The situation is far grimmer than in the middle 1980s. Apart from potatoes and a few heads of rotting cabbage, the only produce available, even at the beginning of the shopping day, consists of oranges at 1.50 rubles a kilo (70 cents apiece) and of very wrinkled apples at 2 rubles a kilo ($1.60 a pound). The only alternative for a wider choice of produce would be the *rynok,* the open farmers' market, where the prices are far higher because they're not government-controlled. There, tomatoes were selling that week at the equivalent of $4.00 apiece, tiny wilted bunches of parsley at $2.00 each.

Keeping in mind that the average Soviet salary is 200 rubles a month ($320, or one third of our median wage) I note further: Sausage, the staple protein of most Russians—$7.00 a pound. Chicken, the luxury protein—$2.10 a pound. The cheapest cut of beef for grinding into hamburgers—$1.60 a pound. Margarine—$1.40 a pound. A can of orange juice imported from Cyprus—$2.60. Milk—50 cents a quart. A jar of stewed vegetables—$1.15 a quart. Canned peaches—$3.00 per quart jar. Rare are the weeks when more than two of these items can be found on the same day.

So even in the government stores, prices for these increasingly scarce victuals are at least 50 percent higher than in the United States. And as I walked toward Lyuda's flat, I wondered how any family within Tamara's circle of friends, in which men earn modest wages while wives sit home with the children, can safeguard their offspring from scurvy or other forms of undernourishment.

Lyuda is a frail, beautiful woman in her middle twenties who graduated from university in economics as an *otlichnitsa*, the equivalent of our summa cum laude honors, but has little hope of ever getting a decent job after having stayed home for three years. She is married to Lev, a doctor. Although Soviet housing conditions have improved in the past years, the family is still crowded into one single room in a communal flat. Since they presently have less than five square meters a person, they are wait-listed for a two-room flat; but they estimate that it may take them another five or six years to get one because "we have no connections to push the request forward."

Sitting with Lyuda and Lev at breakfast that morning, I am awed by the cozy orderliness with which they keep their tiny space, fastidiously labeling the shelves that run from floor to ceiling and hold all of their books and clothing. Lyuda and Lev must share the kitchen with a retired woman of such unpleasant manners that they are not on speaking terms, and can never use the kitchen at the same hours. Lyuda's morale is not boosted when she takes her children out for their airing, and faces the ire of older women in their housing settlement. " 'Spoiled, idle youth staying home instead of working!' " she quotes them as saying. " 'In our day we used to all go back to work after two months, *we* weren't finicky about our day care centers!' "

Lev is employed in a state clinic, where he receives a salary of 230 rubles a month, about half that of a skilled factory worker. Since

SOVIET WOMEN

perestroika made private practice legal he has been trying to earn a bit more by practicing homeopathy in his tiny bed/living room. The demand for private consultations is such that he received twenty calls in the week after he first advertised his services in the newspapers; the standard patient's fee for such a visit ranges from 15 to 20 rubles.

Yet in a one-room communal flat housing four persons (renting an office outside of the home would be exorbitant) how much of a private practice can Lev have? Through lack of space he is only able to receive patients on weekends, when his family can go to spend a night in the country with his in-laws.

Lyuda and Lev attend church weekly and sing in the church choir. When asked how they would like their children's lives to differ from theirs, Lev says, "We would like them to have faith in God, and to practice religion fearlessly from their earliest years."

Lyuda and Lev have applied for emigration papers. They plan to leave for the United States as soon as their papers are in order.

Natalya is a wiry, voluble mother of four who loves painting, poetry, social gatherings. "In another life," she says, "I would have a literary and artistic salon, the way they do in Paris."

Paris, art galleries, glamorous salons are an obsession with Natalya. Her greatest role model, when she was twenty years old, was a woman called Aida, who had five children by five different men—the last two were conceived in Paris, one with a Japanese, one with a black diplomat. When Aida returned to Moscow, Natalya often visited her. "Everyone sang at her home, there were many artists, guitarists, poets . . . all those lovers, all those children, precisely the way I'd like to live. Unfortunately I can't go to Paris and learn to do it the way Aida did . . ."

This Utopia is far distant from Natalya's reality. Now thirty-three, trained as a historian, Natalya sacrificed her career to keep her children out of day care centers. She earns 160 rubles a month doing freelance work at home, writing educational manuals for a trade school which teaches how to fabricate macaroni.

When their fourth daughter was born, Natalya's husband, an engineer, also left work to help take care of the tots (at least that is the excuse he gives) and works as a janitor in their housing settlement. Together, the couple earns some 360 rubles a month (560 dollars). Natalya estimates that 300 rubles of their salary goes to food. The rent on their apartment is 35 rubles, "leaving 25 rubles a month," as Natalya ironically puts it, "to provide clothes and diversions for six persons. How much clothing? A child's winter coat costs 25, 30 rubles, and an adult's, 80 to 100 rubles. Imagine our wardrobe."

But the couple fell into luck with their apartment: Thanks to the fact that Natalya's mother was still living with them, and they were then a family of seven, they qualified for thirty-five square meters and were granted five rooms. This enabled the obstinate Natalya to fulfill one small part of her ambitions and use her flat as an art gallery for "apartment exhibits" (private home showings of unofficial art, the kind that would not be approved by the Artists' Union, are a popular practice in large cities). Natalya does not keep a penny from the proceeds, which she immediately hands over to the artists, and estimates that she sells only some four canvases a year. "But it's a form of community work, and my only recreation—it keeps me sane."

As Nonna and I visit Natalya one afternoon, she proudly walks us through her current exhibition. She has put on her most fashionable outfit for the occasion—faded jeans that tightly hug her muscled, boyish body, a white tennis shirt. Her hair is artfully tousled and teased, her beautiful long-lashed eyes coquettishly made up. The walls of her sitting room are hung with large works of protest art—violent fauve hues, many religious and erotic emblems, tortured human figures writhing under Red Army bayonets in front of gilt-domed churches, an abundance of sword-penis motifs, the letters KGB often twisted into genital symbols. The stark rooms in which the canvases hang, each furnished with no more than a bed, a chair, a cupboard, are of awesome neatness.

Natalya's four disheveled, skinny daughters, who range from three to nine years of age, run shouting through the apartment, brandishing broomsticks and umbrellas in mock battle. *"Dievushki, pazhaluista!* Young ladies, please!" Natalya remonstrates. Undaunted by the children, who continue running, yelling, through the flat, Natalya opens the door of one small room where she hangs her prints and lithographs. A slight, mustached man with meek and terrified eyes sits in the room's only chair, by its only table, reading a book. It is Natalya's husband. "Oh, excuse us for disturbing you!" Natalya says with an edge of irony in her voice, closing the door. "He could have been a university professor," she whispers to us as we move on. "The worst thing about the Soviet system is that it has so diminished our men's self-esteem . . ."

Our hostess closes the door and shows us into her daughters' room, an equally stark chamber with two double bunk beds, one desk, in which she hangs her watercolors. A few toys lie scattered on the floor. "Now this I will not have! Who is responsible?" Natalya shouts out severely to her brood. "I shall punish anyone who leaves toys on the floor and spoils my gallery effect!"

"It's Dasya's fault!" one little voice cries out as the girls continue racing through the flat. "It's Tanya's," another one shouts. "No, it's Masha's," another pipes up. Natalya does not pursue any punishment. "I really should have a governess for them," she says with a sigh as she ushers us into her stark kitchen, denuded of any sign of food save for a few pots of jam.

Natalya puts on the kettle. Her two youngest daughters run in, grab a pot of jam from the cupboard, and sit on the floor, sticking their fingers into the pot and licking their thumbs. *"Dievushki,* you're going to be sick!" Natalya mildly protests. The children continue to glut. There is a soft, shuffling sound of adult feet in the adjoining rooms; Natalya's husband moves aimlessly through the apartment, smoking. Natalya, sitting at her kitchen table, talks about food prices ("One ruble fifty for a kilo of oranges, four oranges a kilo, that means one orange per child every few days.") She returns to another favorite topic, the government's paltry child support legislation.

"Poverty is not supposed to exist in the U.S.S.R., but in effect every family in which the wife sits home to preserve the kids' health lives on the edge of penury. They give you certain privileges when you have more than three children, like discounts on items like refrigerators and sewing machines, and a stamp on your passport that allows you to go to the head of any food queues when you're shopping . . .

"But how often do we use that privilege?" Natalya asks, hoisting onto her lap one of her younger daughters, who is now weeping because her sister stole her jam pot. "We only use it when we're in dire straits, because everyone in the queue starts insulting us with the most vile words in the language. Women with more than two children are resented here; despite the government hoopla about larger families they're seen as anti-social, as . . . *not proper,*" she adds delicately in English.

Natalya's husband has shuffled into the kitchen, still in his bedroom slippers. He sits in a corner, squatting on his haunches, smoking, staring at us with mournful, idle eyes. Natalya has gone on to discuss the sorry state of Soviet gynecology, and is relating the story of her third daughter's birth, when she was so mistreated by doctors that she jumped out of a clinic's second-story window.

"One fine June day my contractions start, it's a month ahead of time but I go to the clinic just to make sure; during the night my contractions stop and I tell the doctor I want to go home. But the doctor doesn't let me go. She inspects me and says, 'Everything's open, you're ready, I'm going to start inducing birth.' 'But it's a month too early,' I complain. 'You're wrong,' the doctor says, 'you're ready.' And she starts giving me shots of some horrible drug they use for schizophrenics; it's supposed to calm me down but it made me beastly. I realized that the doctor wanted to induce birth just to get me out of the way, I kept shouting I wanted to go home. . . ."

"It was my birthday . . ." Natalya's husband butted in.

"No, it was *not* your birthday," Natalya retorted. "I wanted to come home because I wanted to be with my children. Anyway, in the middle of the night I waited until the nurse on duty was asleep, I stole one of the nurses' white housecoats from a closet and tried to get out of the ward, all the doors were locked so there was nothing to do but jump out of the window. I jumped. I hurt my ankle badly but I managed to hitchhike home. I had a quiet two weeks at home and the real contractions came and I went to another clinic, they told me there that the doctor at the first clinic had tried to induce the birth prematurely, my baby was very underweight, I've been trying to fatten her up ever since. . . .

"Haven't I, Mashenka," she says, stroking the head of the child in her lap, who has fallen asleep, her jam-smeared face nestled in her mother's shoulder. "But it's hard to fatten up any child on our diet."

Natalya looks at the clock. "Tanya," she calls out to her eldest child, "time to go to your puppet theater class! Please hurry and go immediately!"

"In another life," Natalya says dreamily, "I'd like to live in Paris, and have all my children be artists."

Defying the system by sitting home, refusing to be the prolifically versatile national heroine, dropping out of jobs and day care programs: Housewife with many children as radical dissenter—that, I mused at the visit's end, would strike American women as a most curious model.

Portraits, Cont.

Svetlana

Forty-two-year-old Svetlana Alekseevna Vereshchagina is the cultural editor of the largest newspaper in western Siberia, *Vostochno-Sibirskaia Pravda,* which reaches a million readers. I look back on her as a particularly striking example of Russian women's powerful filial and maternal bonds.

Svetlana is single-handedly raising her three-year-old granddaughter. Her daughter, who was married at nineteen, attends a university in Moscow with her husband; the young couple must live in one tiny room in a student dormitory; and Svetlana insisted on bringing her granddaughter to Irkutsk to give the child a healthier life and allow the young parents to pursue their studies in peace. The child's mother and father miss her very much. Svetlana makes cassettes of her granddaughter's voice, which her parents listen to when they phone in the evenings.

"I get up before seven and dress my little Nastasya for nursery school," Svetlana told me when I asked her about an average day's schedule. "I wash her and do her braids, and walk her to the day care center. We chat on the way over—she's such a miracle, so very sweet! I return and make coffee for myself and throw on my makeup and go to work.

"In the evening," she continued, "Nastya has to be picked up by seven, and frequently I'm still at work. So I'm saved by my mother. When we have our weekly editorial meeting, for instance, Mother will pick her up and feed her and put her to bed. When I do finish work by seven, I pick Nastya up at school and warm up dinner, which I've usually made the night before. Around nine, after we've watched a bit of television, I put my granddaughter to bed and iron her clothes for the next day—I leave the door open to her bedroom so she can *see* me ironing, that way she falls asleep more peacefully. When she falls asleep, I take a little time off for myself, read a pile of magazines and journals . . .

"Ah, you're probably wondering about what happens to my private life," Svetlana added with her very forthright, candid smile, without any prompting from me. "I can entertain guests after Nastya is asleep. I've reinforced the dividing wall so that if I close her door she doesn't hear a thing. I have a few women friends who often come over, and sometimes I entertain a man with whom I'm on very warm terms . . ."

Svetlana belongs to that generation which came of age during World War II and still looks on marriage as "an important asset." Although she has been twice divorced, she sometimes wishes she had a husband to help her bring up little Nastya. And Svetlana has had many new offers of marriage. But those possibilities seem to have receded before the more powerful ties of kinship and tribal loyalty.

"I turned down a Moscow man, as perfect a gentleman as one could find," she told me. "This is hard to believe . . . I turned him down even though *he has his own apartment and car!* I couldn't do it because my aging parents are here, and the graves of my ancestors, all my kin are in a cemetery nearby, my roots are here . . . without this rough land, these mountains, I can't imagine my life. So I would be incapable of moving to Moscow, even for a great job, even to get married and live in a splendid flat of my own. . . ."

Sitting in her office at the newspaper, photographs of Decembrist heroes hung above her desk, this cultivated, seductive woman looked torn, confused about the drawbacks and advantages of remaining single.

"I still have time to start a new family," she continued with that great candor which I found particular to Siberian women. "I have time yet to offer love, and passion, and temperament, I can give it all to someone who will value it. My husband would not be displeased with me," she added coquettishly. "I have a wide range of interests, I'm a fine conversationalist. All this is also very important to a man . . ."

And then the irrepressible domesticity of Soviet women came to the fore.

"I'll tell you," Svetlana said in a confidential tone, "there's still no better way to reach a man than through his stomach, that's the way most fine conversation, spiritual contact will occur! To please a man, go to the market as soon as the first cherries, the first tomatoes are out, put out your best tablecloth and napkins, set a charming table laden with all the beautiful first produce, your man will be so pleased!"

Over dinner that night at my hotel, I asked Svetlana whether it had been a hard decision to make: single-handedly to bring up a grandchild.

"I never had a moment of hesitation," she answered. "I simply told my mother when Nastya was a year old, 'I'm flying to Moscow and picking her up to bring her back here.' "

Most forty-two-year-old American women, I said, would not find the decision that easy. They would probably look on such a step as a considerable responsibility and sacrifice.

"They would consider it . . . a sacrifice?" Svetlana asked me, bewildered.

Yes, I repeated, a sacrifice.

Svetlana looked shocked.

"How can you say it might even be a hard decision for anyone? It was not even a decision, but an immediate and unquestioned impulse! I must give my daughter what my mother gave to me. When I was a student, my mother enabled me to get an education by bringing up my daughter. Later she stayed with her when I went on every business trip . . .

"How can you Americans even speak of such a thing as sacrifice?" she added, shaking her head with disbelief. "To us, such behavior is nothing more than the normal and absolute return of love, the sacred call of the heart."

Portraits, Cont.

A Letter from Natalya

A few days before the New Year I received the following communication from Natalya:

Moscow, 2/12/89

Dear Francine!

How are you? What about your book on Russian women . . . and is anybody interested in the life of Soviet women?

I live such a way as I did a year ago. But I am in divorce now. But my husband lives here in our flat. He works seldom, but he doesn't like to do it.

It is very difficult to live in our country now. We have no soap, laundry soap not at all. There aren't products in the shops and department stores. And it takes much time to find something to eat there. Ruble doesn't cost anything. All of it is awful. I don't hope it will be better in the future. And I'm afraid, I worry about my children. All changed in this year. If about a year ago majority hoped and waited the changes, but now I think nobody believes them. And it's awful that many countries finished to invite immigrants from Russia.

But maybe it'll be better. Now I want to congratulate you with the New Year . . .

Natalya

XI

Life and Literature: Formidable Women

The relationship of Soviet women to Western Slavists much resembles that of birds to ornithologists: Due to their society's taboo on any form of gender analysis, Soviet women are no more aware of the vast feminist literature being written about them in the West than scarlet tanagers are aware of Roger Tory Peterson. This pool of American, British, Scandinavian research has been focusing on many intriguing aspects of Slavic studies: The powerful matriarchal patterns in early Russian society; the despotic misogyny of the Orthodox Church; the images of women in nineteenth- and twentieth-century Russian literature.

Scholars concur that Russia is a region in which woman-centered cults and social orders lingered far longer than in most other cultures.

SOVIET WOMEN

Early Slavic religion was strikingly lacking in any dominant male gods. Worship of the "Great Mother" and of other self-inseminating female deities common to agricultural societies prevailed far into the Christian era. Russian folklore still remains uniquely rich in Powerful Woman archetypes. *Polianitsy* (from *pole*, "field") are Amazonic heroines of early Russian epics who rival their masculine counterparts in strength and valor. The *Rusalki* we meet in the opening lines of Pushkin's *Ruslan and Lyudmila* are virginal, often malicious water deities who live in streams, lakes, ponds. The most fearsome and pervasive female prototype of all is *Baba Yaga*, an unmarried, prescient, angry old witch, sometimes aided in her craft by a *Rusalka*, who is a symbol of female wisdom at its most wrathful and punitive.

In few other societies, so many historians have noted, did women retain power so long over tribal institutions and maintain a more forceful role in family life. The heroes of Russian epics must obey the orders of their mothers or wives rather than any male authorities; contrary to Latin or Anglo-Saxon custom, a son needed his mother's blessing, rather than his father's, when he left home for war or any quest of honor and success. One of the most popular male archetypes of Russian folklore is Ivan the Fool, a kind, generous "village idiot" figure who lives at home with his widowed mother, and ultimately triumphs over his worldly, questing brothers by retaining the shamanistic powers of the female hearth. To this day, few idioms so forcefully express a country's umbilical spell upon her citizens as the language of "Mother Russia." Many of the nation's major rivers, the Volga in particular, are referred to as *Matushka*, "little mother," while the very noun for "native land" is *rodina*, from the word *rod*, "birth."

Yet there are few cultures in which the sentiment of heterosexual love, on men's part, has been so admixed with dread. The very word for "passion," *strast*, also means "horror, terror"; men's apprehension of women, and that exacerbated tension between the sexes particular to the Russian heritage, remains explicit in the lines of the popular song *"Otchye Chornye,"* "Dark Eyes": *"Kak liubliu ia vas, kak bayus ia vas,"* "How I love you, how I fear you." This blend of awe and aversion may well be rooted in an archaic terror of the forceful female's sexual powers, a terror which the Orthodox Church fully exploited when Christianity finally came to Russia in the tenth century.

An interesting new contribution to Slavic studies, Joanna Hubbs's *Mother Russia*,[27] draws close links between Russia's singularly powerful maternal archetypes and the misogyny of its Orthodox Church. Byzantine Christianity may have been more repressive of women than Roman Catholicism, the author speculates, because the region was more vulnerable to the goddess-centered fertility religions of the Near East, and the Orthodox Church had to contend with unusually powerful matriarchal patterns. Furthermore, its ascetic obscurantism was never counterbalanced by a tradition of chivalric love, or by the liberating secular influences of a Renaissance or an Enlightenment.

And so Russian culture remained totally deprived of that idealization of marital sex which prevails in much of the Roman Catholic tradition. The Orthodox clergy, which referred to women as "those cursed by God," continued to look on the female sex as the source of all spiritual danger. Faithful to Tertullian's view of women as "the devil's gateway," Orthodox theology emphasized women's mental inferiority and their powers of witchcraft. In few Christian countries did the clergy hold more negative views of women, forbidding them access to church services during their menstrual periods, only allowing Communion bread to be baked by females past childbearing age.

The occupation of Muscovy in the thirteenth and fourteenth centuries by Moslem Mongols further intensified these patterns of oppression, particularly in the urban *boyar* classes. Women's social status reached its nadir in the sixteenth century, when an extreme segregation of the sexes prevailed and was a matter of family honor: In those very decades when the salons of Parisian women were the center of France's literary and political culture, virtually dictating men's tastes and restructuring the mores of their nation, Moscow women lived in *terem*—"harems"—on their houses' uppermost floors. They ate separately from men and were rigorously shielded from public view. Until the time of Peter the Great, who outraged many of his subjects by holding Western-style mixed gatherings at his court, women were mostly allowed out of the house to go to church. (One can think of few cultures so replete with sexist folk sayings: "A maiden seen is copper, the unseen girl is gold." "Long in hair, short in brains." "Beat the wife for better cabbage soup." "I thought I saw two people, but it was only a man and his wife.")

The sixteenth century was also marked by the appearance of one of the most crudely chauvinistic documents of the Christian era, the *Domostroi*, or "Law of the Home," written by the monk Sylvester and distributed to all Russian households at the order of Czar Ivan the Terrible. A manual for family behavior which modeled marriage on the monastic ideal (a "perverted" and "abominable morality," the philosopher Nikolay Berdyaev calls it, "a disgrace to the Russian people"),[28] the *Domostroi* offers meticulous instructions on the manner in which husbands must beat their wives ("privately, politely"). It orders wives to "complain to no one" about such abuse, and to remain silent about all domestic problems.[29] And it may well have been responsible for that rigorous habit of privacy concerning all family matters that persists in Soviet culture to this day, presenting a formidable obstacle to psychologists, gynecologists, and most any kind of social worker.

Yet, paradoxically, the power of the Virgin Mary has remained more pronounced in Russian society than in the West. The context of philosopher Nikolay Berdyaev's startling phrase, "The fundamental category [of Russia] is motherhood,"[30] is a discussion of the Virgin Mother's omnipotence. Berdyaev points out that in Russia Mary even "takes precedence over the Trinity," that it was the icons of the Virgin, rather than those of Her Son, which were deemed to be miraculous. The icon of the Virgin—rather than the Crucifix, as in the West—remained the national totem: It was hung in a corner of every Russian home, preceded all armies into battle; before it all oaths were sworn and conflicts resolved.

So Russian culture has been equally marked by men's ambivalent awe and resentment of forceful females, and by a singularly intense worship of the Virgin Mother. It is interesting to trace the imprint of these obsessions upon nineteenth- and twentieth-century Russian literature.

Russian prose fiction is a genre which until very recently remained a predominantly male domain. For of the novelistic traditions that have most enriched Western culture—British, French, American, Russian—Russian fiction is the only one that has not been profoundly marked by the female imagination, the only one in which no novel or short story crafted by a woman has yet endured beyond its time and remained a classic.

Eighteenth- and nineteenth-century Russian literature did yield some marvelous memoirs, diaries, and autobiographies penned by women, notably those of Yekaterina Dashkova and Nadezhda Durova, and a handful of fiction writers briefly in vogue in their day such as Elena Gan and Evgenia Tur. In our own era Russian culture has offered us two of the most sublime poets of the century, Anna Akhmatova and Marina Tsvetaeva; and two of the most admirable memoirs of the Stalin epoch, Evgenia Ginzburg's and Nadezhda Mandelstam's.

Yet until the flowering of Russian women's fiction that occurred in the mid-1960s—Baranskaya's "A Week Like Any Other" was a prime example—the great novelistic tradition of Russia has had no Lady Murasaki or Madame de Staël or Madame de La Fayette; it has had no Aphra Behn, no Jane Austen, no George Eliot or Brontë sisters or Virginia Woolf, none of those wondrous chroniclers of the female sensibility who have transfigured the novel form. And compared with Great Britain, the United States, or France, where popular women's novels, however wretched their quality and transient their vogue, profoundly affected and feminized their nation's cultures, Russian women's prose remained marginal.

As for the images of women in nineteenth-century Russian novels —created by male authors whose genius has seldom been surpassed— they are marked by two interlinked themes which draw on Russia's deep puritánism: 1) An idealization of women's moral virtues which led to the creation of heroines considerably more powerful than their male counterparts. 2) A paradoxically negative, ascetic attitude toward women's sensuality and intellect. For in classical Russian literature sexual union is mostly seen as grotesque; mature, still sexual women must be severely curbed, are only safe when their energies are totally sublimated in that holiest of duties which is motherhood; heroines

SOVIET WOMEN

tend to incarnate perfection in either prepubescent youth, as redemptive presexual virgins, or in advanced age, as admirable, safely postsexual matrons.

These fixations are well exemplified by Natasha of Tolstoy's *War and Peace.* Part of Tolstoy's "implacable hostility toward women," to use Gorky's phrase, is his degrading of their mental faculties, and in particular of their linguistic skills. "Women," so Tolstoy wrote in his journal, "do not use words to express their thoughts, but to attain their goals." In the fifth chapter of *War and Peace,* as we are introduced to Natasha of the tossing curls and adorable little lace-frilled legs, two features of this child-woman are particularly striking: Her forthright, penetrating, all-knowing gaze, and the fragmentary, barely intelligible language in which she attempts to tell her mother about her doll ("Do you see . . . My doll, Mimi . . . you see . . .") Within two pages of her appearance Natasha's very incoherence, coupled with her singular insight into others, endows her with that female gift, already evidenced by Pushkin's Tatyana, which will remain a constant in Russian novelists' rendering of their many young "earth women": An uncanny grasp of reality which is based on pure intuition, a nonverbal keenness which is linked, in turn, to a redeeming, close-to-the-soil Russianness.

But when we take leave of Natasha some twelve hundred pages later in the novel's epilogue she is well on her way to embodying another familiar female archetype of Russian mythology and literature —the Formidable Woman. Now ill-kempt and straggly-haired in her soiled housecoat, grown fat "like a breeding-fish" from incessant childbearing, our heroine has become an omnipotent domestic tyrant. Her husband Pierre, by far the most vital male protagonist of the novel, has capitulated to his wife's primeval force. We are told that he is seriously henpecked ("under her heel," *pod bashmakom,* as the original goes) and meekly submits to her wishes "that every moment of his life belong to her and to the family." Pierre does not even dare "speak smilingly to another woman" or "dine at his club as a pastime," and is confronted with a tantrum of fibs and reprimands when he is a few hours late returning from a business trip. This final Natasha is abundantly praised by Tolstoy for her very slovenliness and enduring plainness of speech, for disdaining the dangerous example of

French women who continue to take care of their appearance after marriage, is extolled, in fact, for having ceased to be sexually enticing to her husband.

The novel, better than any art form that comes to mind, communicates the most unadmitted terrors, the core hang-ups of any society. Throughout much of the Russian tradition, with the exception of Chekhov and Turgenev, women in love, even within marriage, tend to be a force that must in some way be neutralized. As Barbara Heldt puts it in her remarkable contribution to recent Slavic studies, *Terrible Perfection: Women and Russian Literature,*[31] much of the denouement depends on what strategy of suppression various male writers and heroes choose.

Tolstoy, as we see in *War and Peace*'s epilogue, which sets forth his grim view of marital sex as both essential sublimation and inevitable damnation, dooms women to bovine domesticity. Lermontov's leading man Pechorin, of *A Hero of Our Time,* both conquers and fails by deceit. Turgenev's men capitulate to the female's superiority. Dostoevsky, who equates the erotic drive to "the sensuality of insects," offers his women spiritual regeneration. Gogol's men might prefer suicide to the moral perils of copulation or marriage. And all their protagonists must resolve a paradox central to Russian fiction: Woman, whose body is such a threat to man's spirit, becomes his moral superior once her sexuality has been in some way annulled.

The revulsion against women's flesh expressed by Gogol, a devout Orthodox believer, may not be equaled by any other literary genius in history. And in his story "Ivan Fyodorovich Shponka and His Aunt," the author manages to fuse the archetypes of redemptive virgin and admirable Post-Sexual Woman into one Amazonic figure. The kind, magisterial Aunt Vasilia, who governs the life of the orphaned, timorous bachelor Ivan Shponka, "values her spinster's life more than anything else," and transcends all gender in her awesome androgynous skills. Giant in stature and endowed with "very manly hands," she shoots wild game and climbs trees like the ablest sportsman, rows boats "more skillfully than the fishermen themselves." Things go awry when Auntie Vasilia, suddenly craving for a brood of children over whom to extend her rule, orders her tenaciously celibate nephew to get married. Ivan, terrified of abandoning his safely virginal living arrangement, swears to desist marriage to the end. And in the apocalyptic nightmare sequence of the final scene, his hallucinations lead him to see a monstrous, domineering wife in every inch of his room:

> His wife was sitting on a chair . . . and then he noticed that she had the face of a goose. He looked the other way, and saw another wife, and she had a goose's face as well. He looked again and there was a third wife; he looked around, still another . . . He took off his hat—and there was a wife sitting in it . . . He took some cotton wool out of his ear—a wife was there too. . . . Then he had another dream, that his wife was not a person at all, but some kind of woollen material. He had gone into a shop . . . "What kind of material would you like, sir?" asked the shopkeeper. "Have some *wife*, it's the latest thing now! . . . Everyone's having coats made from it." The shopkeeper made his measurements and cut the wife up . . . "That's very poor material," says the Jewish tailor to whom Ivan takes the fabric, "No one uses *that* kind of stuff for coats now . . ."

This landmark of the fantastic prose genre sums up that ascetic, punitive dread of sexual union which marks much of Russian fiction, and grows in Gogol into virtual paranoia. Might the genius, the shamanistic force of nineteenth-century Russian literature be in part traceable to this archaic terror of female power, and of the primeval forces it can unleash?

The sexual exorcism of Lermontov's *A Hero of Our Time* takes a more Westernized form, a jaded Casanovan revenge against every female whom the hero conquers. The most interesting seduction achieved by Lermontov's Pechorin is that of Princess Mary, for it displays several other aspects of Russian anti-heroes' inferiority complex before their female peers: The cynicism, rootlessness, Europeaping decadence, self-defeating introspection already embodied by Pushkin's Onegin. In this particular section of *A Hero of Our Time*, jaded Pechorin conquers the heart of proud Princess Mary, whom he abandons as soon as he is certain that she is in love with him. " 'Why do I so stubbornly try to gain the love of a little maiden whom I do not wish to seduce, and whom I will never marry?' " Pechorin asks himself during his courtship. " 'Why this feminine coquetry? . . . I sometimes despise myself . . . Is this not why I despise others?' " After Pechorin has ravaged Princess Mary's life by killing her suitor and destroying all chances she has for any future marriage, he visits her one last time and absolves himself in a typically Russian form of *mea culpa*, the sensuality of self-degradation: " 'I am base in regard to you,' " he tells her; the curtain falls on this exchange: "She turned to me as pale as marble. 'I hate you,' she said."

Could the forceful Russianness of Pushkin's Tatyana ever have delivered Onegin from his own feckless narcissism? Could any turn of fate have helped Madame Odintsova, the cool, kind aristocrat of Turgenev's *Fathers and Sons*, to rescue Bazarov from his tragic theorizing? Could any seductive woman ever have nudged Goncharov's Oblomov out of the lethargic Russian male's favorite armor, his housecoat? There is one key word which describes the superiority of Russian heroines to a literary community of anti-heroes and born losers. Crucial to generations of Russian literary critics, it is the concept of "wholeness," *tsel'nost.* This rich and loaded word connotes endurance, selflessness, patience, stability, and above all, decisiveness. Female "wholeness" serves as a rebuke to the Hamletic escapism of various classes of Russian males, be he a parasitical *chinovnik* bureaucrat, a lazy country gent, or a disaffected intellectual such as Oblomov.

My favorite of Turgenev's women is Marianne of *Virgin Soil,* through whom the author stages a particularly admirable choreography of kinetic female and born-loser male. Marianne, clearly modeled on that remarkable generation of women revolutionarics who came to the fore in the 1860s, is somewhat of an anomaly among Russian literary heroines. Unusually plain, squat, rather masculine, she is not chaste, nor is she endowed with any of the condescending diminutives

SOVIET WOMEN

of feminine charm that characterize even her noblest sisters (we are always asked to admire Anna Karenina's charming *little* hand, Masha's or Natasha's adorable *little* feet). Marianne, who suffers "for all the poor, the oppressed, the wretched in Russia," has espoused the cause of women's emancipation and the overthrow of the czarist regime. With her lover, the equally militant Nezhdanov, she joins the *narodnik* movement, "going to the people" to prepare them for revolution.

The novel is tragi-comic in its descriptions of how these refined young aristocrats, to the bafflement of the abjectly conservative Russian peasantry, masquerade in laborers' garb and vainly struggle to learn such rustic tasks as chopping wood and planting crops. But *Virgin Soil*'s central theme concerns the vastly different levels of vitality and decisiveness with which Marianne and her lover dedicate themselves to revolution. Instead of roughening his hands with labor, as Marianne does, Nezhdanov lies in bed pondering on his lack of will; and part of his torpor is rooted in his deep sense of inferiority before Marianne. Seeing her as "the incarnation of everything good and true on earth—of fatherland, happiness, struggle, freedom!" he berates himself for being "a corpse, a half-dead creature . . . an honest, well-meaning corpse!" Finding himself unworthy of her, and of the Revolution, Nezhdanov commits suicide out of a genuine and perhaps realistic despair at being another "superfluous man," at the impotence of his class, at the futility and doom he senses concerning any genuine political change. Resilient Marianne survives, marrying a true man of the people, of the virgin soil.

Leafing through Dostoevsky for a statement of his own beliefs in the natural superiority of the female, I find few more eloquent than the following excerpt from his journal: "In her [woman] resides our only great hope, one of the pledges of our survival . . . Barbaric Russia will show what a place she will allot to the little sister, the little mother . . . that self-renouncing martyr for the Russian man." Women's suffering as a source of national redemption: Few prototypes of nineteenth-century Russian fiction better illustrate this central theme than Dostoevsky's idealized, curiously defleshed, virtuous prostitutes—characters limned by just about every nineteenth-century Russian writer—who confront men with the following paradox: "Look how far nobler than men all women remain, even in their most degraded state!"

Along with Dostoevsky's fallen women, the theme of the redemptive, suffering female is best embodied by Marya Timofeyevna in *The Possessed*. A kind, feebleminded cripple who is whipped and beaten by her degenerate brother, Marya Timofeyevna is given several mystical and divine attributes. She is an incarnation of Sophia, the principle of Divine Feminine Wisdom, a concept which would become crucial to Blok, the entire Symbolist movement, and to Bulgakov and Pasternak. Like many of the "holy fools" of Russian tradition, Marya Timofeyevna is also endowed with the gift of prophecy and vision. This enables her to bear her misery with the knowledge that through their very suffering women bear "the hope of the human race"—an ideal that the Soviet state would amply exploit in its female Logo of the dedicated, all-enduring mother/citizen/worker/wife.

Chekhov is perhaps the most humane portraitist of female character in the national pantheon. It's worth noting that the heroine of his "Lady with a Dog"—Anna Sergeevna—bears the same Christian name as the most beloved heroine of Russian literature, Tolstoy's Anna Karenina. But Chekhov's Anna, created a generation after Tolstoy's Karenina, is allowed to triumph over the tyranny of convention, and her adulterous liaison is described in as noble a light as marriage. Here as in many other works, Chekhov, along with Henry James, is perhaps the first great Western writer to forego any form of biological determinism, and to praise—with what subtlety and compassion—the courage of women who leave the roles prescribed them by society. It is in part this sense of wasted energy, of a constantly thwarted female potential, which gives his work its sense of irony and impending doom, of an empire's end.

Since the Revolution of 1917, when Moscow the Third Rome was transfigured into Moscow the Third International, the Russian literary heroine has passed through roughly three phases: 1) The brief bacchanal of artistic freedom that lasted until the late 1920s, during which her struggle to be reborn as the New Soviet Woman was turbulently portrayed. 2) The period of Socialist Realism (jargon: *lakirovka*, "the Great Varnishing"), which lasted until the death of Joseph Stalin, throughout which most of the heroine's psychological conflicts were carefully shielded from view. 3) A growing acknowledgment, first expressed during the Khrushchev thaw, and stated with increasing rage and despair in our own day, that the revolutionary ideal of women's equal rights was a paper equality at best, perhaps a pipe dream and a lie.

In the refreshingly depraved years which immediately followed the Revolution, that long-suppressed Dionysiac, erotic trait of Russian culture which had come to fore in the first decades of the century had its last Indian summer. And it is worth noting that during this period—the 1920s—the classical Russian motif of devouring female sexuality grew to more monstrous proportions than ever. It is typified by the grotesquely sluttish widow who engulfs the protagonist of Yury Olesha's *Envy* (1927), and by the constantly pregnant slut of Isaac Babel's fable *The Sin of Jesus* (1921). In Babel's tale, the female's lechery is so fiendish that she suffocates (in bed, of course) an angel sent to her by God to protect her from her own lust and that of mortal men.

For Soviet heroines of the 1920s had many promiscuous incarnations which a decade later might have doomed their creators to the Gulag. The drugged, alcoholic ingenue of Sergey Malashkin's *The Moons on the Right Side* (1926) can't even remember how many dozens of lovers she's had—as she explains, saying "no" to the *tovarishchi* might be considered bourgeois. The heroine of Nikolay Bogdanov's *The First Girl* (1928) is a member of Komsomol, the Young Communist League, who has spread venereal disease "in the performance of duties to the comrades," and is murdered by her best friend in order to save the organization from scandal.

Incarnations of the Amazon Woman are not solely negative in this decade. In Aleksey Tolstoy's *The Viper*, a pampered, aristocratic debutante grows to be a tough, disciplined soldier who handles guns and horses better than any man in the regiment. The Amazon is valorous in the fictions of the first and last great Soviet feminist, Aleksandra Kollontai. She is tragic in Fyodor Gladkov's *Cement* (1925), whose protagonist, Dasha, immolates her life so totally to the state and to the emancipation of women that she sees even the death of her daughter in a government children's home as a valid sacrifice to the revolutionary ideal of abolishing the nuclear family.

But the redomesticization of women imposed by Stalin in the 1930s was amply reflected in the renewed chasteness of Soviet literary heroines. The model for all Socialist Realist portrayals of women was Maxim Gorky's *Mother:* An ironic prototype indeed, seeing that it was written in 1906, much of it during a trip to the United States, two decades before the author resettled permanently in the U.S.S.R. after many long forays abroad. However clumsy as a novel, *Mother* is made riveting by its recycling of archaic Orthodox ideals of woman's mission into Communist state propaganda. "Mother" is an illiterate working class woman of saintly kindness who survives the brutal beatings of her alcoholic husband, and who in her widowhood is "raised from the dead" by the revolutionary activities of her charismatic bachelor son, Pavel, "Paul." He gathers about him a band of apostles who all refuse marriage because "No revolutionary can adhere closely to another individual without distorting his faith." As Pavel is sent to exile— perhaps to death—in Siberia, the heroine, Mother, states that she has gained "a resuscitated soul they can not kill" by becoming, herself, a socialist militant.

It is with the aid of these curiously mystical ideals that the literature of a militantly atheist state, in the Stalin era, forged its images of women: The notion that all citizens' personal joys and problems must be sublimated into that holier maternal unity which is the socialist collective; the precept that one's true spouse and parent is the Party and the nation-state. Under these premises, the heroine could be portrayed only as the resilient arch-nurturer who serves her nation by holding a job as well as any man and taking care of the family as only a woman can. No chink in her armor was ever allowed to show, we were barely even permitted to enter into her home; the only truly uplifting fiction about this self-abnegating superachiever was to be set in the work collective, preferably on immense construction projects. During this hydroelectrification of Russian literature, all family conflicts were taboo; our heroine's traditional mate—the spineless anti-hero of *ancien régime* fictions—had been reborn as the provident, dedicated "positive hero," Socialist New Man: No more depressions, no more romantic Hamletic indecision, no more Oblomovian housecoats. And all endings had to be happy, for women's life in the socialist state, as the old Russian saying goes, was "a river of milk amid fruit-jelly shores," *"Molochnaia reka, Kissel'nye Berega."*

These lacquered sweets began to go sour as our heroine entered Phase Three of her incarnations, under Khrushchev's thaw: The ideological soul-searching of industrial and *kolkhoz* novels gave way to more personal life-problems. Particularly in the writings of Vera Panova, perhaps the most popular woman writer of the postrevolutionary years, we were offered fictional forays into the home which admitted —oh, revelation!—to difficult housing conditions, juvenile delinquency, even adulteries. Archetypal plot: The young careerist in love with her older colleague, such as the heroine of Galina Nikolayeva's *A Running Battle*. After trysting for a few months in a cockroach-infested suburban room, the lover, declaring that "the era of socialism is ill-equipped for adultery," returns to his wife. The abandoned ingenue accepts a post in some distant province and nobly dedicates her life to work and the nation-state.

The case of Vera Panova, a faithful slave of Party doctrine whose domestic settings were nevertheless censured by male critics as being overly "feminine" and "naturalistic," calls for a mention of Soviet attitudes toward women authors: Notwithstanding its official policy of equal rights, the U.S.S.R., in literature as in life, remains a very oriental society which segregates women into various forms of ideational harems. And so sexist biases against women writers on the part of Soviet male authorities, the crude gender stereotypes and the abusive language in which these biases are couched, have been chronically abysmal. (No other society that comes to mind more direly needs to heed Henry Adams' saying, "A proper study of mankind is woman.")

Chauvinism may now be less overt than in 1946, when the Writers' Union expelled the sublime poet Anna Akhmatova with a motion of censure that labeled her "a nun and a fornicatrix." But to this day, praise offered women authors by male critics in the Soviet press is often accompanied by the following accolade: "This is fine writing, as if accomplished by a man's hand." And as of 1986, there were only a dozen women holding executive posts in the Writers' Union, as against 360 men—even though a sizable group of gifted women writers, for the previous two decades, had been altering the landscape of Soviet fiction.

This new wave of women authors who came to the fore in the mid-1960s gained their place, in part, by stating some of the more subversive views put forth since the 1917 Revolution: The notion that full-time employment is not the panacea for citizens' problems which the founding fathers had promised it to be; that the average Soviet workplace, in the recent words of novelist I. Grekova, is "a heart attack factory," *"fabrika infraktov."*[32]

I. Grekova and Natalya Baranskaya, the author of "A Week Like Any Other," are among a score of women authors, most of whom tend to work exclusively in the short story form rather than the novel, who have greatly feminized Russian letters. Much of their writings, particularly those of I. Grekova and of Tatyana Tolstaya, have already been widely translated and published abroad; and most of these authors are included in a half-dozen important collections of Soviet writing issued in the United States in 1989 alone. The most striking single trait shared by this new generation of women authors is that they have returned with a vengeance to the nineteenth-century duet of Formidable Woman-Weak Male once tabooed by Socialist Realism. The male protagonists limned in these Amazonic fictions are often endowed with those odious diminutives which nineteenth-century writers used to bestow on their heroines—they tend to have "limp little hands," "frail little feet," "thin little chicken necks." They are quite as superfluous, as Oblomovian, as lethargic as the heroes of nineteenth-century fiction, and far less complex.

The indecisive lover of Viktoria Tokareva's short story "Nothing

SOVIET WOMEN

Special"[33] admits to "his essential and beloved inertness," confessing that he will never be able to know happiness because "you have to work for it." Lyudmila Uvarova's "Be Still, Torments of Passion"[34] is the chronicle of a successful actress whose one lover was such an ineffectual wimp that she has chosen to live out the rest of her decades with two devoted women friends. The larger-than-life heroine of Grekova's novella *The Hotel Manager*,[35] who is left a widow conveniently early by her petty husband, finds fulfillment in the love of her own widowed mother and of the resilient unwed mothers she befriends. The male protagonist of Nina Katerli's "Between Spring and Summer,"[36] a gentle cardiac patient who is the only male employee in a work collective of bossy women engineers, offers the following meditation: "Equal rights . . . had turned out to mean . . . that a man was no longer the master of his home . . . that he was the least important person in it. What had happened to men? And where had these women come from who ran everything, whether at home or on the job?"

Contemporary Soviet women writers break totally with their classical male predecessors, however, by their creation of radically deidealized heroines: Perhaps they have learned that men place us on pedestals in order to keep us in our place, the better to admire our suffering. Their female protagonists—be they alcoholic actresses, harassed single mothers, or widowed surgeons—project an unsparingly critical self-image of Soviet women as tough, modest, vulnerable, often vain, often embittered, and frequently at the end of their tether. They have a striking lack of verbal communication with whatever males hover in their lives; they are chaste only through dearth of adequate men; they are self-sufficient, yet like many of their American peers, they are very lonely. Their melancholy, curiously loveless landscape is suffused with a Chekhovian mood of disillusionment; it is a requiem for a romantic happiness once dreamed of but never achieved. If there is one quote from classical literature that might serve as these contemporary fictions' epigraph, it is the lament of Elena in Turgenev's *Rudin:* " 'We can't live without love . . . but who is there to love?' "

Women's literature in the U.S.S.R. currently shares many striking features with contemporary women's letters in the United States. Their fictions, like ours in the 1990s, are obsessed with filial and maternal attachments, which are inevitably portrayed as far more precious than romantic ones. For the harassed young housewife of Baranskaya's "A Week Like Any Other" tends eventually to become a single, divorced woman whose life is concentrated on her child, her parents, her career, and (with luck) a few women friends. The middle-aged heroine of Baranskaya's recent story "The Kiss,"[37] for instance, a single working mom with a grown, married daughter, is offered her first romantic interlude in over a decade. While setting a festive table for her longed-for lover she receives a phone call from her beloved daughter—the baby is sick, please, Mama, I need you; and without a pang of regret or of hesitation, ten minutes before her date is scheduled to arrive, Mom packs up the dinner goodies into a shopping bag and takes the subway to attend to her darling Natasha. This literature is more than Amazonic; it is downright parthenogenetic.

Another similarity between Soviet women's writing and ours is that it tends to be familial and intimist, obsessively focused on *byt,* the minutiae of everyday domestic life. Like our own shopping-mall realism and name-brand fiction, Soviet women's writing is strikingly bourgeois, extremely concerned with the acquisition of comforts and personal belongings (seeing the decades of dearth, heaven knows their consumer obsessions are far more pardonable than ours). And as in our own literature, Soviet women's fiction is thematically far less ambitious than that of our male peers. Such grand Slavophilic motifs as salvation-through-Russianness, or women's suffering as a source of national redemption, have remained an exclusively male domain, best embodied by Rasputin's heroic old villagers, and most sublimely so by the protagonist of Solzhenitsyn's "Matryona's House" (Soviet women are not entranced by the theme of redemptive suffering).

There is one striking feature of Soviet women's fictions alien to ours: A prevalence of hospital settings. The American Slavist Elena Goscilo interprets the hospital syndrome as "a metaphorical microcosm of an ailing, segregated society in which women, its quintessential victims, join forces to struggle . . . against colossal incompetence, shoddiness, general indifference to their plight."[38] The hospital

and maternity wards repeatedly portrayed in the writings of
I. Grckova, Lyudmila Uvarova, Inna Varlamova, Viktoria Tokareva,
Lyudmila Petrushevskaya, and particularly in émigré writer Julia
Voznesenskaya's remarkable *Women's Decameron*[39] indeed offer
these authors an oblique way of criticizing the scandalously corrupt
state of Soviet medicine and other human services, the indignities
which they particularly inflict on women. But these segregated ward
settings are also literary ploys which enable literary protagonists to
speak with utmost candor and sarcasm on a popular Soviet topic—
how to effect the *perestroika* of Russian men. And by consciously
depicting women as a separate, underprivileged sector of Soviet society, they may also mark the nascence, at last, of some form of feminist
consciousness.

However fascinating and unprecedented they are as social documents, Soviet women's fictions can not yet be admired for their formal innovations. Like their creators, their heroines are often overly
sentimental and lacking in irony; their authors still tend to be confined to a rather archaic realism, and a breathless use of flashback gives
the impression that they never heard of the technique until last year,
which they may well not have. For whom do Soviet women writers
have in the way of models? They work in a culture which has long
been denied access to its own remarkable modernist tradition; in
which the very forgers of European modernism—Joyce, Kafka, Beck-
ett, Stein—are only beginning to be officially available; in which such
universal classics of women's literature as Edith Wharton, Virginia
Woolf, Colette, Doris Lessing, Simone de Beauvoir remain untranslated or virtually unobtainable.

To use Simone de Beauvoir's paradigm of Woman as the Other, as
the alienated creature solely defined, throughout history, by men's
standards and men's needs: In life as in literature, the female may still
experience a greater alienation and Otherness in the Soviet Union
than in any other advanced nation that comes to mind. But the current vigor of Soviet women's prose gives reason to believe that they
are finally gaining a voice and a room of their own in the creation of
those uniquely redemptive worlds we call fictions; and that the freedoms of Gorbachev's *glasnost* will soon enable them to express life's
most quixotic lesson: The irony and anxiety of true freedom.

XII

In Central Asia

Following the itinerary charted for us by the Soviet publisher sponsoring my trip, Nonna Volenko and I had traveled from Moscow to Latvia, to Leningrad, to Georgia, and to Uzbekistan before flying on to Siberia for the last stage of our journey.

Uzbekistan was a region I particularly looked forward to visiting. For in the last decade before the Revolution, when it was still known as Turkestan, the father of a close friend of mine had been governor of this region, which was only brought into the Russian Empire in the 1860s when the local *khans* capitulated to the Czar.

My friend's accounts of his romantic childhood in Tashkent had incited me to read more about Uzbekistan than about most other regions of the U.S.S.R. I had been particularly interested in the impact of its Moslem heritage on women's lives, and in the violence provoked by their emancipation at the time of the 1917 Revolution.

In the first decade of the Bolshevik regime, several thousand Uzbek women who obeyed state orders to discard their traditional veils were put to death by their government-defying fathers, brothers, or husbands. In one particularly famous case, the male relatives of a young girl who had discarded her veil to join the Soviet revolutionary troops had punished her by cutting off her hands, her ears and her tongue. Assuming she was dead, they had thrown her into a pit from which she was rescued by Red Army soldiers. She eventually found shelter with a group of charitable Moscow citizens who took care of her for the several decades she lived on as a deaf-mute cripple, dressing and feeding her like a small child.[40]

The continuing oppression of Uzbekistan's rural women into our own times was exposed in 1987 in a *Pravda* article,[41] with a candor toward national inequities which would have been unthinkable before Gorbachev's *glasnost*. In an essay entitled "Living Torches," *Pravda* reported that three women in a rural area of the republic, that very year, had committed suicide by self-immolation in protest against the slavery imposed upon them by archaic Moslem customs. Still bought for marriage in their early teens, forced to live with their husbands' families and to work twelve-hour days in the cotton fields, submitting to the tyranny of often sadistic mothers-in-law who refused to feed them unless they obeyed their every whim, suffering yearly pregnancies through ignorance of any birth control measures, they lived in a state of crude feudalism—apparently overlooked by three generations of Soviet leaders—equal to the most primitive regions of Iraq or Iran.

The suicides described in that *Pravda* article confirmed that the status of women in the more backward areas of Soviet Central Asia had changed little since the glorious October Revolution. "After seventy years of Soviet rule," the *Pravda* article raged, "can we not mobilize public opinion to redress such archaic injustices?"

In the past decade, the *glasnost* press had revealed Uzbekistan to be not only the most abidingly feudal of the Soviet republics, but also its most flagrantly corrupt. One of Gorbachev's first steps upon assuming power in 1985, in fact, was to purge the Central Committee of Uzbekistan's Communist Party; as exposed by his regime, the network of graft and racketeering which had thrived for two decades during the rule of Uzbek Party Chairman Sharaf Rashidov—a lethal gangster worshiped like a medieval *khan* by the Communist Party's local hierarchy—made the Gambino family's scandals seem like kindergarten candy sales.

It was in the context of these historical particulars that I observed the details of our stay in Tashkent, and the caprices of our exotic local guide, Hociat Abdullaevna. Hociat Abdullaevna (so I shall call her) is one of the more narcissistic Communists of the many Communist narcissists I've met. And she led me to understand, as clearly as any other Soviet citizen has, the various forms of corruption, self-indulgence, and inertia which Mikhail Sergeevich Gorbachev has set out to reform in the U.S.S.R.

An employee of the local *Goskomizdat,* the government publishing committee, Hociat had appeared at our hotel the morning we arrived in Tashkent to give us our first tour of the city. Dressed in a sleek turquoise silk suit, her face as whitely, thickly powdered as a kabuki dancer's, her plump mouth deep ruby-red, her hennaed hair teased into a very tall, gleaming beehive whose protection was evidently the first priority of her day, Hociat, who claims to be in her middle forties, immediately struck me as a distinctive product of the local Party system.

For reasons we could not at first decipher, our guide had arranged for us to be lodged forty minutes out of town, in a mysteriously luxurious residence whose vast terrains were circled by a high metal gate and a half-dozen guardhouses staffed by militiamen round the clock. This hostelry's lavish rose gardens and immense marbled bathrooms, its vast mahoganied suites eerily equipped with Baccarat crystal and china services for twenty-four guests, recalled the opulence of the Marcos family.

Nonna and I had instantly asked our mentor why we hadn't been put up at the standard Intourist hotel in downtown Tashkent, where most travelers had been lodged for over a decade. "Why should you suffer all the noise and heat of midtown?" Hociat exclaimed. "I only wanted the best for you," she added with that regional pride for which her republic is noted. "This was a residence of our ministers, only taken over by Intourist a month ago!"

We rode into Tashkent in the chauffeured car provided for us by Hociat's *Goskomizdat* office; our guide crouched like a halfback in the front seat to protect her coiffure from brushing the car's ceiling, alternating laments concerning her hair with a stunning display of local propaganda. "Ai, ai," she would moan at every heave in the bumpy road, sheltering her beehive with a red-clawed hand. She would then continue to boast about her lifelong work for Uzbekistan's Central Party Committee; would resume praises of the patriotic zeal with which Tashkent had rebuilt itself after the earthquake of 1966, which had destroyed all of its ancient monuments; of her republic's paradisal climate, of its fabled abundance of cotton, wine, fruit, and beautiful women, of its legendary hospitality and respect for elders ("I hear that in America you let your own *parents* starve to death").

As Hociat accompanied us to our first round of meetings with lawyers, doctors, and other local citizens, I was surprised to observe that despite the misogyny of the Moslem past, contemporary Uzbek women of the urban professional class now enjoy some of the most privileged lives in the Soviet Union. In Tashkent, a sprawling, gleaming modern town that has become the U.S.S.R.'s fourth-largest city, the percentage of women employed full time is only slightly lower than the Soviet average; they comprise some 70 percent of the republic's doctors and lawyers, and over half of its engineers. An abundance of farmers' markets, stocked almost year-round with lavish produce, spare families the horrendous food queues common to northern cities. Alcoholism—the plague of many Russian families—is almost nonexistent in Uzbekistan, and its rate of divorce is one of the three lowest in the Soviet Union.

Although it is overwhelmingly secularized, whatever Moslem traditions abide in Uzbekistan's urban population seem to work to women's advantage. Even the custom that once forbade women to exit their houses has had a curiously beneficial effect: it is still the traditional task of Uzbek men to do the family shopping. ("My wife," several Uzbeks boasted to me, "doesn't even know where the market is.") In striking contrast to European Russia, where the great majority of men shun all child-rearing and household duties, many domestic tasks—such as the cooking of the traditional lamb *shashlik* and of *plov*, the Uzbek variant of our "pilaf"—remain masculine prerogatives. Male authority also extends to the moral education of children, the supervision of schoolwork, and all issues of family discipline.

Amid this curious blend of patriarchy and male domesticity, women seem to thrive. Soviet Central Asia having lost relatively few men in World War II, the matriarchal patterns of European Russia are far less evident here. Yet there is something about the Soviet system which encourages a dominating character among its working women, regardless of ethnic origins. I felt it upon my first morning in Tashkent, when Hociat, readjusting her hairdo every few minutes with the aid of an eight-inch wide pocket mirror, took us to Uzbekistan's Ministry of Health to visit a psychiatrist who specializes in family counseling problems.

It was a quintessential Uzbek meeting in its blend of profligate hedonism and of archaic Party discipline. A stifling density of busts and photographs of Lenin pervaded every nook and cranny of the office, as it pervades every private home, kindergarten, public corridor in the republic. In a typically exhibitionist display of local abundance, the table at which we sat was laden in mid-morning with foot-high mounds of cherries, strawberries, fresh apricots, pastries, and chocolates which could have fed a northern Russian family for weeks (we would be presented with similar displays several times a day, upon each visit we made).

The psychiatrist we were appointed to meet with was flanked by Uzbekistan's Assistant Minister of Health, a dour fellow with a chest full of patriotic decorations which in the north are worn only on two or three state holidays a year; he was evidently there to ensure the orthodoxy of the psychiatrist's views. But the two men were also joined by a woman gynecologist with whom we had an appointment scheduled for that very afternoon. Upon hearing of our morning visit to the Ministry of Health, she had simply barged in, uninvited, upon her male peers. "So eager was I to meet our American guest," she explained, "that I didn't want to wait until after lunch."

This genial intruder, Dr. Shakhista Islamovna Mirzaeva—the exotic custom of blending Russian patronymics with Moslem names prevails—was a trim Uzbek beauty with a friendly smile and the array of gold teeth still considered classy throughout Soviet Central Asia. (The vogue is explained by yet another remnant of Moslem tradition which enabled a husband to divorce any of his wives at whim and thrust her out unto the street with no more possessions than she wore at that moment; upon such a misfortune, a mouthful of gold was often the only way she had to pay her way back to her own relatives.) Overlooking the fact that we had officially come to visit the psychiatrist, our gilded trespasser, Dr. Mirzaeva, instantly launched into a paean on recent improvements in the field of Uzbek gynecology ("I can't wait to show you our new East German spirals"), and confronted me with a barrage of astute questions about the state of her art in the United States. Constantly splurging on the array of sweets and fruits spread on the table, for the two hours of our visit at the Ministry of Health this Uzbek-Soviet superwoman barely let the men put in a word, answering three out of four questions I asked them, and upstaging them at every turn.

I shall always be grateful to have had Hociat Abdullaevna as my guide to Tashkent. For in her own self-assertiveness, in her combination of pre-Gorbachevian Party orthodoxy and intense hedonism, she was as exemplary an Uzbek woman as I could have hoped to observe. Hociat loved to impress us, for instance, with the total dominance she enjoyed over her husband, a handsome, sad-eyed employee of the local Ministry of Public Works. Although he was of half-Russian, half-Ukrainian descent, Hociat had so well indoctrinated him into local habits, she boasted, that she didn't remember once ever clearing the table in their fifteen years of marriage. "He washes all the dishes, and his mashed potatoes are a dream."

Yet like the gynecologist who dominated our meeting at the Ministry of Health, and the majority of Uzbek women, Hociat combined an amazonic temper with a deeply conservative view of women's roles. During her subtly stated but frequent diatribes against *perestroika*,

Hociat inevitably expressed her disapproval of Raisa Gorbachev's pre-eminence. "She shades him too much, she's too visible! She'd better remember that her primary role is to take care of her household. Our central duty as women is to be *khozyaiki,* 'housewives.' "

Hociat often hinted that she had been a ranking member of Uz-bekistan's ill-fated Central Committee, and had suffered a heartbreak-ing demise during Gorbachev's purge of its racket-ridden cliques. And there were many ways in which our vain, sloganeering Hociat re-mained an exemplary Party careerist of the Brezhnev era: In her re-solve that not one flaw in the Soviet system should ever be noticed, in her greedy materialism, and above all in the helplessness which she evidenced in most areas of daily life when deprived of the Party's cradle-to-grave nurturing. Never have Gorbachev's words on develop-ing citizens' "initiative," on curbing the extent to which they can abuse Party privileges, seemed more prescient than during the days I spent with this prehensile yet astoundingly helpless creature. For de-spite her considerable innate shrewdness, Hociat remained so depen-dent on Party offices, Party cafeterias, Party banking systems, Party phone lines, guided Party trips through the U.S.S.R., that she was innocent of most survival tactics mastered by the average Soviet citi-zen at age eighteen.

A typical day with Hociat: Over breakfast Nonna and I realize that we are out of money, and must cash the simplest Soviet equiva-lent of a travelers' check. But the only banking system Hociat has ever used is her Party savings accounts; and we waste a morning following Hociat's swaying blue-silked hips and gaudy lacquered head, the click-ety-clack of her spike heels, through the streets of Tashkent in search for a branch of the Central Government Bank.

As we wander through town our guide continues her customary prattle about the acquisition of various domestic and cosmetic ser-vices: The East German sewing machine (some four hundred dollars, with the help of Party acquaintances) her husband has promised her as a birthday gift; the health cure she takes every summer at a spa on the Black Sea (travel coupons still provided by the Party) where she applies a variety of mud packs to her face to regain her "best form"; the pair of pale blue shoes essential to the completion of her favorite costume, which only I can buy for her at one of the city's foreign-currency stores (Hociat's lust for similar commodities consumed a precious part of our crowded schedule in Tashkent). After a morning of alternately exploring the city's *beriozki* for such shoes and searching for a source of cash, we finally find a branch of the desired government bank a mere block away from Hociat's own *Goskomizdat* office.

We return to her office during lunch break to pick up some books. I urgently need to call a friend in Moscow to make some appointments for the following fortnight. And although Hociat is very eager for me to get through to Moscow—she has already asked me to ask my friend whether a certain brand of face cream which I could eventually send her is available in the capital—she has no notion of how to dial an intercity call. "Ai, ai," she moans from her desk as she reapplies her mascara, flashing her pocket mirror as she dials several wrong digits, "in the good old days at Party headquarters all such communications were made for me by our central switchboard. . . ." She never does learn how to get through to Moscow during the duration of our stay.

Next comes the matter of our plane tickets to Siberia. A car must be ordered two days ahead of time to go to the airport, and it's one of Hociat's principal duties as our local guide to arrange such details. Travel through the vastness of the Soviet Union is much complicated by the nation's twelve time zones: All plane schedules are listed in monolithic Moscow time. Nonna and I show Hociat our tickets, and ask her at what hour, Tashkent time, our plane leaves for Siberia. "It says 4 P.M.," she says didactically, "so it must be 4 P.M." "That 4 P.M. is *Moscow* time," we tell her, "we're just not sure of the exact time-zone difference between Moscow and Tashkent." Hociat anxiously smooths her beehive, calls her husband at the Ministry of Public Works. "Even he doesn't know what the time difference is between us and Moscow." She adds, in a defiant nonsequitur: "He, too, has been a Party worker all his life."

The following morning, Hociat's self-indulgence, and her ignorance of even her own republic's geography, almost leads us to miss our trip to Samarkand. We are an hour late to the airport because after forty-five years of living in Tashkent Hociat does not know that there is an hour's time-zone difference between the two cities; and because she insists on stopping at her office clinic on the way to the plane to get her daily, Party-paid vitamin E shot, which she claims is "the best recipe for an absolutely perfect skin."

One of the most popular current words among liberal Soviet intelligentsia is *veshchism*. Derived from the noun *veshch'*, "thing," the term was coined in the first decade of the Brezhnev years to express the gross materialism and moral degeneration characteristic of that epoch. As described in a recent article in *Moscow News*, *veshchism* denotes "the whirlpool of all-embracing corruption and careless work" of that era,[42] and, most particularly, the flaunting of material privileges by an increasingly powerful class of party sycophants. Our guide Hociat, the prototype of Party careerist-as-insatiable-consumer, was a microcosm of *veshchism*. And few idiosyncrasies of hers would be more instructive to us than her need to flaunt the splendor of Uzbekistan life before Gorbachev's interference, when that republic's *apparatchiks* had abused their privileges as few citizens in the Soviet Union had ever dared.

Which leads me back to why she had decided to lodge us in that mysteriously luxurious guest house that was nearly an hour from town in peak traffic; the arrangement shortened our working schedule by a good two hours a day, and piqued our curiosity from the beginning of our stay in Uzbekistan.

Upon arriving in Tashkent at 5 A.M. from Georgia, Nonna and I had been met by a driver from Hociat's *Goskomizdat* office and taken to a green enclave in the city's suburbs which was surrounded by a high, forbidding metal gate. Upon a password given by our chauffeur, a policeman standing at a guardhouse at the entrance of the compound had opened the portal. We drove into a park filled with luxuriant tropical foliage, and were ushered into a large villa which looked newly refurbished and underpopulated. A few Indian tourists were bringing down their bags to catch an early flight; the reception personnel consisted of one lonely, friendly young woman who sat on a sofa in the marbled entrance hall, watching television.

Later that morning, when Hociat had informed us that we were

SOVIET WOMEN

lodged in "a former residence of ministers," we had questioned her further. Had this been one minister's private residence? A conference center for ministerial groups? She had been evasive, instantly shunting the conversation to matters of kitchen blenders and herb facials; Nonna and I were not able to satisfy our curiosity until the end of the day, when we took an after-dinner walk into what had first looked like a few acres of garden.

The domain we found ourselves in was more akin to an Asiatic Blenheim. Taking a path from the villa's parking lot, we found ourselves walking down oak-lined alleys banked by splendid rose gardens, over delicate Chinese-style bridges that surmounted man-made ponds filled with water lilies, through meadows dotted by marble gazebos and stucco follies; the verdure was everywhere overgrown, as if upkeep had been stopped a few seasons ago.

After twenty minutes of walking we suddenly came upon another large villa, approximately the size of our own lodging, through whose windows there still sparkled the crystal of many chandeliers. Walking on, we came in sight of an immense swimming pool, more rose gardens, more follies and gazebos, more lily ponds flecked with carp, and saw in the distance still another palatial villa. . . . "What *is* all this?" I kept asking Nonna. "It is a place," she said with her ironic, never-failing wisdom about all Soviet state matters, "which I'm certain they'd rather we not see."

Hardly had Nonna spoken when a young Uzbek policeman biked up to us, and courteously asked us who we were. "We're guests of the new Intourist residence," we answered. "I fear you'll have to go right back there," he said. "But no one told us not to take a walk," we protested. "They just haven't had the time to post any notices," he replied. The policeman silently accompanied us to the entrance of the hotel, walking his bike beside us. He saw us to the steps of our hostelry, said with an embarrassed smile, "Sorry, such are my orders," and rode away.

Before going to my room, I asked the lonely hotel clerk about the nature of the vast estate in which we resided. Who, precisely, had owned it before Intourist had acquired it? "This was a *dacha* of our former Party chairman," she answered pleasantly. "You mean Sharaf

Rashidov?" I asked. "Yes, yes, you are well informed about us," she said with pride.

I went to bed, my curiosity sated: Due to my abiding interest in a friend's colonial childhood in Tashkent, I knew a few things about the former Uzbek Party chief, Sharaf Rashidov, who during the Brezhnev years had accumulated a multimillion-dollar fortune through a vast network of graft and corruption. His reign of terror had led to the largest government scandal of the post-Stalin era, one that reached to the uppermost hierarchy of the Brezhnev regime, and directly implicated members of Brezhnev's own family.

Under Sharaf Rashidov, government awards and ministerial posts, *dachas,* Party membership cards, literary prizes, every possible form of reward and privilege, even places in cemeteries, were sold to citizens of Uzbekistan by the Republic's Central Committee in return for cash bribes that ranged between ten thousand rubles (the directorship of a school) and several million (a seat on the Central Committee itself). Uzbekistan is the U.S.S.R.'s largest provider of cotton; and one of Rashidov's favorite forms of embezzlement was to distort the amount of cotton grown in his republic by millions of tons, putting an equivalent number of rubles into his own pocket.[43]

Another example of Rashidov's *veshchism* (he is described by survivors of his regime as "a gray, very neutral man, not your typical flamboyant dictator") was his obsession for gold. Some of the most striking artifacts found by Gorbachev's investigators, when they swept into Uzbekistan in 1985, were life-size gold statues of Rashidov placed in his numerous palatial *dachas;* several hundred gold-embroidered fur coats custom-made at Rashidov's order as presents for Brezhnev; and thousands of trunkfuls of gold watches, jewelry, and coins from czarist times *(chervontzi,* or ten-ruble prerevolutionary coins, the most valued form of gold available in the U.S.S.R., are an illegal possession particularly prized by Party bigwigs). As my companion Nonna astutely observed, "It's in the local Moslem tradition to worship a *khan,* an absolute ruler. Their need to be tyrannized is even deeper than the Russians'."

Brezhnev's "Stagnancy" era had been replete with many similar instances of profligate decadence: In the late 1970s, for instance, the Party chief of Azerbaijan built an opulent white marble palace overlooking the Caspian Sea—complete with indoor swimming pool, sauna, and movie hall—for the exclusive purpose of lodging Brezhncv during a two-day stay. After the leader's weekend in Baku the residence was locked up and never used again until 1987, when the Gorbachev regime started revamping thousands of such "guest houses" into kindergartens, sanatoriums, and Intourist hotels—the history of our own lodgings in Tashkent.

But Rashidov's reign was marked by far more murderous fetishisms: He commanded a personal guard of several thousand men that amounted to a private army and a network of underground jails into which several hundred Soviet citizens considered too inquisitive vanished forever. Rashidov also disappeared from sight in 1985—the very year Gorbachev's prosecutors swept into Uzbekistan—in circumstances as grim and bizarre as the ones under which he had ruled: His body was never found; some think that he committed suicide; others believe that Rashidov was poisoned by members of his private army, who feared that he might reveal their roles in his crimes.

The demise of this oriental Party *khan*, however, made his local cult all the more fervent. A few months after his disappearance, the Central Committee of Uzbekistan's Communist Party erected an immense memorial to the dead leader; it also passed a "Resolution on Perpetuating the Memory of Sharaf Rashidov," which forced all Pioneer groups to stage monthly celebrations at his shrine, and ordered city officials to take all tourists to the site. Despite Moscow's official protests against these observances the rituals prevailed for several years, until the Kremlin passed a severe law banning all manifestations of honor or respect for the tyrant. The Rashidov cult went underground, and took on symbolic forms which are said to be still observed to this day.[44]

The Rashidov case became increasingly notorious because of the high-ranking Moscow officials, accused of taking million-dollar bribes to keep silent about the Uzbek chieftain's crimes, who finally went on trial in the autumn of 1988. Named in the indictment were Brezhnev's Minister of the Interior, who committed suicide during the investigations; and Brezhnev's own son-in-law, Yuri Churbanov, an inept lug who had used his family connections to fawn and fake his way to the number-two job at the same ministry. And although she did not testify in court, the trial was made all the more lurid by the character of Churbanov's wife, Galina Brezhnev, a flamboyant *high-life-itsa,* as Soviet jet-setters are called, with extravagant tastes in foreign clothes and jewelry, reputed links to the U.S.S.R.'s vast network of organized crime,[45] and an erotic preference for circus performers. (She is also rumored to have used circus animals as a means of transporting jewelry in and out of the Soviet Union, hiding diamonds in certain orifices of elephants' bodies.)

At the trial's end in the last days of 1988, Churbanov was convicted and sentenced to twelve years in a labor camp on charges of accepting six-figure bribes to protect widespread fraud in the Uzbekistan cotton industry. His Uzbek co-defendants, former high-ranking police officials under Rashidov's regime, received similar sentences. The Churbanov case became a symbolic indictment of the entire Brezhnev era, and the day before the trial's end the Soviet government announced that it was stripping Brezhnev's name from all public sites throughout the U.S.S.R.—streets, schools, factories, naval vessels.[46]

So it was in one of the hundreds of luxurious private *dachas* built by Rashidov on his racketeer's fortune that our guide Hociat Abdullaevna, a dedicated Party worker during the gangster's tenure, decided to house us during our stay in Tashkent. It is interesting to decode the blend of cheekiness, regional chauvinism, and extreme naiveté which might lead an ultrafervent Communist to offer a foreigner such intimate details of Party corruption, and of her nation's moral debacle. Might this form of exhibitionism have been a tribute, even subconsciously, to the dead tyrant so adulated in her republic?

Hociat tried to flaunt the splendors of Uzbekistan until the last minute of our stay. The night before our departure, she arranged a dinner feast at the home of a "Party colleague" which made even the most fabled Georgian banquets look like austere church breakfasts.

Our hosts were a couple in their late thirties with five beautiful children. At center table, the traditional bowls of apricots, strawberries, cherries, were flanked by assortments of greens worthy of the most lavish Mediterranean feasts: bunches of tarragon, parsley, dill, fennel; zucchini squash, lettuces, green peppers, and tomatoes, many *zakuski* of still other fresh vegetables—grated carrots with mayonnaise and walnuts, puréed beets with garlic. The menu proceeded to *lagman,* a thick soup of lamb shanks, potatoes, chick-peas, and noodles; steaming bowls of *manty,* or meat-filled dumplings, an Uzbek variant of Russian *pelemeni;* a *shashlik* of lamb and onions; abundant desserts of varied honey-and-nut sweets.

I kept recalling the last meal I'd had in a friend's house in Leningrad, at which the menu consisted of a scrawny chicken, a few cucumbers, radishes, and apples, for which I'd stood in line with my hostess for an hour and a half in three different stores. I thought back to the various diseases caused by vitamin deficiencies in the U.S.S.R.'s northern regions—rickets, anemia, rotting teeth. And I wondered again, as I had in Georgia, what massive malfunctions of technology, what phenomenally backward transportation systems, what further forms of local and central government corruption prevented the health-giving bounties of Central Asia from ever reaching the nation's other regions.

To my right sat Hociat's husband, a handsome and obviously henpecked Russian with kind, sad eyes who had taken up jogging after reading our own Dr. Fixx while he was being "retrained" at a Party school, and now ran fifteen miles every morning after rising from his wife's bed. He alternated vodka and cognac, Russian style (our Uzbek hosts abstemiously drank mineral water) while Hociat questioned me relentlessly about American domestic habits. Was it true, she particularly wanted to know, that some American women allow their husbands to handle family finances? Such a custom was unknown in the Soviet Union. I had to admit, didn't I, that 80 percent of Americans were homeless? We spent an hour arguing over this statistic from a decade-old issue of *Izvestia,* which she still looked upon as the Bible of universal truth.

In front of me sat our host, an expansive, jovial *apparatchik* who was waited on at table by his cheerful, gold-toothed wife and sister-in-law. "Up to five years ago," as he nostalgically put it (I mentally registered all such dates in terms of Rashidovian, pre-Gorbachev times) he had yearly enjoyed Party-organized boat cruises on which he'd visited most every Western nation: France, Ireland, Italy, Scandinavia. During my stay in Tashkent, it had become obvious to me that Hociat and her pals were once members of that bloated, 2-million-strong corps of full-time Party workers which Gorbachev has begun to whittle down to one tenth of its prior size. Throughout my months of travel in the Soviet Union, this Uzbek feast would be the only social occasion at which not a single mention was made of Gorbachev or *perestroika.*

We watched the year's most popular television show, the *telemost,* or television-bridge, between the "paired" cities of Seattle, U.S.A., and Tashkent, U.S.S.R. More dead than alive, we rose from the table at half-past midnight, five hours after we'd sat down, ending the visit with those ritual compliments to Uzbek hospitality which are customary to this profligate republic. Driving back to Sharaf Rashidov's former *dacha,* Nonna and I speculated about which oblique channels of the Uzbek Party apparatus had helped in financing our feast: it must have cost the equivalent of three hundred dollars.

Despite the precious time Hociat wasted with her coquetry and helplessness, I have remained indebted to her for offering me precious insights into the mind of an exotically archaic, un-*perestroied* Soviet woman's mind. I have been filled with gratitude for the blundering way in which she led me to the very heart of Brezhnev's *Zastoi:* of that era during which an indolent leader who gloated on his dozens of hunting lodges and his seventy foreign cars permitted the chieftains of distant republics to run their fiefs like medieval war lords, and allowed his entire nation to lapse into that Stagnancy which will label his tenure for centuries to come.

For the eighteen years of the Brezhnev era were also those in which the original Bolshevik ideals, already betrayed by Stalin, further degenerated into widespread graft and self-contented torpor; when national productivity declined to one third of its former capacity, consumption of alcohol quadrupled, absenteeism on the job and black-market racketeering reached unparalleled heights; when the growth of personal savings grew from 11 billion to 200 billion, a rate unique in history, and a spiraling greed for consumer goods was accompanied by a tragic decline in human services; when the rate of infant mortality

SOVIET WOMEN

grew by 50 percent, and the Party apparatus pilfered the citizenry with a materialism unequaled since the glorious October Revolution, breeding a mood of cynicism which poisons the nation to this day.[47]

I glimpsed the reality of that era most clearly in Soviet Central Asia, thanks to the chauvinism and very feminine vanity of one of its former beneficiaries.

XIII

Women at the Edge

Fatima Kerimovna, a warehouse worker of the Tartar nationality, talked constantly about suicide in the months following the death of her seven-year-old son. The child had been vacationing with his father in the Caucasus. The father fell asleep at the side of a lake during an afternoon outing. Left unattended, the boy drowned.

After the funeral Fatima left Moscow with her baby daughter and returned to her hometown, Gorky, to live with her mother. Fatima's husband pleaded with her to come home. But she blamed him harshly for the tragedy. She said she could never trust him with a child again.

"He was such a good husband, he never drank, he earned 250 rubles a month as a construction worker," Fatima says many months later, while being treated at a psychiatric clinic in Moscow. "But after

SOVIET WOMEN

it happened I couldn't bear the sight of him, I threw everything in his face, I was ready to kill him. And even during my first months here at the clinic I refused to see him. Now I'm calmer, now I just keep silent, he can come once a week. He wants to visit every day, but I would get sick again. Yet I understand how much he also suffers, his hair turned gray in the one week after our boy died. . . ."

Fatima is a small, compact woman with high cheekbones and grieving brown eyes. She rubs her hands together many times as we talk, smooths a hand over her bun of dark hair to compose herself.

"On top of all that, there were other griefs," Fatima says softly. "We'd been living in a communal flat; after my daughter was born, since we were a family of four, we were wait-listed for a two-room apartment. But when my boy died and we were three again, the authorities immediately took us off the waiting list and told us we had to stay in our communal flat. I was too weak to fight the bureaucracy back. And imagine! The two room flat we almost got even had a balcony!" She shakes her head in disbelief.

(The graduation from communal lodgings to a two-room apartment is a potent symbol of status and achievement. A balcony—a place to sit and hang out wash in summer, to use as an extra icebox in winter—remains a lifelong Utopia for many citizens.)

"And then, and then," Fatima adds with a sigh. "Just two weeks ago, I almost lost my youngest brother, I may still lose him. He's a policeman and as a hobby he plays jazz guitar in a club. One night a group of *rockers* burst into the place on their motorcycles, went right through the doors and windows of the club, and started beating up everyone right and left. They wounded a half-dozen people, critically. My brother's still unconscious, there's a hope he might live, but he might be an invalid, a vegetable. A beautiful young man, just thirty, with a new family of his own . . ."

Fatima looks down at her hands, biting her lip.

"The youngest brother is especially dear in Tartar families," she whispers. "The *rockers* were all arrested, but does that allay my grief? My mother has come back from Gorky with my daughter to take care of my sister-in-law, to take care of all of us."

She collects herself, looks up at me again. "Soon I'll be able to return to my husband, I think. We want another child. He feels great guilt."

Masha, seventeen years old, attempted suicide shortly after one of her two boyfriends was drafted into the Army and she was refused admission into the Moscow Hairdressing Institute. Her father is a truck driver. Both boyfriends are factory workers. There were other extenuating circumstances. Masha's mother, to whom she was very close, died of cancer two years ago. Her father immediately took up with another woman, who moved into their flat a few weeks after Masha's mother died.

What confuses Masha further is that the first of her boyfriends, Igor, was "a tough unfeeling guy," the second one, Sasha, is "a gentle, kind one." So gentle that he could not put an end to the intrusions of the tough guy, who kept trying to break up Masha's new love affair.

"And now that Sasha's gone into the Army there's no one to defend me from Igor, there's no one to take care of me," Masha says.

Masha is slender and very pretty, with short brown-and-red streaked hair combed up in a brush cut and elaborately long bangs. Every minute or so, especially when she pauses for an answer, she blows upward provocatively at her bangs.

As she states her fear of being at the mercy of "the tough guy," Masha looks at me with a sideways glance that is flirtatious and defiant. Trying to end her life, she says, she swallowed every pill and syrup she could find in her father's apartment—cough medicines, sedatives, laxatives, all that remained of her mother's cancer medications.

It has been Masha's obsession since childhood to get into the Hairdressing Institute. It is a prestigious profession; the *konkurs*—competition—is very tough, offering only one place for every six applicants. Her father opposed her studying hairdressing, he wished her to attend the Culinary Institute, so when she didn't get into hairdressing school she spent a few unhappy months at the Culinary. Next year she will try again to get into hairdressing school—the evening sessions, this time—and support herself by working daytimes in a restaurant.

SOVIET WOMEN

I ask Masha how she used to spend her leisure time when things were still okay, when she was out with the tough guy, or, later, with the kind guy. "We hung out with pals in bars, listening to rock," she says. I ask her who her favorite bands are.

"Michael Jackson," she answers with her first smile of pleasure, "Billy Joel, Durand Durand. But of course it's all over so early. We've got to get there by 8 or 9 and everything closes up at 11 P.M. And we can't drink there until we're twenty-one. There's nothing interesting in this country on television," she adds as if to explain the vacuum in the lives of her peers.

I ask Masha if she's taken drugs. She nods her head casually. "Sure, we inhale a lot—glue, resin, turpentine." How long is the high? I ask. Is there any depression afterward? "No, two or three minutes of euphoria, then it's all back to normal. I like it. I always take it in groups. We also smoke *anasha*, hashish." I ask her where she and her friends get money for hashish. "It's not that expensive," she answers, blowing up defiantly at her bangs. "They try to hook you on it, so they give it to you for free."

I ask Masha whether she belongs to political youth groups. "I'm a *komsomolka*," she says with a certain pride. "At the age of fourteen I took it very seriously, I was the leader of my group. But then I realized that the Komsomol has lost all its prestige, how meaningless it is."

There is a silence.

"My generation has no values," Masha adds. She thinks a bit, blowing up at her bangs again. "Igor, the tough guy, is also scheduled to be drafted into the Army soon, so then I'll be rid of him and I can quietly wait for Sasha to return."

"Maybe when that happens you'll get well enough to go home," the psychiatrist in whose office we are meeting suggests. "Maybe," Masha answers, casting her eyes coquettishly toward the doctor. "You've helped me a lot."

I ask Masha if she ever discusses *perestroika* with her friends. "Oh yes, a lot. We constantly try to retain our hope in it. We're particularly excited by the idea of cooperatives." What kinds of cooperatives does she find most interesting? "Pastry-baking cooperatives, clothing cooperatives."

I ask if there were any sex education classes in Masha's school. She gives me a jaded smile, as if to say, you know the answer to *that*. "Zilch," she says. "Nothing to read about it, no manuals, nothing. Many girls start sex when they're eleven or twelve."

I ask her at what age she'd started. She looks at me more defiantly than ever. *"Ia yeshcho ne zhila,"* she answers, "I haven't lived yet." ("A hundred and forty times she's a virgin," the psychiatrist at my elbow whispers caustically.)

Ten years from now, Masha tells me later, if she could choose her ideal life, if she could "play God" and get everything she wanted, this is how it would be: She would be married to a "beloved man" and have two children and a two-room flat with a balcony. She would have her "beloved work," hairdressing. Thanks to the new laws on privately owned cooperatives she would have a little hair parlor in her own home—two hair driers, one washbasin, a manicure table. She'd live in the vicinity of Lenin Prospekt, in the very same district where she was brought up, she wouldn't think of living anywhere else.

Elena, a twenty-eight-year-old mother of two who works in an electrical appliances factory, has twice attempted suicide because of her husband's infidelities.

"I'm here at the clinic," she tells me very forthrightly, "because I'm constantly terrified that someone at the factory will talk about his unfaithfulness. I'm ashamed. When I was told he went with other women he half denied it and I knew he was lying. It's the shame at my work collective that I fear most. Better death than scandal at the collective. I love my work, I verify electric outlets and lamps, it's very careful, responsible work. I began to be sleepy at the factory because I cried so much at home, they started scolding me, that's when it became unbearable and I tried to hang myself . . ."

Elena is in her second marriage. She was first married when she was twenty-two, divorced that husband even before their child was born because he was a schizophrenic; even without drinking he had fits, hallucinations, broke everything in sight. Her present husband is a friend from childhood, "a good man who helped a lot at home, did the child's laundry, even washed dishes." But somehow their relations went bad after their baby died.

I ask Elena which of her friends have been most supportive since she's been at the clinic. "Men friends from my work collective," she says assertively. "The guys have been fantastic. I only have one single woman friend whom I can trust, but many close men friends—at least half a dozen."

"Our Elena Maximovna has great success with men," the psychiatrist says with a gentle smile. Elena looks at her fondly. "Aina Grigoryevna understood and cured me so well that I'm happier with myself now, I'm going home on Friday."

For Elena finally seems ready to go home and face life without a man. "I have a mother and a five-year-old daughter whom I love, I live with them in a two-room apartment," she says. "My mother brought me up to think that an unmarried woman is a nothing, 'neither fish nor fowl,' but I'll give it a try. I have my beloved work, all work in the soviet Union has become much more rewarding in the past years. We all have to struggle, we have to work very very hard to help Mikhail Sergeevich."

I ask Elena how she conceives her ideal life ten, fifteen years from now.

"I'd like to have exactly the same work as I have now," she answers. "I think I want my husband to return. I'm happy with the flat I have now, I don't want any more possessions. But above all, throughout my life I want to maintain close bonds with my daughter and my mother—my grandmother and my mother were very close and lived together, and that's how it should remain from generation to generation, mother-and-daughter bonds must remain intact."

"Like a *matrioshka?*" I suggest.

Elena clapped her hands and laughed. "Yes, yes," she agrees, "like a *matrioshka!*"

I wished the two other patients were as ready to go home as Elena was. I was awed by the rootedness, the frugal modesty of such women's expectations: No car, a two-room apartment, the same beloved job, the same pay, the desire to live on in the very same part of the city in which they were brought up—ideally, in most cases, with Mother, and a child of their own.

The clinic in which these women were being healed and probably saved, Moscow's Center for Suicide Prevention, is the only institution of its kind in the Soviet Union. Dr. Aina Grigoryevna Ambrumova, its founder and director, is as visionary a scientist as I have met in that country.

For before her pioneering work, the discipline of "social psychology"—the treatment of "healthy" persons suffering from borderline neuroses caused by some life crisis—barely existed in the Soviet Union. There was only "big psychiatry"—the treatment of epilepsy, schizophrenia, genuine insanity. As Dr. Ambrumova puts it, "until a decade ago our government still believed that a Soviet person didn't have the right to weep out of love or suffer from loss, that he had no rights at all except to stand stoically under all of life's circumstances in the service of his country. And if he didn't fulfill these conditions he was considered useless, locked up in a psychiatric ward with the truly mad, and rendered mad in the process."

Aina Ambrumova is a frail, coquettish, indefatigable militant in her early seventies. She has a taste for Solzhenitsyn, English furniture, and religious discussions, and a peppery wit. When I first visited her at the Center for Suicide Prevention, it was shortly after she had suffered a concussion in an almost fatal car accident; but three days later she had valiantly returned to work, a trim blond wig set over her bandaged skull, her cashmere sweater gleaming with garnet jewelry. She toured me proudly through the clinic, which is one of the most cheerful interiors in Moscow: walls freshly painted in tones of rose and blue, four-bed wards filled with fresh flowers, airy sitting rooms furnished with handsome sofas and armchairs donated by a British supporter.

Dr. Ambrumova was born of Armenian parents in Baku, Azerbaijan. Shortly after obtaining her degree in medicine, during World War II, she was assigned to Georgia to work with wounded Red Army soldiers who had suffered psychological trauma in the battlefield. It was during this fieldwork that Ambrumova began to be interested in "what happens to normal people under extreme situations," and in the importance of "talking things out" in any process of therapy. It was in the decades following the war years, after she'd moved to Moscow and begun to teach psychiatric medicine, that she became obsessed by the problem of suicide, whose incidence was to triple in the U.S.S.R. during the Khrushchev and Brezhnev years.

Until very recently, Soviet medicine assumed that any person who made a suicide attempt was a schizophrenic, and could be healed only in psychiatric hospitals. But Ambrumova had long ago learned that 75 percent of suicides are "normal" persons suffering from borderline mental problems; she made it her life's mission to heal and eradicate suicide's root causes.

In 1970, with great difficulties, at a time when the Soviet Ministry of Health was still staffed with "nightmarishly backward people of medieval ignorance," Ambrumova opened her first psychological counseling center in a wing of a Moscow hospital, and staffed it with her graduate students. Perhaps because it was the first medical service of its kind where citizens could be treated anonymously, without fearing that a psychological "problem" might stigmatize their career, it was filled to overflowing. Within a few years, under a somewhat more enlightened Ministry of Health, Ambrumova was able to enlarge the service to a network of twenty-one such centers throughout Moscow.

By the mid-seventies, Ambrumova had expanded her program to a score of cities in the U.S.S.R.—Tallinn, Leningrad, Vilnius, Minsk, Riga, Dnepropetrovsk, Kazan, Rostov. She had started another service unprecedented in her country: A "Phone Crisis Center," staffed around the clock by forty-four psychiatrists, which enables Moscow citizens to talk out their problems at any time of day or night. Due to the rising rate of divorce, the decline of the three-generational family, a vast increase in the number of persons living alone, the legendarily communal Soviet citizen seems to have discovered solitude. And although the average telephone call lasts forty-five minutes, the compassionate psychiatrists manning the crisis center's phone lines sometimes let their callers ramble on for two or three hours. Many callers are simply lonely, and merely call to discuss some book or article they've read—such citizens might be enthusiastic but confused about the new freedoms of *glasnost,* and have no one to discuss it with.

The service is widely advertised in newspapers and street posters.

The center averages some seven hundred calls a day. Seventy percent of the callers, whose ages range from fifteen to eighty, are women. Common problems: Teenager-parental conflicts, the death of loved ones, old-age loneliness, single-mother family worries, concern about incipient alcoholism and narcotic addiction, love quandaries concerning change of partners—betrayal, lack of trust. Adolescent pregnancy is another increasingly frequent issue. Ambrumova's staffers advise abortion if the girl is under fifteen; if she is older they counsel her to talk about it to both her mother and her grandmother—a *babushka*, curiously, tends to be far more liberal, and often is more willing to take charge of the baby.

According to Ambrumova, her counseling network has cut Moscow's suicide rate to one ninth of its 1970 level. The strength of her Phone Crisis Center is that its psychiatrists are well trained to estimate whether their callers need more personal psychological help. One out of four callers mention suicidal impulses, and are immediately referred to Ambrumova's network of counseling centers; if the crisis seems acute they are asked to report instantly to the in-patient clinic in which Fatima, Masha, and Elena were treated.

The in-patient branch of the suicide prevention network, which she looks on as "a halfway house," is Ambrumova's pride and joy. It accommodates thirty persons and is lodged in a wing of Moscow's Public Hospital No. 20., which has full surgical and emergency facilities. A great majority of its occupants, at any time, are women—the first time I visited it, there were twenty-eight women and two men. Ambrumova attributes this disproportion to the fact that four times as many Soviet men as women are successful in their suicide attempts.

During one of my several visits to Ambrumova's clinic, over the festive lunch of caviar, roast goose, and sweets which she insists on serving to her visitors, Aina Grigoryevna spoke of her religious beliefs —she never stopped going to church, even in the Stalin years. She has recently started to invite Orthodox priests into her counseling program. "An intelligent priest is a philosopher and healer. He can work with our doctors, offer his compassion, give the patients his blessings to have a good life and a happy road ahead. Religious faith is ineradicable in our people, you'd be surprised how many soldiers wore crosses around their necks in wartime, they were never reported. Our people

SOVIET WOMEN

have been ruined through their inability to practice their faith. This is the first country in history built without spiritual foundations . . . it's only now, thanks to Mikhail Sergeevich, that we can return to normal life. But it may just be too late."

Like most Soviet citizens over sixty, Ambrumova focuses quite as much on Stalin as on Brezhnev's "Stagnancy" (the butt of the younger generation's hatred) when analyzing her country's misfortunes. "Stalin was a profoundly diseased, psychiatrically ailing man, and he induced true schizophrenia in us: We used to publicly heap praise on our successes and internally weep about our flaws, there was a total contradiction between our interior and exterior lives—why do you think psychological services such as ours are so needed?

"Brezhnev's legacy was of a different order of evil," she added. "It bred cynicism, which has far more terrible effects in women than in men. Our women seemed to have taken two paths as a reaction to the Stagnancy: The healthier part of them retreated into a cloying domesticity, indulged in tasks their mothers never had the time for, sewing, baking, knitting. But the rest—those who became cynical—turned to drugs and alcoholism . . . And in Russia female alcoholism is much uglier and more destructive than men's, it carries a far greater stigma and isolation than in other nations, it's more devastating to the family structure than anywhere else because of the absence of fathers in our society . . ."

I once told Ambrumova that one of the more curious aspects of Moscow life, for a woman traveling alone, is to walk through the city late at night, ride its subways into the early hours of the morning, without any threat of assault or robbery. She looked at me very skeptically.

"We now have everything you have in the U.S.A., prostitution, Mafiosi, narcotic addiction," she retorted in her peppery voice, "and we're so diseased that it's growing very fast. Soon there'll be ten times as many *rocker* gangs like the ones who almost killed Fatima's brother, ten times as many girls like little Masha sniffing glue and worse, soon we'll be like New York, you won't be able to walk in the streets of Moscow past 6 P.M."

XIV

Why They Dress Up

She was the floor attendant at my hotel in Tbilisi, a plump, tired-looking woman in her thirties who earned a hundred rubles a month working three twenty-four-hour shifts a week. And she came into my room one morning to show off a skirt of faded blue jean material (a current Soviet fad that has replaced the vogue for trouser jeans), which she had just bought for a hundred and fifty rubles, or 12 percent of her year's salary. "A bargain!" she exclaimed, "an absolute bargain!"

She had bought it the night before, she went on to explain, from one of the Polish contrabandists who cross the Soviet frontier by the thousands every weekend, their suitcases filled with Western goods from West Germany, France, Italy. Poles enjoy an exchangeable currency, and have been obtaining visas to travel abroad with increasing ease. News of the Polish teams' arrival, my acquaintance informed me, spreads in a matter of hours in any Soviet city. Parties are held in hotel rooms or private homes at which the goods are displayed and bought. The contrabandists, in turn, go on to purchase Soviet commodities not findable in Poland—electrical household appliances, gold—which they resell at high prices in their own country.

"And what a bargain," the floor attendant repeated, twirling in front of the hall mirror in her new skirt, "seeing current black-market prices!" She went on to recite a familiar litany about the uselessness of Soviet-made clothes: Why pay eighty rubles for those shoes you see in our windows, which will fall apart in three months, and you've already had to bribe the salesgirl with a bottle of cognac to put them aside for you. So better wait for the Poles to bring you a decent pair of Austrian ones, a hundred and fifty rubles—an entire month's pay, but how are you going to keep up your morale except by dressing up . . .

(However exorbitant these sums may seem, they fit quite accurately into the demented range of the Georgian black market. It is a region whose high standard of living, the highest in the U.S.S.R., encourages a particularly developed system of *blat.* The worst curse you can speak to a Georgian is "May you have to live off your salary." In Tbilisi, a pair of American shoes, "Topsider" brand, can bring seven hundred dollars; a wool outfit from Pierre Cardin—three thousand dollars, four times the Paris or New York price. The sums were given me by my friend Kakha, an ever impeccable source of information who was proud of his own two-thousand-dollar West German suit.)

As the floor attendant proudly displayed her bedraggled new swath of denim, I asked her for whose sake, in her opinion, Soviet women made such sacrifices to fashion. To heighten their self-esteem? To be more seductive to men?

The latter notion struck my acquaintance as hilarious. "For *men!* Do you think they ever get out of their selfish little brains to *notice* what we wear?"

She twirled again before the mirror and added: "No, no, you see, life is bleak, and this is one of the few inner joys I can buy, and the girls at work . . . *they* will be so impressed."

To achieve some inner joy, as my Tbilisi acquaintance put it, by being festively attired; to rise in the esteem of the predominantly female members of one's work collective; and above all to impress them with that highest status symbol of Soviet life, a foreign label, or *firma*—these are the major reasons given by our Soviet peers for their pathological obsession with fashion. I've met few who will not readily admit, with a certain pride, that they put greater importance on outward appearance than any other community of women in the world. And any American who lives for a while in the U.S.S.R. is in turn amazed, appalled, and awed by the passion and energy her Soviet contemporaries exert in their search for imported clothing and cosmetics.

Amazed and appalled, at first, that highly educated women should dedicate so many hours of the day to what most of us look on as frivolous trifles. Awed, after the first weeks, when it becomes clear that this addiction for an impeccable, coquettish appearance has little or nothing to do with narcissism; that it is more akin to the compulsive grooming instinct of a healthy cat or bird; that it may be the only way of cheering the uniform drabness of Soviet life, and of establishing a status in its complex hierarchy.

The fixation on costume, the constant scrutiny of every other woman's way of dress, plays a major part in what I've come to call the Dreadful Soviet Gaze, that blend of safety detection, ethnic pigeonholing, and status-definition with which Soviets devastate each other in all public places.

One might divide the Dreadful Gaze into three separate components: Conditioned by decades and centuries of political state terror, it immediately sizes up whether a person is trustable or not, potential enemy or friend. Almost simultaneously, the Gaze swiftly classifies the citizen's ethnic components—that dash of Tartar or Byelorussian blood, that blend of Jew, Moldavian, Georgian, or any of the other hundred nationalities fused in the Soviet melting pot. These two estimates—the first loaded with survival value, the second fairly neutral—

are made at lightning speed. It is the third component of the Dreadful Gaze that is the most time-consuming, particularly among women: the decoding of a person's social status through his or her way of dress.

Sitting in any Soviet research library, for instance, one is struck by the hours its women occupants spend looking up from their texts, dedicating their attention to scrutinizing other women in the room. In any such public space, as my Soviet friends describe it, women's thoughts tend to run on in somewhat this manner: "This one's Italian skirt must have been bought in that new consignment shop off Petrovskaya Street . . . that one's blouse is French and she may be the girlfriend of a foreign diplomat, nice little detail on the collar, I must reproduce it on my sewing machine . . . as for those shoes and pocketbook they must have been bought from the latest Polish team, or even more likely on a recent trip to Hungary, so she must be a member of the Party . . ."

So powerful are these obsessions, my informants estimate, that the average woman scholar at the Lenin Library, say, will spend at least half her study time involved in such perusals.

The Soviet woman with whom I recently traveled throughout the U.S.S.R.—Nonna Volenko—is a forty-year-old honors graduate of her country's most competitive linguistic institute, a brilliant literary scholar who can recite by heart thousands of lines of Russian, British, and American poetry. Her vocation is to translate Russian poetry into English. Married to a man of equal intellectual gifts, she is selfless, beautiful, generous to a fault, a person of religious bent constantly obsessed by the needs of others. I came to love Nonna during our weeks together, and was all the more fascinated that even this spiritual a creature was imbued with the national fashion fixation. Like most of her peers, Nonna can spend many hours of the month scouring Moscow consignment shops for that little blouse or skirt with an air of *firma,* many hours of the week at her sewing machine attempting to reproduce the line of some seductive item glimpsed in *Vogue, Burda,* or *Elle* (Western fashion magazines sell for some fifty dollars a copy on the Moscow black market).

Impatient, like all her peers, with the pathetic quality of Soviet goods, Nonna even makes her own coats, fur hats, and jewelry, pasting and twisting and threading beads onto gold or silver wire. During our weeks together, there was not one hour out of twenty-four when my scholarly companion was not put together with cover-girl fastidiousness. Hair washed daily and blow-dried into a seductive bob, subtly highlighted eyes freshened every hour, lacy stockings cunningly matched to a festive skirt of home design and alluring shoes, she remained, like my mother, my aunts, all the White Russian women who'd brought me up, voluptuous yet curiously prim, a model of decorous matronly elegance.

From the first day of our trip, Nonna began to scrutinize my getup as carefully as she did her own, turning her Dreadful Soviet Gaze upon me every morning to examine me head to toe for a few difficult minutes. Not even my fashion-obsessed Russian mother had ever stared at me so searingly. And I knew that my gentle, saintly friend needed to be constantly reassured that no detail of her American traveling companion's clothing, sparse makeup, or deplorably casual hair would make a "bad impression" (crucial phrase) on the Soviet citizens we were scheduled to visit with that particular day.

Such was the intensity of Nonna's scrutiny, in fact, that one evening in Riga she unwittingly detected in my right eye the result of cataract surgery; barely visible to the naked eye except to medical specialists, it had gone unnoticed for four years by my relatives or closest friends. "There is a tiny, tiny golden fleck on your right eye," she observed, "which makes it a *trifle* different from your left eye." She was cheered to hear that the reflection was caused by a plastic lens implant rather than by faulty makeup, and continued to sear me head to toe with the Gaze until she detected a one-inch tear on the bottom of my raincoat. She insisted, almost by force, on taking it to her room to mend it, declaring: "I will not *allow* you to leave for Leningrad in such a state of disorder."

One surprising result of this obsession with outward appearance, I discovered during my travels, is that Soviet hairdressers are among the best in the world. It can be very difficult to even *get* into such an establishment in a nation so obsessed with cosmetology: The queues begin at six-thirty; as I reached the beauty parlor nearest my hotel one morning at seven-thirty, I was advised that there would be a minimum of two hours' wait. But be it in Leningrad or Irkutsk, whenever I was able to talk myself into an appointment I enjoyed some of the swiftest, most skilled hands I've ever experienced in the coiffure business; first-rate Hungarian and East German products; and, for the equivalent of about three dollars for shampoo-and-set, an aura of amiable competence which would put to shame many beauty parlors in Paris or Rome.

A central factor in the national fashion fixation is the feudalism which prevailed in Russia until well into the nineteenth century, far later than in Western Europe, and the sumptuary laws that inevitably attended it. Until my own *babushka*'s generation very specific clothes were assigned to specific classes, specific hairstyles distinguishing married from unmarried women. Until the liberation of the serfs in 1861 peasants could be sent to prison for putting on noblemen's clothes, and in turn it was considered shocking for a nobleman to dress as a peasant (the uproar caused by Tolstoy's plebeian costume is a case in point). Equally central is that deep sense of inferiority toward the West, that groveling for European style, which since the eighteenth century has led Russian women to look on Paris (and later, Rome, Berlin, New York) as the only reliable sources of *chicarnost'* (elegance, derived from the French *chic.*)

In the late 1950s, a few decades after the Revolution had imposed drab, undecodable clothing upon the Soviet masses, a new sumptuary feudalism was created by those high-ranking party officials who were allowed to travel abroad.

"From the time I was a small child, you could recognize Party bigwigs and their families from a mile away because they were so proud of wearing foreign clothes," says forty-year-old writer Tatyana Tolstaya, great-grandniece of Leo Tolstoy and one of the shrewdest observers of Russian society I know. "They simply recreated the costume hierarchy we had under the czars."

This Party-based sumptuary code, this greed for Westernness, was greatly reinforced during the "Stagnancy" of the Brezhnev decades, when a new middle class thriving on rampant graft and corruption bought foreign black-market goods on an unprecedented scale. A pathetic current instance of this toadying to the West is the thriving Moscow underground dedicated to the fabrication of false European labels—false *firma*. The counterfeiters copy Dior, Cardin, Calvin Klein, Valentino labels, sew them on Soviet-made clothes, and resell them to consignment shops for exorbitant prices. Within a few weeks, the Soviet fakes fall apart.

Soviet women are very candid about their fixation on costume.

"It's due to our terrible sense of bleakness," said a program director at Riga's central television station, "everything about us is as drab as our apartment houses—anonymous, breaking down the year after they're built. So decorating your outer surface is like bringing flowers inside of you, it's your only way of cheering up . . . Well," she added wistfully, "it may also be due to the fact that our men don't seem to value us, don't behave toward us with any *manners*."

"The fashion fixation may be a key to Soviet women's special strength, a source of self-esteem that men are deprived of," says Riga magazine editor Monika Zile. "How are you going to keep your morale up if you work all day long and have a family and no mother to help out at home, and your combined work load is sixteen hours? Your only way not to fall apart is to put on the prettiest things you have every single morning of your life."

Tatyana Grigoryevna Agafonova moved to Uzbekistan from her native Siberia in order to attend Tashkent's Institute of Costume Designers (there are only a half dozen such full-fledged faculties in the U.S.S.R.). She married an Uzbek man, and now directs the city's largest fashion design collective, *Dom Modeli.*

"For decades of our century, a person wearing a bright green skirt to the office, or, say, an imaginative homemade hat, was singled out for reprimand, could even be sent to prison for such unorthodox dress," says Agafonova, whose favorite foreign couturiers are Pierre Cardin and Thierry Mugler. "This uniformity simply robbed women of their youth . . . So now we dress up every morning as if it were a feast day."

Talking to members of Agafonova's fashion collective, I learned that the career of *Khudozhniki-modelieri*, or artist-designers, as they are called, is one of the most remunerative and rigorous vocations a Soviet woman can pursue. State enterprises pay fashion collectives up to a thousand rubles for each design which they buy to copy for the mass market. Added to their base pay of two hundred and fifty rubles a month (already equal to that of the average doctor or lawyer) the premiums designers receive for each model they sell to state enterprise place them in the income bracket of high civil servants or skilled engineers.

But the career must be preceded by seven years of demanding training in a succession of specific institutes. A two-year university degree in "artistic learning," which demands thorough mastery of draftsmanship and painting skills, is the first step. Next comes a very competitive entry exam into a Faculty of Fashion Designers, which tends to accept only one applicant out of fifteen, and whose five-year course includes command of a foreign language and thorough grounding in Russian art history and culture.

This elitist training is an accurate indicator of the enormous importance which Soviet society has placed on fashion in the past decades. Perhaps because it is one of the few professions which always allowed exposure to Russia's ancient artistic traditions, the exalted state of Soviet *couture* is reflected in the high intellectual level of its designers, who include some of the most cultivated and spiritual women I met in the Soviet Union. It is telling, for instance, that the philosophically inclined Aleksandra Sokolova, Leningrad's star designer, is more harshly critical of her nation's fashion fixation than any other Soviet citizen I've met.

"When there is such a prolonged dearth of basic commodities, the problem of dressing takes on ridiculous, monumental proportions," she says. "It's tragic that it drains us of so much energy which should be directed into more important issues. Can you imagine the silliness: We Soviet women, who have so little leisure, should spend hours on such empty-minded trifles as finding a secondhand blouse with a fake St. Laurent label!"

Sokolova's critique reminded me of a comment by a forty-year-old avant-garde writer, a star of Moscow's most progressive "Golden Youth," who once took great pains telling me why Soviet women have no time to start any kind of a women's rights movement. "They're too busy trying to survive?" I suggested. "Forget about surviving!" he retorted. "They're too busy trying to get well dressed."

Throughout my trip to the U.S.S.R., as I saw my women friends— linguists, sociologists, psychologists, who had once burned midnight oil to obtain high academic credentials—bent for hours over the sewing of a blouse, as I observed women on subways and schoolgirls on buses preening themselves with their hand mirrors several times an hour, I reflected that costume may be an extension of the Russian tradition of *pokazukha,* a crucial word meaning "false show."

There has long been a national tendency to erect cosmetic facades with the purpose of hiding the drabber reality that lies behind them: Some of the most legendary *pokazukha* are the portable villages which Catherine the Great's courtier Potemkin devised during the Empress's triumphal tours so as not to expose her to the misery of the Russian people. So I began to think of fashion as the spiritual side of Soviet *pokazukha.* Here we have the bleak, ever so monotonous outside world; the bleak, solitary inner world; and in between them, the costumed cosmeticized facade of feigned cheerfulness, care, and color which provide the interface between the two, the solace for both. And talking to the czar of Soviet fashion, Vyacheslav Mikhailovich Zaitsev, I was also reminded that any system of "Beauty" has long had religious associations to the Russian mind.

XV

Some Artists

Zaitsev

Fashion designer Vyacheslav Zaitsev, "Slava" to his friends and to the thousands of adoring Soviet women who come to Moscow to admire his creations, is a dapper man in his late forties with a punkish mop of brush-cut brown hair and soulful green eyes who traces his inspiration to "God and my sainted mother." Among his trademarks are flashy diamond-and-onyx cuff links, emerald-green wool jackets, and a gift for the media-wise phrase ("I am the first spring swallow of Russia's aesthetic renaissance"). He presides over a nine-story building on Moscow's Prospekt Mira, *Dom Modi,* where with the help of two assistant designers he produces the first Soviet-labeled clothes in fashion history to be exported abroad.

Although Zaitsev's clothes range from the equivalent of three hundred to a thousand dollars, far out of range for most women anywhere, his firm is well patronized by members of the Soviet intelligentsia—writers, dancers, musicians, actresses—whose income can be a hundredfold the national average; and also by clients from the wealthier Soviet republics—Georgia, Armenia—who have begun to value the Zaitsev *firma* almost as much as Valentino's or Dior's. This support has enabled Zaitsev to emancipate himself totally from state control, making his business into a model *perestroika*-era cooperative.

Zaitsev is yet another Russian who never knew his father. The son of an indigent laundress who has only had one vacation in her seventy-two years, he was brought up in a rural poverty redeemed by those qualities of his mother's which he still finds central to Soviet women: "Heroic patience, and a saintly capacity for self-sacrifice." As passionate a Gorbachev fan as can be found, the concepts of "individualism," "beauty," and "spirituality" are to him indissolubly linked.

"We were taught to forget the word 'I,' " he says about the Stalin and Brezhnev years. "We lived in an apotheosis of tastelessness, a bacchanalia of anti-aesthetics. But as individualism now reflowers, our people will find a new spiritual harmony by looking more beautiful. For the individual cannot attain spirituality without knowing beauty. . . . I'm a Communist and I believe in justice, equality, etc., but I'm also a Russian, and spirituality for me comes first."

Zaitsev thus brings an almost pastoral sense of mission to his fashion crusade. Off-the-rack clothes displayed on the ground floor of his *Dom Modi* are in tall, slim sizes, part of Zaitsev's campaign to improve Soviet women's figures. He offers free consultations to some fifteen women a day who come to seek his advice on how to "find their individuality" through a choice of fabrics, silhouettes, and cosmetics. ("Soviet women must develop their spirituality by being constantly *exposed* to beauty.")

"In the West fashion is a matter of money," Zaitsev says patriotically. "Here it is a matter of bringing people joy." Zaitsev's crusade for fashion-as-spirituality is not confined to the fair sex. Alongside his women's couture line, Zaitsev, with the help of his twenty-eight-year-

old son, also designs some one hundred items of men's wear a year—
Soviet men's clothing, he declares, has been for decades "one of the
worst pollutants of our environment."

The Zaitsev innovation that has been most influential in the Soviet Union, however, is the fashion show. In the four-hundred-seat
auditorium of Zaitsev's *Dom Modi,* such spectacles are held three
times a week most of the year. Entrance, again, is free, though tickets
must be requested weeks in advance. Microphone in hand, Zaitsev
plays the show to packed houses like a Las Vegas emcee, offering
explanations for each of his models, acknowledging his deep debts to
Balenciaga, Sonia Rykiel, Montana, and Kenzo but always stressing
that "God and my sainted mother are my chief sources of inspiration."

Zaitsev travels indefatigably through the Soviet Union with his
spectacle, covering dozens of cities a year, and his gospel of redemp-
tion-through-beauty has spread through his country like wildfire. In
Tbilisi, Tashkent, Leningrad, the staging of fashion shows down sleek
mirrored runways, inevitably accompanied by deafening American
rock music, is barely distinguishable from the ones on Seventh Avenue. Across the nation, the hems of any autumn or spring collection
are approximately as many inches above the knee as they are in Dallas,
Paris, or New York. The legs of the newly athletic, diet-conscious
young Soviet women who model such spectacles are as splendid as any
in the world, a reminder that the fabled White Russian beauties of
the 1920s immigration provided Paris couturiers with their finest
models. And a growing ethnic pride in the design traditions of each
Soviet republic—the sumptuous striped silks of Uzbekistan, the bold
primary colors of Georgian folk art, the liturgical Muscovite ornateness that inspires Zaitsev's evening clothes—makes these Soviet displays far more eccentric and entertaining than any to be found in
prosperous Western cities such as Lyons, Barcelona, or Frankfurt.

Everywhere, the auditoriums are packed with women who have
come to listen to that "bird song of individualism," in Zaitsev's words,
which can gladden the drab anonymity of Soviet life; and also to glean
ideas with which to inspire their incessant occupation of sewing, sewing, sewing costumed joy into their often dismal lives.

"Dostoevsky was right, we shall never be redeemed by suffering," philosopher Aleksandr Sivak once lectured me during one of those late night talk fests on God, history, and salvation which make me prefer Russian conversations to all others in the world. "Russia can only be redeemed by Beauty."

Some Artists, Cont.

Kossenkova

A dozen young Soviets sit or lie on the floor of a room in an abandoned Moscow schoolhouse, performing one of the earliest classics of Russian literature, *The Lay of Igor's Campaign.* They are declaiming the text in the original twelfth-century Slavonic, an idiom which only a few hundred scholars in Moscow might understand. Their audience of some thirty persons sits on folding chairs at one side of the stark space.

The actors half mime, half dance the action, writhing on the floor in moments of pain or sorrow, leaping acrobatically across their makeshift stage to mimic the aggression of battle. They are dressed in the ragged tunics of medieval mendicants. Their performance is interspersed with ancient Russian games and songs, strains of Orthodox Church music litany. As they speak or shout or wail out their lines, their voices rise and fall by two octaves into often unintelligible trills, whimpers, growls, laments, recalling, in turn, calls of tropical birds, parodies of dictators exhorting crowds, ecstatic chants of shamans performing an archaic rite.

In a battered chair in back of the audience sits the group's director, Veronika Kossenkova, a woman in her late forties with a scrubbed, impassive face who scrutinizes her actors with minute attention, often closing her eyes to concentrate on the nuances of their diction. She is the founder of *Tembr,* the most "off-off fringe" of the several experimental theater groups that have recently been allowed to flower in Moscow's *glasnost.*

Tembr is the closest blend of Judith Molina, Grotowski, Robert Wilson, John Cage, and Peter Brook any Soviet theater troupe has yet dared to venture. And Kossenkova's staging of *The Lay of Igor's Campaign* is a boldly subversive performance of the hallowed national classic. Russian schoolchildren have been taught to venerate Prince Igor as one of their first heroes and patriots; *Tembr's* actors present him as a sexist, sadistic tyrant who wastes his subjects' lives for his greedy motives, as an ego-tripping warmonger whose pompous, stentorian diction could be, as Kossenkova puts it, "that of any of our past dictators."

Like much of Moscow's cultural avant-garde, one of the principal aims of Kossenkova's group is to "plumb our Russianness," "rediscover our lost or hidden roots," by recapturing the shamanistic power of ancient national rituals. Simultaneously, it aims to reappropriate an almost forgotten tradition of Russian modernism: The visionary explorations that took place in Russian drama in the 1910s and 1920s, before Stalin's ban against all experimental art desiccated Soviet culture, when Meyerhold and Stanislavsky staged productions that would change the course of Western drama.

Like those predecessors, Kossenkova believes that the "meaningless" sounds her actors often vocalize can have a deeper effect on the spectator's subconscious than any rational idiom. She aspires to create a universal theater which could communicate its intent anywhere in the world, "a system of moving mirrors through which Russian and all other languages would lovingly recognize each other." (In 1913, the Futurist dramas of poet-playwright Velemir Khlebnikov had resorted to a "trans-sense" language, *zaum'*, to reinvigorate contemporary speech and create a universally intelligible discourse.)

Kossenkova maintains that every one has a "real voice" which is as unique to each of us as a soul; that this search for the true voice must be carried out in a spirit of charity and selflessness; that if honestly used, our own real voice will lead us onto a path of self-perfection. (Stanislavsky stated that in refining his stage technique each performer heightens his integrity of character; his contemporary, drama theorist Vyacheslav Ivanov, claimed that only theater could replace religion in a faithless age, that the spiritual community created through drama's "collective action" has ennobling effects on the lives of all spectators.)

Kossenkova's disciples live and work in deliberate poverty, with no permanent locale or site, no established source of funding. They perform free, and accept whatever donations spectators can offer. As nomadic as they are tightly bonded, they depend on the charity of schools, churches, trade unions, other small theaters, for an occasional space in which to stage their productions. Like Meyerhold, who resurrected ancient traditions of street theaters and wandering minstrels, *Tembr* performs Shakespeare for crews of highway construction workers in the steppes of northern Russia, stages Tsvetaeva plays for Afghanistan veterans in Odessa hospitals, plays benefit performances of *The Lay of Igor's Campaign* for victims of the Armenia earthquake. In summertime members of *Tembr* take to the outdoors for what Kossenkova calls "pirate actions," assembling hundreds of spectators by wandering barefoot through the streets of Soviet cities and leading them toward a performance space in some nearby park or forest.

It is in her method of voice training that Kossenkova may most differ from the traditions of Russian modernism. Her technique is based on Yogic Tantric doctrines which teach that our voice is our most direct link to the Cosmos, that every major vowel is associated with a certain element of the universe (air, water, fire, ether) and with a specific part of the body. In Kossenkova's adaptation, the voicing of "a" must emanate from the extremities—palms, soles of feet; "o" originates in the groin; "u" from the spinal chord. Kossenkova was led to this esoteric science by tragedy and providence.

Born into a Russian family which had lived in Tashkent for two generations, trained as an actress and singer at the local Institute of Dramatic Art, Kossenkova was left destitute by the powerful earthquake which destroyed much of the city in 1966. Homeless and penniless, she moved with her actor husband and their two-year-old child to the barren Siberian town of Magadan, a former site for some of Stalin's most brutal concentration camps: The Soviet government was offering free housing there in its efforts to populate the northeasternmost reaches of the nation.

In Magadan, Kossenkova earned her living as an actress with the regional theater. It was in part staffed by former convicts who had been imprisoned under Stalin, and who had played in the amateur prison groups which camp directors prided themselves in founding. Their lives broken, their families having disappeared in the purges, some of the former *zheks* had remained in Magadan to earn their living on the stage. They became Kossenkova's mentors, engaging her into stage experiments on the Meyerhold and Stanislavsky models which, in the 1960s, would have been severely censured in the U.S.S.R.'s large urban centers.

It was also in Magadan that Kossenkova made friends with a young actor of the local Chukchi tribe; the Chukchi, one of the U.S.S.R.'s smallest ethnic minorities, have an ancient tradition of Shamanistic rituals related to the Tantric Buddhist practices of Tibet. Kossenkova's Chukchi friend had learned tribal rites from his father, who was himself a shaman; but he could not practice them, all such religious cults having been suppressed. He trusted Kossenkova, and taught her the doctrine of Tantric breathing which would become central to her vocal technique. In her extensive later studies, Kossenkova would assimilate these Yogic doctrines to Pythagorean teachings about the human voice being a link to "the Music of the Spheres"; and to St. Thomas Aquinas' theory of vowels, which resurrected the ancient Greek teaching concerning the sacred powers of the human voice.

I participated in a *Tembr* rehearsal one afternoon to get a more intimate sense of its workings. Standing in a circle with eight of the young actors, our hands linked to one another's, we engaged in the Tantric exercises which are an obligatory warm-up for every rehearsal; we shouted two-octave range chants on the vowel "ee," concentrating on the shoulder area from which, according to Tantric teaching, that sound is supposed to originate. We went on to groan and hum five-minute modulations on the vowel "o," concentrating on our groins.

How familiar it all seemed! I could have been participating in one of John Cage's happenings of the early 1950s, in some liturgical protest of the Vietnam years, in a Buddhist liturgy of the same era led by Allen Ginsberg, in any of those rituals of our own counterculture which for the past three decades have equally satisfied our search for renewal and brotherhood. But my Russian friends seemed infused with a compassion, selflessness, and serene patience that I had seldom experienced in the United States; and also by one of the most striking features of current Soviet society—that unprecedented sense of solitude which is leading many citizens to search for new forms of community.

Kossenkova rejects the traditional separation between professionals and amateurs. She chooses her actors solely on the basis of their "purity of heart" and on their ability to find their "true voice." Linked to my left arm was wan, gentle Sergei, a literary critic by profession who has joined the group because the "micro-climate" created by Kossenkova helps all its members to resolve their conflicts with society and become better persons.

Linked to my right arm was twenty-six-year-old Oleg, a slender youth with shoulder-length blond hair and a proliferation of Western anti-nuclear buttons pinned to his T-shirt, who was trained as a theater director. "All of our griefs and joys are shared here. We may need a group like this more than ever because we're in a historical period filled with ethnic divisions and broken families, with much of our traditional sense of community lost." In front of me was Oleg's wife, Elena. Penniless, like most of their colleagues, they survive by living two and a half hours north of Moscow with Elena's mother and their four-year-old child. They spend five hours of each day commuting to the capital to rehearse with *Tembr*.

On my right also stood Igor, a factory worker who has chosen to work the 4 A.M. to 3 P.M. shift in order to suit his schedule to *Tembr*'s daily rehearsals; and Dima, an engineer and physicist in his thirties, who left his job because "this is the first true sense of community I'd felt; the group has become a family."

Kossenkova lives alone in a one-room flat an hour and a half away from the center of Moscow—reachable by a combination of trains and buses which cease functioning at midnight—where rents are the cheapest. When her rehearsals run late she depends on the hospitality of friends for a bed. She is one of the few women in Soviet theater who have achieved recognition as a director, and she is eloquent about "the paper equality" offered women in the U.S.S.R., and the "oriental forms of misogyny" that still prevail. " 'It is not evident that the director is a woman,' " she paraphrases several typical critics who have praised her work.

Kossenkova was divorced when her child was very young, and admits that the only loves she's known in life are for her work, her mother and grandmother, and her son, who now has a family of his own. She does not practice the Orthodox faith but believes in "the Logos, and the life after death." The ambition of Veronika Kossenkova and of her *Tembr* colleagues is eventually to share a country house near Moscow where they can live together, invite friends to performances, and continue to work "not in a spirit of self-promotion but in dedication to a cause and a belief in its truthfulness." Until then Kossenkova's community will survive, in the words of its own members, on "bread, water, faith, and love."

Some Artists, Cont.

Tolstaya

Tatyana Tolstaya, a novelist in her early forties who is considered at home and abroad to be the most gifted woman writer of her generation, is a great-grandniece of the author of *War and Peace*. She is the granddaughter of Aleksey Tolstoy, the writer who emigrated during the Revolution but returned to the Soviet Union after five years abroad and became one of the most esteemed artists of the new regime.

Tolstaya, a tall, statuesque woman with an ironic smile and long black hair which she wears in a thick bun, thinks, dresses, and speaks very differently from other Soviet women I've met. The stark stateliness of her bearing, her iconoclastic disdain for fashion and many other national obsessions, the purity of her Russian diction are proof that a small segment of the prerevolutionary aristocracy remains alive and well unto the fourth generation.

One of seven children of an eminent physicist, Tatyana grew up in Leningrad and received her university degree in classical philology. Her dissertation theme was "The Myth of the Phoenix in Ancient Literature." She was married at the age of twenty-three to a fellow philologist whom she'd met at university, and has two teenage sons. Fluent in English and French, Tolstaya can also read Latin and classical Greek, and is the only Soviet woman I've met who enjoys discussing Plato, Aristotle, and other founders of Western thought.

Among contemporary Soviet women writers, Tolstaya is perhaps the only one who can be called a postmodernist, or even a modernist. Her idols are Trifonov, Platonov, Nabokov; she read the latter's oeuvre in *samizdat* long before it was allowed into the Soviet Union. Her own work centers on the classical themes of nineteenth-century Russian literature—womanly self-sacrifice, the weak, mother-dominated male —and turns them into parody. The heroine of her classic story "Sonya" is a homely spinster whose saintly generosity is exploited and ridiculed by her cynical friends. The hero of "Peters"[48] is tyrannized by an archetypally powerful mother, and after a few decades of attempted bachelorhood ends up being dominated by an even more suffocating wife.

However progressive she may be, Tolstaya has a darkly ironic view of Gorbachev's revolution. "We have more *glasnost* than we can handle, but we'll never have *perestroika,*" she told me during one of our talks in Moscow. "*Glasnost* is a spiritual category; but *perestroika* is a material achievement, and we Russians are a spiritual people who disdain material advancement . . . which is not an ounce better than being materialistic.

"We are people who tend to apocalypse," she continued, "and the newest apocalypse has already begun for us. People in our country have begun to hate each other more than they've ever hated each other before. Of course this began with the distrust bred in Stalin's time, but it's a far worse and different hatred now, look at the way our ethnic groups are using weapons against each other . . . Our empire can not withstand such divisions between a hundred nationalities, can not survive in its present form, it will have to destroy itself and be

SOVIET WOMEN

reborn and reshaped on a totally new model, perhaps on something akin to the British Commonwealth . . . But you know, like most of my compatriots I always see an apocalypse, I can not have enough apocalypses!

"All of our history is one of slavery and oppression," Tolstaya continued. "Under Gorbachev, for the first time in our tradition we have freedom. But all may go wrong because we don't know what we really want, we're in love with this new freedom but after love comes marriage and that's a totally other matter, and anyhow Russians are terrible at both love and marriage, even at friendship."

We went on to discuss love and friendship. And I sensed again, in Tolstaya, the solitude at the core of many Russian women.

"Friendship is a most important and dangerous thing in our country," she said. "Of course it's far more valuable in our culture than in yours—Russians have little else, even if we have money there is nothing to buy with it, only friends can help you locate decent food, clothes, basic comforts, friendship is a central aid to survival. But in the Soviet Union friends become too close to each other and begin to ruin each other's lives, they want to know everything about the tiniest movement of each other's souls. We have a word adapted from the French for this state, *amicochonstvo*. When Russians become friends they think that they can burst into your house at any time without a phone call, if they have a problem they make you feel responsible, you must immediately give money, help, everything, they totally invade you. That's why I dislike having close friends, when I have some grief I have to boil it over in my soul by myself.

"There is a strange tendency to destruction in the Russian soul," she added. "There is some strange desire in them to even destroy their families; men and women collaborate in that, the women perhaps more than the men, with their voracious demands and will to power . . ."

Like the overwhelming majority of even the most progressive Soviet intellectuals, Tolstaya has only hostile feelings toward the concept of a "women's movement." Soviets' primitive understanding of Western feminism, as I've noted before, is caused by cultural isolation, by the fact that they've only caught echoes of the outdated radical voices of the 1960s "movement" without ever having had access to basic feminist texts such as Virginia Woolf, De Beauvoir, or even Colette.

"I used to know an American graduate student in Leningrad who called herself a feminist," Tolstaya once stated to me. "This American tried to explain this feminism to us because we don't really understand what it is. And sure enough, in time we found out she was a lesbian, she told us that she only began to be happy in the Soviet Union when she met a few other American women students with the same tastes. This confused all of us because lesbianism is not very widespread here, homosexuality is forbidden . . . So it's always like that, when women say they are feminists they look like men, they try to dress like men, they don't like men . . ."

She shrugged her shoulders, and added: "But how *can* we understand your American feminists? The few I've talked to tell me that they're fighting for the right to work in coal mines. My dear, Russian women are fighting *not* to work in coal mines!"

Tolstaya went on to deny virulently that the lives of Soviet women are any harder than those of Soviet men. "I refuse to see any difference between men's and women's problems," she said. "In many ways men's life is far harder than women's. They are weaker, they die younger, they can take far less stress than we do."

I remarked that according to Soviet statistics women in the U.S.S.R. get two hours less sleep a night than men.

"But that's just the way it should be!" she exclaimed. "Men need that extra rest, otherwise they would die far too young. Women are the roots, men are just the leaves."

I once asked Tolstaya if she shows her work to any friend or relative before she sends it out to be published. The answer was wonderfully tribal.

"I make nine carbon copies of everything I write," she answered, "and I give a copy to my husband, my parents, and to each one of my six brothers and sisters. Usually every one of them has a different comment, but if every one of my siblings has a unanimous opinion on the detail of a story then I know they're right.

"You know," she added, "when my parents and brothers and sisters gather together in Leningrad, we feel closer to each other than we do to our own husbands or wives, blood ties are just closer than any other bonds. If I had another life to live I'd have five children so they could enjoy the same extraordinary ties I've had with my siblings. But it's not possible because I'm too ambitious for my sons, they must have the best piano and skating lessons, the best English and French teachers, I would become like Shiva with thirty-seven arms . . ."

Even this most sophisticated of Russian women is obsessively domestic, and structures her working schedule totally about her children's. She can work well only at night after supper, "when the children are fed and in bed and reading," because she is too anxious about them when they are out of the house. She writes until three or four A.M. and rises at noon, in time to warm up her sons' lunch when they come home from classes. They could have their midday meal at school, but their mother doesn't trust the school diet. Tolstaya refers to her husband as "an excellent educator but a kitchen idiot." Her only household helper, curiously, is her father-in-law; he is a retired military man who adores her children, lives nearby, does much of the family's shopping, and stays with the children when Tatyana and her husband are away.

In the afternoon, when the children settle to their homework, Tatyana Tolstaya prepares the family supper, fixes the next day's midday meal, and goes about her housework, ironing, sewing, dusting, tasks she considers conducive to literary inspiration. "My eyes see the dust, but my soul is somewhere else."

Like most progressive Russian intellectuals of the Gorbachev era, Tolstaya feels great nostalgia for prerevolutionary Russian values, for the heroism, asceticism, spirituality of her grandparents' generation.

"Those almost disappeared people who are over ninety now—they had another psychology, they were a generation with great soul. My mother's mother, for instance, who committed suicide a few hours after her husband died, and was buried in the same grave: Throughout her life she had only one dress, and when it got old she bought or sewed another one, she simply thought it was indecent to have more than that when other people were starving. What did she do with the little savings left from her husband's earnings? She sent it every month to friends and relatives in exile, after her death my parents found that she had sent over six hundred thousand rubles to people abroad. That was her debt to society, not unlike the English Victorian notion of duty, how egotistical, materialistic Russians seem now in comparison . . ."

I once asked Tatyana Tolstaya whether she believed in God.

"But of course," she answered, as if I were asking an idiotic question. "Every Russian still does, in his or her own way. And we believe in life after death. And we like to do little else but speak and care about the whole universe. And there is a Russian notion that it is a sin to have, to possess material things, which is perhaps why we're going to be so bad at *perestroika*, why we're bad at most forms of progress . . . You see, you Westerners think that the best life includes happiness, money. We do not, because there is a deeply monastic streak in our culture, probably brought on by the asceticism of our Orthodox Church, which leads us to believe that happiness and material possessions are wicked, should not be had, that they corrupt us and should only lead to guilt . . .

"Please do read a story by our great writer Nikolay Leskov called 'Chortogon,' 'The Exorcist,' " she added. "The protagonist is a modest merchant who suddenly makes a lot of money. In the West you think that one must always earn more money to have a better life; but the Russian response to material gain is 'So what?' This 'So what?' felt by Leskov's hero is a very dark, very Russian emotion, perhaps our deepest form of shame. He goes to a French restaurant in Moscow— palm trees, women in beautiful dresses—and tells the owner to make everyone leave. And then after eating and drinking all alone the merchant takes a sword and starts to destroy everything about him. It is the pure pleasure of destruction, a very Russian feeling . . . that dark feeling that comes upon us, the desire to destroy. . . .''

XVI

Family and Work; Turning the Clock Back; *Perestroika*

"Greetings, my name is Lyubov," one of the cheerful, bespectacled factory workers said as we sat down to tea. "I'm a member of the Machine Builders' Union, my salary is about four hundred rubles a month. I live with my husband in a two-room apartment near Kolsomolskaya Station, our daughter is grown and has a family of her own."

"My name is Rimma," her friend said, "I also make about four hundred rubles a month. I'm a member of the Construction Workers' Union. I live with my husband and son in a two-room apartment with a balcony in Kuskovo, about ten miles from Moscow."

My friend Elvira Novikova had arranged the gathering a few days before the end of my last trip to the U.S.S.R. We met over tea at the *Zhensoviet* headquarters, a magnificent neoclassical nineteenth-century building off Gorky Street that was once a palace of the Volkonsky family. *Zhensoviet* is a government-controlled women's organization modeled on the *Zhenotdel* founded by Aleksandra Kollontai in the 1920s. (The original *Zhenotdel* was eventually abolished by Stalin, but was resurrected in the 1960s in somewhat different form as *Zhensoviet.*) Like many industrial workers, the two *tovarishchi* Elvira introduced me to are very active in this women's council, which has branches in most every factory and town of the Soviet Union.

The two women, who as members of the *Zhensoviet* serve as ombudsmen for the women employed at their respective plants, described some of the "women's issues" they lobby for throughout the year: They verify safety precautions and make sure that their colleagues are not lifting too heavy loads, inspect offices and production rooms to check that lighting is efficient and the ceilings are properly painted, strive to improve the diets of their factory cafeterias. They have recently started an anti-smoking campaign—a considerable problem in any site where Soviet men are employed. And they have devised an ingenious system to ensure the quality of child care in their factories' *yasli:* the care-givers' earnings depend on how well their charges fare; each *nyanya* gets extra pay for every youngster who doesn't get sick during the year; conversely, a sum is subtracted from her salary for every child who falls ill. "You should see our kids," Lyubov said. "They're fed like kings, they thrive like flowers!"

Lyubov's *Zhensoviet* group has obtained a cultural center in which workers can stage their own plays. Rimma's group takes pride in having obtained free meals for its employees, and resting facilities equipped with VCR's and audio-visual cassettes "designed by psychologists to relax you beautifully during a half-hour break." Rimma and Lyubov's respective *profsoyuzi*—"trade unions"—have special funds to draw on for emergency cases, and they also interview women who apply for such support.

"We have an increasing amount of single mothers," Lyubov said. "We had one recent case of a pregnant gal who threw her husband out in the fifth month saying, 'I can't stand him, I hate him.' That was courageous, after all, she's pretty old . . ."

SOVIET WOMEN

"Well, not *that* old, twenty-six," Rimma retorted. "I know that girl in your collective—who can blame her, perhaps her life was beautiful and stopped being beautiful when she got married."

As the three women chatted, I was impressed by the abundance of privileges enjoyed by industrial workers which are denied to the intelligentsia. Beyond having solved that central problem of the working woman—child care—Lyubov's and Rimma's trade unions offer their members a wide choice of resorts to choose from for their vacations, enabling them to pick a spot in just about any part of the U.S.S.R., from Smolensk to the Black Sea. The unions also have their own clinics and sanatoriums (part of a network of some three thousand institutions of that kind in the U.S.S.R.) to which any worker can go for a rest cure upon a doctor's referral without using up any vacation time.

"Ah, *tovarishchi*, what privileges you have," Elvira sighed. "Your benefits will always be far greater than ours because of collective bargaining; that's never worked for professors. Well, the working class feeds the country, they do everything for us, whereas the world will survive if I don't lecture all year."

"Oh, we *do* need your lectures," Rimma said genially. "And there are many problems we haven't solved yet."

Lyubov and Rimma went on to discuss one dilemma which trade unions or *Zhensoviet* councils have not begun to solve: It is very difficult for many Soviet families to go on vacation together. All Soviet citizens must obtain a *putyovka*—a government-assigned coupon—for any vacation they take. Since most spouses work at different factories, a special dispensation must be obtained from the ministry that runs the husband's plant to enable his wife to obtain an *putyovka* to the same vacation resort, and such bureaucratic tangles can be insoluble. But the problem did not seem to bother the two women much. "In our plant," Lyubov blithely said, "we're beginning to solve these family situations in 50 percent of the cases."

As we discussed the issue of family vacations, I was struck again by the extent to which many women of the working class look on their workplaces rather than on their homes as the center of their lives. This priority was beautifully summed up by Lyubov, with a very Soviet emphasis on the single mother: "Every factory is a self-contained unit in which you can give birth, bring up and feed your child . . . of course we're not going to get fur coats, but we get what we strive for, an independent woman."

"After all," added Rimma, "it's at work that we spend the best hours of our lives."

That same evening, I had invited Elvira to dine with me at a cooperative restaurant in the company of our friend Olga Voronina, a philosopher and feminist whose writings have been one of my most precious sources of research. Our meeting was preceded by an eerie incident which illustrated the fragility of many Gorbachev era achievements.

In mid-afternoon, I had dropped in on the restaurant to check it out and secure a reservation for dinner. It was a tiny café on a narrow side street in northern Moscow whose substantial prices, like most of the new privately owned eateries, were far beyond the reach of the average Soviet citizen. After I'd chatted with one of the proprietors, a genial half-Greek, half-Georgian citizen who described his fare as "eclectic Mediterranean," he accompanied me to the door with a flourish of "Madames" and kissing of hands.

As I was about to step into the street, six menacing, thuggish-looking men burst into the tiny space, shouting, "Where's the manager?" They looked like carbon copies of villains in 1930s American gangster films, down to their sinister, scarred faces, mean eyes, and slouching fedoras. The restaurateur looked properly terrified. With a whispered command to get out of the way instantly and avoid trouble, my taxi driver, who had been standing at the curbside, whisked me into his car. During the ride toward my hotel, he reported that the gang of six had emerged from a police van, adding that it was customary for many racketeers to fake militia credentials.

Who will ever know whether these lugubrious intruders were plainclothesmen on a genuine checking tour of the city's privately owned ventures, disgruntled citizens resenting the restaurant's flourishing business, racketeers demanding protection money, or corrupt police demanding the same? The last three alternatives are by far the most likely. For similar incidents are said to be proliferating at lightning speed in Soviet cities. At a time when *perestroika*'s concrete promises remain unfulfilled, and food and commodities are scarcer than ever, such harassments have to do with the bitter envy felt by less privileged citizens toward the wealthy new entrepreneurs of the Gorbachev era. They may also be motivated by that archaic, ascetic "disdain for material advancement" which Tatyana Tolstaya says is a constant of the Russian psyche. On the part of many older citizens, such onslaughts are also abetted by a nostalgia for the austere, more egalitarian, more orthodox Marxism of the pre-Brezhnev decades.

But if the intruders were indeed racketeers, the incident points to one of the darkest sides of Gorbachev's *perestroika:* The phenomenal recent growth of a Soviet Mafia which exploits the citizenry's and the police's resentment of capitalist-style ventures, and is able to amass vast private fortunes through criminal and often violent means.

I was still unnerved by the incident when I returned that evening to the restaurant to meet my dinner guests, Elvira and Olga. I was relieved to see that the manager was still alive—looking wan and shaken, he sat a few tables away from us with a group of whispering, anxious-looking cronies. As my friends and I began dinner, our conversation, like many between Russian women, was a real-life replay of Baranskaya's novella "A Week Like Any Other." Looking back on our afternoon with Lyubov and Rimma, we discussed the many psychological perils of finding "the best hours of our lives" in the workplace. We analyzed the many other covert ways in which the Soviet system discriminates against the family, against most personal relationships— how many affordable cafés were there in Moscow, for instance, where one could quietly sit and unburden one's soul to a friend?

"Collective, collective, all the emphasis is on the collective, all the privileges are in the workplace," Elvira said. "It's the socialist way to center life on the production ethic. It's been hammered into us since we're children that the work collective is our true home."

"And the horrendous housing conditions make our workplaces all the more important," Olga concurred. "So where does that situate the family in our system of values?

"And just try to get yourself a *putyovka,* a vacation coupon, to the same place as your husband," Olga added. "How many women manage that? One in ten. You're lucky if you can bring your child along. Families are even divided during their only leisure time of the year."

"Friendships outside of the collective are made equally difficult," Elvira said. "It's almost a matter of town planning. There are no restaurants, no cafés to meet a chum in, and only foreigners can afford the new cooperatives. Do you realize that this is only the third time in a decade I've been out to a restaurant?"

"And the first time you and I have ever been to a restaurant without a man," Olga added. "Our society is so sexist that when women go out together the way we have, every man in the joint will assume they just want to be picked up."

"We sure could use more outings like this one!" Elvira exclaimed. "What kind of a condition are we in when we finally get home after an hour or more of commuting from work, after another hour of being pushed around in the bus, the subway, the food queue?"

"That's when we take it out on our husbands," Olga sighed. "The man is the one we've been shopping, cooking, scrubbing, darning the socks for all week, so in our exhausted state we see him as the most immediate enemy, we start shouting, yelling, breaking up the family again . . ."

"One of the problems is that men are like big children," Elvira said, turning to me, "and in our country they don't have any toys. Over in the States your men have a car, community groups and bars and coffee shops where they can meet their friends. Here they have no clubs, no cars to play with, no decent apartments where one can either be private or receive friends properly . . ."

"And so all our anger and violence are always brought back to the home, the family," Olga said. "To the essential, terrible, beautiful family."

How fragile, how vulnerable the Soviet family seemed to me toward the end of my journeys to the U.S.S.R.! During one of my flights back from Moscow, as I was rereading Solzhenitsyn's *Gulag Archipel-*

SOVIET WOMEN

ago, I realized that the Soviet family's frailness is not only traceable to the abiding "production ethic"; that its very fabric had already been ravaged under Stalin's rule.

Official rhetoric, in this case, was more deceptive than ever. In the orthodox view which prevailed until the *glasnost* era, Stalin was upheld as the family's most loyal champion because he outlawed abortion, made divorce difficult, reinforced the traditional Russian cult of Motherhood. But in reality few twentieth-century leaders have so destroyed parental, filial, marital bonds. From the late 1920s on, all social institutions were geared to a particular cult of youth—the creation of the new Revolutionary Being.

Young citizens' true spouses, so the first Bolshevik generation was instructed, were the Army, the Party, the state, which they were taught to look on as their ideal kin. Their true parents were presented to them as suspect, as still infected with the viruses of the *ancien régime.* Children's newspapers of the Stalinist era ordered youngsters not only to beware of their parents but to spy and report on them, sacrificing any filial emotion to the welfare of the state. It is only in 1987 that the central role model imposed on three generations of young Soviets—Pioneer Pavlik Morozov, the twelve-year-old who sent his father to death on trumped-up charges—was expunged from history books and exposed as an idiotic little coward.

A new emphasis on family relations occurred in the mid-1960s, when demographers' panic about a dwindling labor force led to vigorous new propaganda in favor of more offspring. But that is also the time when the Brezhnev regime began its degenerative impact on Soviet society. And if I were to choose the single most shocking social flaw in the contemporary Soviet Union, it would be the plight of the nation's most underprivileged citizens: the children that Soviet mothers, in the past two decades, have felt forced to abandon to orphanages and welfare homes. The number of state orphans has grown awesomely in the past decades. Even during the years when the U.S.S.R. was recovering from the tolls of collectivization, World War II, and Stalin's purges—tragedies through which it lost 40 million men—the number of homeless children was only about one third of its present level.

One of the most admirable new magazines of the *glasnost* era,

Semya, "Family," is dedicated to exposing the many injustices that plague Soviet women and children, and particularly its state orphans. *Semya* reports that there are an estimated 1 million children in the Soviet Union living without parental care. Some seven hundred thousand of them are in government-assigned guardianship; some three hundred thousand live in foster homes in often appalling conditions. A recent article in *Semya,* for instance, estimates that only one fifth of orphanages are "even adequate" in their physical conditions, not to speak of their total lack of effort in allaying the kids' loneliness, offering them any recreational facilities or psychological support. Describing the appalling conditions of seven children's homes in the Taka region, a remote area of Siberia in which a very large number of such institutions are concentrated, a *Semya* article states that these facilities are devoid of indoor toilets or showers and that their maximum daytime temperature is 7 degrees centigrade, dipping far below freezing at night because most of their boilers are not working.

Semya has also noted that notwithstanding the desperate need for male role models among Soviet youngsters, a number of dedicated, well-trained young men with university degrees in pedagogy who applied for work at such homes were rejected—always by the decision of a female bureaucrat—on the rationale that "We don't need men for these jobs." In this society which is already unbalanced by a severe stereotyping of gender differences, all vocations associated with the bringing up of children continue to be seen as "women's work"; and of the some five thousand children's homes in the Soviet Union, there is only one with a male director.

The deterioration of the Soviet orphanage system in the past decades is also made evident by the following data: In the 1930s over half of the nation's orphans went on to higher education. Whereas in 1986 only four hundred out of the hundreds of thousands of young men and women brought up in foster homes in the Russian Federation, the U.S.S.R.'s largest republic, even finished high school; and only fifty made it to the university. These days, orphanages automatically transfer their wards to vocational schools after secondary schooling, whatever their intellectual gifts.

The plight of orphans in the U.S.S.R. is made all the more tragic by the Soviets' curious prejudices against the practice of adoption.

SOVIET WOMEN

The traditional excuse given by women for this bias is that "They are all children of alcoholic prostitutes"—a glaring untruth, seeing the number of infants abandoned because of mothers' poverty and lack of government support. The truer reason is that there is something sacred and cultic in the Russian ethos about the concept of *rozhdene*, the natural birth process, which casts a pall of shame upon any infertile couple. The few families who choose to adopt do so in great secrecy, and habitually move to another province for a year, claiming upon return that the new baby is their natural offspring.

Over the last two decades many of the infants abandoned at birth have been born to the tens of thousands of unskilled women workers in their mid- to late twenties who teem into Moscow every year for better jobs, and live in often dire straits in communal dormitories. In the past few years, an increasing amount of illegitimate babies (often referred to these days as "disco children") have also been born to high school students. But there is a category of foundlings given a far more frightening name: "Orphans with two living parents."[49]

"Orphans with two living parents" are infants rejected at birth by their married mothers because of alcoholism or drug addiction; because of low salaries, insufficient living space, insufficient government support; or out of a crass materialism and a level of moral depravity seldom witnessed in earlier decades of Soviet life. *Semya* magazine has documented some particularly extreme examples of such debasement: Hundreds of parents are known to have conceived offspring for the single purpose of obtaining a two-room apartment; immediately after being assigned the desired housing, they have abandoned their children on sidewalks or sent them to orphanages. One more proof (as my philosopher friend in Leningrad points out) that suffering will not redeem the world; that nothing returns us more thoroughly to the jungle ethic than a half-century of communal terror, hunger, suspicion, and a relentless dearth of basic necessities still being blamed four decades later, with chauvinist hypocrisy, on the patriotic sacrifices of a devastating war.

In this outsider's view I have tried to document some of the obstacles which have stood in the way of Soviet women's self-fulfillment, and which until the Gorbachev era remained more silenced than in any other developed nation: Misogyny, the double burdens of work and family, a scandalous insufficiency of child support measures, a vastly deteriorated health system, a dearth of basic commodities that *perestroika* has not even begun to assuage. These somber aspects of contemporary Soviet life help to explain the mood of despair and confusion in which citizens are currently trying to reevaluate the importance of the family and the home.

For upon the seventy-third anniversary of the October Revolution, Soviet society seems to be engaging in a powerful backlash against the emancipation of women brought by that very event.

Oppressive patriarchal attitudes (always latent in the Soviet Union) were greatly reinforced during the Brezhnev years, when a new cult of bourgeois goods and values resurrected images of the ideal woman as a sweetie-pie housewife. Men feel increasingly threatened by women's slow rise to positions of greater power at the workplace. They are distraught at home by the war of nerves caused by the overburdening of their wives. Like my real-life protagonist, Yuri Krassin, they are seduced by the Utopia of a housewife-spouse yet remain tormented (sometimes, I feel, to the verge of schizophrenia) by the substantial loss of income such an option would incur.

It is in this perplexed state of mind that Soviet men are airing their long-silenced distaste for "the liberated female." One of the many ironies of Gorbachev's *glasnost* is that it allows citizens to voice a vast spectrum of archaic patriarchal prejudices earlier banned as bourgeois or counterrevolutionary. With increasing frequency, men are taking advantage of this new freedom by publicly stating such views as "Women shouldn't get involved in politics at all,"[50] or "If a woman is nicely dressed, looks beautiful, is taken good care of, loved, and in high spirits, and if she doesn't have to earn her living, it means society is healthy."[51] These are opinions, obviously, for which a citizen would have been booed out of any public forum in the first half-century of the Soviet state.

Meanwhile the state-controled media, without suggesting any concrete programs for improving the plight of needy families, continue to

SOVIET WOMEN

cite the "overemancipated, masculinized woman" as responsible for a vast variety of social flaws, and plead for a return to healthily dichotomized male and female personalities. This propaganda is serviceable in many insidious ways: It enables public opinion to blame women for the numerous social ills that afflict the U.S.S.R.—hooliganism, alcoholism, the rising rate of divorce, the abandonment of children—and diverts attention from those structural flaws that are their true cause.

Even General Secretary Mikhail Sergeevich Gorbachev, who has shown deeper concern for women than any national leader since Lenin, has offered only one concrete program I know of to ease young mothers' lives: His regime has legislated that beginning with the next Five Year Plan, in 1991, women will get six extra months of *tenured but unpaid* maternity leave, allowing them to stay home until their child's second birthday without the risk of losing their jobs. As my friend Olga Voronina says, *bolshoye spasibo,* "thanks a lot."

And Gorbachev himself has made some alarmingly ambivalent statements about the future of Soviet women. "It is imperative to more actively involve women in the management of the economy, in cultural development and public life," he writes in his book *Perestroika.*

But a mere three paragraphs later, we come upon the following sentences: "Engaged in scientific research, working in construction sites, in production and in the services, women no longer have enough time to perform their everyday duties at home—housework, the upbringing of children and *the creation of a good family atmosphere.* We have discovered that many of our problems—in children's and young people's behavior, in our morals, culture, and in production—are partially caused by the weakening of family ties and slack attitude to family responsibilities . . . we are now holding heated debates . . . about the question of what we should do to make it possible for women to return to their *purely womanly mission.*"[52]

Thus even this most enlightened of Soviet leaders seems to remain trapped in the rigid ideological division between "masculine" and "womanly" mission which has characterized his society for centuries, and is unable to resolve a dilemma that has confronted his state from its very beginnings—how to reconcile women's dual roles as producer and reproducer. And one wonders if Soviet women can ever be liberated from this patriarchal ethic that neglects the most precious gifts of Western feminism: a pluralism of choices in our styles of life; our refusal of patriarchal stereotypes concerning gender roles; and the ultimate gift of self-determination.

In this laboratory of emancipation offered us by the Soviet Union, in this epochal experiment which has engaged women in the work force longer and more fully than any society in history, the paradoxal "equality" between the sexes may well symbolize a central dilemma of the human condition: the female's secret and ambivalent desire both to lead and be led, the male's confusion and resentment before her mysterious force and her often awesome versatility.

For even on the part of many women, the many bourgeois freedoms of *perestroika* seem to have set off an explosion of nostalgic longings for those days when, as my protagonist Maya Krassin put it, "we were just a little bit subordinated to our men."

"Did we win anything from our emancipation?" asks thirty-four-year-old Narchiza Gargankhedze, one of Georgia's most gifted film directors. "I rather think we lost the most important thing, happiness. We would all be happier in this country if wives were calmer, more peaceful and relaxed."

"In our country too many a woman is masculine in character and behavior," a young television editor in Riga says. "She goes about with her huge shoulder bag, racing to and fro between family and work, not enough time to do either properly, always late everywhere. . . . I have three daughters and I only want to teach them to be lovely women, lovely wives, that's my most important duty."

In few conversations, these days, can one avoid the newly popular theme of women's predestined, so-called "immutable nature." The world's leading woman chess player, Nona Gaprindashvili of Tbilisi, Georgia, gave me a particularly poignant insight into the limitations imposed on women by these alleged gender traits.

It is a centuries-old custom for Georgian brides to receive a chess set as part of their dowry and to continue playing the game into their late years, teaching the game to all their children and often beating the men in their families. Nona Gaprindashvili started playing chess tournaments when she was ten, and by the age of fifteen was ranked seventh in the U.S.S.R. She married a doctor and had a child, and was enabled to pursue her career by an unusually supportive husband who used to "literally chase her out of the house" when she had to fly to international tournaments.

A world-class player for the past three decades—she says she is the only woman with whom Bobby Fisher refuses to play without his knight—Gaprindashvili admits that women's performance in chess tournaments has vastly improved in the past years. But she believes that the "immutable biological differences" between the sexes will never allow women to play as well as men, not even after centuries of emancipation and equal rights.

"Along with scientific research," the champion told me, "chess tournaments take a longer span of concentration than almost any other human activity, for the smallest tournaments last three weeks. During that time you simply can't afford to think of anything else, and women are absolutely incapable of concentrating that long with the necessary intensity . . .

"For we're biologically determined to think about domestic issues, about nurturing others," she continued, "so it's not even a matter of being a mother, of having a family. I think that even a *nun* could never become a chess champion: Over the span of three weeks there would too frequently recur the concern for someone who needs her.

"That's the way women are created, this is our immutable constitution," Gaprindashvili added with a wry smile. "That's our beauty and our strength, and no centuries of emancipation will ever cure that imbalance. There can be great women poets, yes, because poetic inspiration comes in lightning strokes, it's of very great intensity and relative brevity. But to remain exclusively concentrated on one chessboard or one scientific experiment for weeks at a time . . . impossible!"

I asked the champion which domestic concerns have most intruded upon her concentration when she has played her matches. Worries about her husband? About her son, now a university student? Her answer was archetypal.

"Oh, I never worry about *them,*" Gaprindashvili exclaimed. "They can take care of themselves marvelously well, especially now that they can buy ready, hot meals at the new cooperatives. . . . No, it's my mother I worry about, only my beloved sixty-seven-year-old mother, who of course lives with us and is my abiding concern."

Her eyes were imbued with that adoring gaze that comes upon most Soviet women when they speak of Mother. "If I've reached the top of the chess profession it's because my mother did so much for me. And I'm filled with guilt each time I leave her, I'm terrified something might go wrong with her health. . . . And so when I phone my family from abroad to ask for news of her, even if she has the smallest illness they lie to me and tell me she's just fine, because they know I'd drop everything and rush back if I knew the truth."

So much for the original principles of Marxist psychology, which taught that social conditioning can transform all innate biological factors. So much for Lenin's dictum that ". . . the building of socialism will begin only when we have achieved the complete equality of women."[53]

Yet because of their far more arduous lives, because of their greater optimism (a state of mind always based, in good part, on self-esteem), women seem considerably more supportive than men of Gorbachev's revolution.

Among the Soviet Union's male intelligentsia, there is a fashionably macho attitude toward Gorbachev which expresses itself somewhat this way: "Don't tell me about his *perestroika,* don't give Gorbachev all the credit, I was already *perestroied.* . . ." (The end of the sentence might go: "I was already *perestroied* in '68 when I was suspended from university for joining a Christian Democratic group" —philosopher Aleksandr Sivak. "I was already *perestroied* when I tried to open birth control clinics and was forbidden to publish for three years"—Dr. Archil Khomassuridze.)

In this particular milieu of men, there also abides the negativism, the brooding Hamletian pessimism so abundantly expressed by male protagonists of nineteenth-century Russian literature. *"Perestroika and*

SOVIET WOMEN

glasnost will never work because we've always been a nation of losers," one often hears the fellows say in that mood of chest-beating introspective despair which remains a form of Soviet macho. "Throughout history we have lost all battles, all good causes, we are a people bent on self-destruction . . ."

But this skepticism prevails far less among women, perhaps because, as Riga editor Monika Zile movingly put it, "We tend to retain more faith in the sacred future." Women go out of their way to stress, for instance, that *perestroika*'s cooperative systems are creating better work incentives, and offering more flexible schedules that particularly benefit women. Their enthusiasm for Gorbachev remains centered on practical issues of family, on easing their double burdens, and on their desire (this seems crucial) to have more children.

"Women support Gorbachev because he'll help us stop working a double shift!" a factory worker in Moscow says. "He's promising us shorter work days, tenured maternity leave until our children are two years old; even if it brings some economic hardship, a child must be with its mother for the first two or three years . . . it may be that we can finally have larger families again."

"Our waitresses automatically get a share of our co-op's earnings," says Raisa Arhinova, the owner of an ice cream cooperative in Irkutsk, which in its first six months claims to have served two hundred thousand persons, one third of the city's population. "That means four hundred rubles a month working three days a week—is any schedule more ideal for a woman with a family?

"I'll tell you the finest thing Gorbachev will do for our country," she added. "He will enable us to recover our femininity at last, to become true women again."

Although many of them express mixed feelings for Raisa Gorbachev because of her "high lifestyle," Soviet women's personal affection for Mikhail Sergeevich tends to be expressed far more ardently than men's.

"How can I not admire even Raisa Gorbachev, seeing the way she supports and values our Misha!" my Siberian journalist friend Svetlana exclaimed when I asked her opinion of the General Secretary's wife. "To think she's his first censor, the first barometer for his ideas! How can one not revere her, seeing she's the first soul our Misha opens up to!"

To Aleksandra Sokolova, the wise and learned Leningrad fashion designer, *perestroika* even implies a new metaphysics, a new perspective of historical time.

"Gorbachev has at last liberated us from that sense of impending catastrophe that has plagued us for decades. Now we live with a different sense of time, a sense that beyond us there will be many generations which will continue our work and our culture."

But I keep remembering, above all else, the radiant optimism and dedication of the university students I met with in the company of Elvira Novikova at the Moscow Lenin State Pedagogical Institute.

The students had been engaged in a discussion concerning the need to take courses in the history of Russian religion. "It's appalling that for three generations we weren't even allowed to study the Bible and our own Orthodox tradition. How can you be a decent philologist that way?" asked Tatyana, the young woman who looked forward to supporting a child all by herself." "How can you understand Dostoevsky, and Gogol, and Bulgakov?" the ardent Komsomolist Ira concurred. The university's rector and the entire group assembled that morning under the portrait of Vladimir Ilyich Lenin, all fervently nodded their assent.

The young women agreed that the current religious awakening was a crucial part of the nation's "new beginning," and the discussion had inevitably proceeded to the theme of *perestroika*.

"I've gone through three phases in my attitudes toward *perestroika*," Tatyana said. "First, enthusiasm; then, last year, loss of faith. But now I'm in the third phase of the dialectic, realizing that it may take a long, long time, perhaps a generation, and that it's our duty to do all we can to help. We have to fight the negativity of our parents, who constantly complain that nothing is getting better."

"I look on our parents' generation as 'the lost generation,' " said Ira. "They were ruined by the cult of personality under Stalin, and then by the passivity and moral decay of the Brezhnev era."

"We must make our parents understand that what we're suffering through today is not the result of *perestroika*, but of *Zastoi*, the Stagnancy," said Sveta, a young mother and aspiring zoologist. "It's as if

SOVIET WOMEN

our country were one huge room which for decades was kept in a state of extraordinary, increasing disorder, with no light bulb in the ceiling. And suddenly Mikhail Sergeevich comes in and puts in a light bulb, and we finally see the mess . . ."

"Tovarishchi!" the energetic Ira called out. "I was never disillusioned in *perestroika* because I always knew it would entail great sacrifices, much effort. It's only a minimal part of our beloved Komsomol that's building *perestroika!* We must *all* pitch in and help!

"It may even take two generations to build it, the way it took forty years to build our Revolution!" Ira turned around to exhort her peers. "All we can do is fight, fight, fight! Work, work, work!"

"Listen to that word they constantly use!" exclaimed my companion Elvira. *"Barotsa,* fight! During our parents' youth no one was ever able or willing to fight . . . What a time of ferment, what radical reexaminations! How proud Lenin would be of us!"

It is on the fervor of this generation of Soviets, and on the Utopian optimism perhaps essential to any social change, that the survival of our own children may depend.

XVII

Going Home

Visiting Lake Baikal, an hour's drive from the city of Irkutsk, Siberia, I learned an interesting detail about the fabled purity of its six-mile-deep waters, which are said to remain as pristine as they were on the day of creation. It is in part due to the billions of microorganisms endemic to the lake which filter the water's impurities through their digestive tracts and excrete it in its original, immaculate state.

This ecological trait strikes me as symbolic of a certain purity of character, of valor and dedication, possessed by those Soviet women whom I have most admired—Elvira Novikova, Aina Ambrumova, the students at the Pedagogical Institute. I also found it among some of my acquaintances in Irkutsk, the final stop on my last journey through the U.S.S.R.

SOVIET WOMEN

The largest settlement in Central Siberia, Irkutsk is a picturesque city of six hundred thousand inhabitants, whose ancient wooden houses, graced with shutters and dormers of exquisitely eccentric pastel hues, re-create nineteenth-century Russia more faithfully than any other city in the nation. Walking by Irkutsk's tiny two-floor wooden houses, snugly decorated with lace curtains and potted flowers which frequently recall decors of our own Nantucket, one experiences Mother Russia at her most seductive and smothering, a past reality preserved as if in amber from the chaos and disillusionments of the last century. It was here that members of the 1825 Decembrist uprising were exiled after their aborted coup to depose Czar Nicholas I and create a constitutional monarchy. Even in Imperial times, Siberia was the only region in the empire in which serfdom was never imposed. And the citizenry of Irkutsk—a town then heavily populated with Russians wishing to flee serfdom, and other dissenters from the czarist regime—had welcomed the Decembrists with open arms.

The city remains, to this day, a shrine to the valor of those first revolutionaries. Few sites in Siberia are more venerated than the house in which Decembrist leader Prince Trubetskoy was allowed to live with his family after his fifteen years of forced labor camps; it has now been made into a beautiful little museum, complete with the hero's original furniture, piano, books. Few nineteenth-century graves, beyond those of the country's great writers and musicians, are more revered than that of his wife, Elena Trubetskaya, who along with two other of the Decembrists' spouses chose to follow her husband into Siberian exile. And few nineteenth-century poems are better known to Soviet citizens than Nekrasov's "Russian Women," which, describing the women's arduous journey toward their husbands, celebrates the mission esteemed for centuries as Russian women's noblest goal—redemptive self-sacrifice. "My true place is not at sumptuous balls, but in the grim, distant desert of exile," another Decembrist wife, Princess Volkonskaya, muses in Nekrasov's poem as she abandons the splendor of her St. Petersburg life. "Let me hasten to him! Only there can I breathe freely! I who shared all joy with him must now share his emprisonment . . . such is the will of heaven!"

It was in Irkutsk that my travel companion Nonna and I were to glean our last spectrum of opinions, from 1917-progressive to 1989-conservative, on the "woman issue." The latter were offered us by a professor of American literature at the local university, Alla Aleksandrovna Karnauhova. We met in Irkutsk University's bleak American studies classroom in the company of one of her colleagues and of our local guide, a genial Leningrad-born *Goskomizdat* executive named Valery Isakovich Tenenbaum.

The classroom's peeling walls were solely cheered by a large map of the United States and drawings of comic strip faces that said "Welcome to Hemingway!" and "Say cheeeee-eeeeese." Like many residents of Siberia, Alla Aleksandrovna and her colleague, Vladimir Feodorovich, are the descendants of criminals and political exiles (in mid-nineteenth century one third of Irkutsk's population were of the latter category) and enormously proud of their ancestry: Alla is descended from a Buryat herdsman and from a Muscovite woman who was banned to the steppes for anti-czarist activities, Vladimir from an Ukrainian bandit who had murdered his brother.

Meeting with these two cordial Siberians, we learned that Soviet views of the United States can be made eccentric by the citizenry's very quirky tastes in American books. The professors concurred, as had all teachers of American literature we met during our trip, that Margaret Mitchell's *Gone with the Wind* (so popular in the U.S.S.R. that a copy of it sells on the black market for sixty rubles, one hundred dollars) is the "greatest modern masterpiece of American literature, along with Faulkner and Hemingway."

Our Irkutsk colleagues also described the very curious way in which our literature is taught throughout the U.S.S.R.: In part because of a dearth of books, in part because of the authoritarian nature of their system, Soviet professors "describe" certain American texts to their classes without the students ever once seeing a copy of the work discussed, either in the original or in translation.

"There is only one copy of John Updike or Sinclair Lewis assigned

SOVIET WOMEN

to any university," Professor Karnauhova explained, "and that belongs to its library. Since private copies of such books can only be purchased on the black market they're far beyond our students' financial means . . . occasionally we can make two or three photocopies of a little passage, a page or so, and pass it around for the students to share so they can get the original flavor. But how far does that go, with fifty, sixty students in each class? That'll just have to do," she explained apologetically, "until we're far deeper into *glasnost* than we are now."

The Irkutsk professors went on to state their esteem for a weirdly mixed list of twentieth-century American favorites—John Updike, Jacqueline Susann, John Dos Passos, Leon Uris, Erskine Caldwell, Flannery O'Connor, Arthur Hailey, and J. D. Salinger, in whom they detected "a great Buddhist influence."

In one of those exotically irrational outbursts of opinion typical of Soviet conversations, Professor Alla Aleksandrovna, a woman with cornflower-blue eyes and the amber-hued Eskimo features of her Buryat provenance, expressed her particular admiration for a strikingly progressive group of American authors—Toni Morrison, Henry Miller, Hubert Selby, and the "radical Lesbian feminist" Adrienne Rich. But then, launching on the issue of her country's working women, she spent an hour trying to convince us that "any woman who becomes independent loses her charm."

"When a woman assumes a high post it becomes the foundation of her life," she asserted. "The husband and the family just don't exist, she loses her femininity, she becomes domineering and bossy, no one likes this! She loses what has been assigned to her by nature. If she has a child, she doesn't take care of him; we call such children half-orphans. . . ."

"Well," I said, "if you think women shouldn't be in positions of power, then there is no true equality in your society."

"Yes, woman must lead, but . . ." Alla Aleksandrova hesitated, ". . . but if she assumes masculine qualities she loses her essence."

"What if she mixes the qualities of administrator *and* good wife and mother?" My friend Nonna entered the fray.

"But that's not possible!" Alla Aleksandrovna exclaimed. "That's against nature!"

"I'll give you a historical example," our local guide, Valery

Isakovich, proposed. "Our great revolutionary leader Aleksandra Kollontai. She took on a masculine job and she seemed to be a good mother . . ."

"She was *not* a good mother," Professor Alla Aleksandrovna said adamantly. "She didn't look after her son at all, she kept leaving the country. Of course women must *try* to participate in the work collective while retaining their femininity. . . . But this is a very complex problem, not to lose our womanliness . . ."

Alla Aleksandrovna rubbed her forehead, looking totally perplexed. "She must remain charming, pleasant, attractive . . ."

"But you're overlooking a fine example right here in our own collective!" Professor Vladimir Feodorovich suggested. He turned to Nonna and me and explained:

"Our boss is one of the only two women in the Russian Federation who is the rector of a university. And we have better material conditions than other universities, more dormitories, more comforts."

"I'm not sure about how well she brought up her children," Alla Aleksandrovna ventured.

"I happen to know she's a good grandmother," our guide Valery Isakovich retorted.

The conversation then turned to one Galina Petrovna, a local factory manager, who, along with the vice-rector of the university, seemed to be looked upon as the most highly ranked woman executive in Irkutsk. Valery Isakovich and Vladimir Feodorovich could not say enough about her firm but gentle manner, the outstanding efficiency with which she ran her plant, the way she balanced her power with compassion and tenderness.

"She's very flexible as an administrator, we call her mini-Thatcher," our Irkutsk guide said. "Like Thatcher deciding Common Market problems, Galina Petrovna has typically female shrewdness; she gently approaches and decides all problems, and she's never criticized."

But Alla Aleksandrovna was not convinced by the example of Galina Petrovna either, and continued to wallow in the perplexities of the women-in-power issue. "The men working under a woman executive may look on her as noble, but to the women working under her she becomes a monstrous non-woman. . . ."

SOVIET WOMEN

Overlooking the professor's reservations, Nonna and I immediately asked to meet "the most important woman in Irkutsk," Galina Petrovna, to resolve the issue for ourselves. And our acquaintances arranged for us to meet her the next day at her place of work.

Galina Petrovna, a heavy-set woman in her fifties with thoughtful brown eyes and a gentle, retiring manner, directs the largest book-distributing plant in central Siberia; it employs about a thousand persons, nine hundred of them women. The factory handles several hundred thousand tomes received yearly from Moscow publishers, and distributes them to some two thousand libraries and several hundred bookstores in central Siberia. Like most Soviet executives we visited with outside of Moscow, Galina Petrovna was courteously waiting for us at the appointed hour outside of her factory, and led us immediately to the production line, an immense space where several hundred women hovered over slow-moving conveyor belts, overseeing the packaging and labeling of books.

The women at this plant struck me as a particularly cheerful and high-spirited lot, a result, perhaps, of Siberia's relatively high standard of living. For as a way of luring more citizens to its underpopulated steppes, the Soviet government has been offering Siberia's residents wages 20 percent higher than the national average, often extravagant bonuses, double vacation time, and ready access to private cars.

Yet it was the privileges they'd fought for and won in this particular plant with the aid of their local *Zhensoviet* council that Galina Petrovna and her employees were eager to boast of. Talking or rather yelling to each other over the din of the machines, we discussed the various services they enjoyed at their work collective: a food commissary where they can buy many domestic staples without any tiring queue; periodical visits from general doctors and gynecologists at the factory site; the poetry readings regularly held at the plant; the seamstress who reserves her services for the factory's employees, charging twenty rubles, or thirty-five dollars, for a made-to-measure dress (the biggest bargain I'd yet heard of in the Soviet Union, one third the price of the dismal apparel in state-owned clothing stores).

I asked the workers about their leisure time, and was struck by their almost chauvinistic dedication to Siberia, the tight bonding of their friendships, and the frugality of their tastes: they talked of their love for fishing, hiking, and camping in the nearby taiga, of driving to their grandmothers' *dachas* or their own collective plots outside of town to grow their vegetables.

"For years, my husband and I have been getting together with two other couples to hike and camp with our children," one worker said. "For holidays the six of us have masquerade parties with the kids . . . our most popular costumes are Cinderella and *Baba Yaga.*"

"We all have cars, so we take our tents and camp out by Lake Baikal with our families," another said. "Siberians love their land like no other Soviets you'll meet." (I thought back to another Irkutsk acquaintance, Svetlana, the journalist who was bringing up her three-year-old granddaughter and who would never leave Siberia, even for a husband with a gorgeous apartment in Moscow, because she must remain "by the side of sacred Lake Baikal.")

I asked the workers how, in their view, they most differed from American women. "Soviet women are prettier," one young mother of three said with great assurance. I also asked them what the major benefits of *perestroika* might be for Soviet women. "We've been struggling to restructure our men for decades," one said, "so we're all ready to go with *perestroika.*" The gathering dissolved into the raucous laughter habitual to Soviet women's talk of men. The lunch siren hooted. We disbanded with warm greetings, and Galina Petrovna, who had been standing quietly at the side of the group as I talked to the women, invited me to her office for lunch.

Galina's stark style of dressing is similar to the one seen in Soviet magazines until the early 1950s—flat, almost masculine shoes, a plain white shirtwaist and navy skirt, straight graying hair pulled back in a flat, simple bun, no trace of makeup. I had not yet met a Soviet woman more impressive in her simplicity, her calm, her idealism, her stoic satisfaction with whatever life had brought her.

Over a frugal lunch of black bread, sausage, and delectable blackberry jam, which we shared with a few of her assistant managers,

SOVIET WOMEN

Galina Petrovna told me that she had married early, and earned her graduate degree in economics at night school while holding a full-time job. Like most of her generation, she'd returned to work when her son was three months old, placing him in a *yasli*. Like the industrial workers I'd met with at Moscow's *Zhensoviet* headquarters, and most women of her generation—members of the first revolutionary decades —Galina Petrovna's work collective held priority over her family and every aspect of her private life.

"When everything's all right at the collective, then all is pure pleasure. My family is not the most important thing for me—and not for my husband or my son, either. We're probably all like this in Siberia, it's in our genes. The most important thing is for everything to be okay at work . . ." (There was a chorus of agreement from her associates—"Yes, yes, that's the way it is for all of us.")

"I bring home the joy I receive from my work," Galina Petrovna said, a smile irradiating her pale, kind face. "I hear that many American women stay at home and don't work! That's unthinkable to me. If you forced me to sit at home I'd rather not go on living." (I kept thinking back to Maya Krassin's talk of "self-expression." The very word would have been like Sanskrit to Galina Petrovna.)

We talked of leisure and books; we had a spirited discussion about whether or not *Gone with the Wind* is the "modern American masterpiece." "The most important woman in Irkutsk," as Galina Petrovna is called, dislikes television, and has no recreations at home beyond reading fiction and history for several hours every night. For years her favorite weekend pastime had been to drive to a friend's house in the country and enjoy a *banya po chornomu* or "black bath," the Siberian sauna, but she'd had to discontinue the saunas because of heart trouble. Upon hearing that Nonna and I had never experienced this regional pleasure, Galina Petrovna and our local guide, Valery Isakovich, instantly began making arrangements to drive us to the country the following day for a Siberian sauna.

It was the afternoon before Nonna and I were scheduled to return to Moscow, four days before I was planning to fly back to the United States. And I remain grateful that my last days in the Soviet Union were marked by the unique warmth and hospitality of our Siberian friends.

When Galina Petrovna and Valery Isakovich picked us up at our hotel for "the world's greatest sauna experience," we were puzzled to see that our expedition consisted of some six persons and three cars: Galina Petrovna was so excited by the prospect of foreign guests enjoying their first Siberian sauna that she had invited along a group of friends and associates, who left their jobs at 2 P.M. to join the excursion. We drove an hour outside of Irkutsk, and reached a little settlement where a friend of Galina Petrovna's and Valery Isakovich's had recently built, with his own hands, a tiny two-room *dacha* and an accompanying sauna.

Our host, a burly, genial man who could not enough praise the health-giving properties of this local custom ("Whenever you've got bronchitis and are running a high temperature, an hour in the steamroom, a big roll in the snow, and you're all cured!"), met us at the door of his minuscule house. As he gave us a tour, "the most powerful woman in Irkutsk" bustled about the sauna that stood a few yards away, across a vegetable patch, to get everything ready for Nonna and me. After twenty minutes she handed Nonna two immense bath towels which she'd brought us from town, and accompanied us to the sauna to gave us precise instructions on how to proceed.

How cozy, thoughtful, and quintessentially Russian it was in that tiny, dark, burning-hot space! In the daintily curtained resting room, between two cots, stood a lace-covered table with a vase of fresh flowers, a pot of hot tea, a jar of jam provided by Galina, and a pail of fragrant, birch-scented water with which to douse ourselves during the treatment. Our mentor told us to undress and showed us into the *banya* itself, a still smaller, darker, far hotter room, which was heated by a mound of bricks burning in a black iron stove, and equipped with four large planks of pine wood to lie on. "But be careful," she chided. "Careful, it's all very new to you, you must get up every few minutes and douse yourselves with the water . . ."

She left us alone. Nonna and I lay on the wooden pine planks,

SOVIET WOMEN

whose fragrant heat was at the limit of our endurance, perspiring greatly, following the directions of Galina, who every few minutes peered into the sauna to shout, "Careful, dear ones! Time for the birch water now and a little tea!"

Coddled in that dark maternal warmth, inhaling the dry, hot smell of pine and eucalyptus and birch leaves and of the smoldering stove, the perfume of the tea and jam in the room next door, I was transported to the arms of the Russian women who had cared for me so well when I was a small child, my great-grandmother, my great-aunt; to the fragrant intimacy of the tiny icon-filled rooms of their Paris exile, to memories of their own nurturing warmth, cheer, gentleness, selflessness, stoic patience—qualities which have given me whatever strength I've had in life. Lying that afternoon in the mother-hot darkness, I sensed that Galina Petrovna, along with my beloved travel companion Nonna, my *tovarishch* Elvira, still enshrined all these precious traits of my Russian forebears, blending them with the ascetic zeal, the dedication to a new and better society, which had been the noblest features of the Revolution my relatives had fled . . . that, too, is why I might have wished to write this book.

Nonna and I dutifully followed Galina Petrovna's orders; every few minutes we rose to douse ourselves; to "awaken the blood" we gently slapped each other's backs, laughing like schoolgirls, with the traditional bunches of birch leaves. When our mentor told us our time was up we obediently rose from the fragrant searing pine planks. We doused ourselves for the last time, got dressed, and were escorted out by Galina Petrovna, with exhortations to stay very warm for the next hour, and to eat plentifully at the meal she had provided in our host's little house.

It was then the men's turn to go to the bath. We three women feasted by ourselves at the table, which "the most powerful woman in Irkutsk" had spread with cold chicken, bread, cheese, a variety of cucumber and tomato salads, a cake she had prepared for the occasion. Over tea Galina Petrovna turned to Nonna and me with pensive eyes and asked, "Are you religious? I so envy people who are. My mother and grandmother still go to service, I envy their faith."

We told her yes, we were, each in our own unorthodox ways; we suggested that if she partook of the liturgy her faith might awaken, too. . . . As we rose from the meal she took my hand in both of hers and said, "How sad that you must leave tomorrow! Here I am, just getting used to our friendship." I kept thinking: How totally wrong many Soviet women had been—Maya Krassin, that professor in Irkutsk, scores of others—maintaining that women can not achieve power without losing their tenderness.

As we prepared to leave, Galina Petrovna offered me some presents to take back to the United States—two sumptuously illustrated books on the Decembrists' exile in Siberia, several pots of the blackberry jam I had admired during lunch at her office the previous day.

Before our procession of cars left for the hour's trip back to Irkutsk, Galina Petrovna made us sit down on the little wooden bench that stood outside on our host's tiny porch, under a clump of birch trees. "It is an old Russian custom," she said, "to sit down very quietly on a bench before taking a journey." We held hands as we sat on the bench, chatting a little, mostly keeping silence.

Years from now, I shall recall Galina Petrovna as an embodiment of the qualities I most treasure in Soviet womanhood; as one who personifies all that the world's most heroic community of women might yet become.

Notes

1. *Harriman Institute Forum*, July 1988. This essay states that in terms of "socio-cultural infrastructures" (electricity, purity of water, numerous other human services), Moscow is ranked in the *third* decile among Soviet cities. Levels of education show equal disproportions; republics of the Caucasus area and of the Baltic States, for instance, have considerably larger ratios of university students per population than do citizens of the Russian Federation.

2. *Population Briefing Paper*, no. 19, October 1987 (published by the Population Crisis Committee, Washington, D.C.). Data provided by The World Bank and the United Nations Fund for Population Activities.

3. *Moscovskie Novosti*, "She and We" column, January 1–8, 1989.

4. Barbara Holland and Teresa McKevitt, "Maternity Care in the Soviet Union," in *Soviet Sisterhood,* edited by Barbara Holland (London: Fourth Estate Publishers, 1985).

5. *Moskovskie Novosti,* "She and We" column, January 1–8, 1989.

6. Natalya Baranskaya, "A Week Like Any Other," *The Massachusetts Review,* Autumn 1974.

7. V. I. Lenin, *A Great Beginning,* excerpted in *Not by Politics Alone, the other Lenin,* edited by Tamara Deutscher (Westport, Conn.: L. Hill, 1973).

8. The official translation of *Goskomizdat* is "State Committee of the U.S.S.R. for Publishing, Printing, and Book Trade."

9. *Novoye Vremya,* July 1987.

10. Olga Voronina, "Zhenshchina V Muzhskom Obshchestve," in *Sotsiologicheskaia Publitsistika,* no. 2, 1988.

11. Ibid.

12. E. B. Gruzdeva and E. S. Chertikhina, *Soviet Sociology,* Winter 1987–88. See also Mary Buckley, "Women in the Soviet Union," *Feminist Review,* 1981.

13. Gail Warshowsky Lapidus, "Occupational Segregation and Public Policy: A Comparative Analysis of American and Soviet Patterns," *Signs,* Summer 1976.

14. Voronina, "Zhenshchina."

15. *Moskovskie Novosti,* "Angry Women Demand Change," June 15, 1988.

16. Quoted in *Moskovskie Novosti,* "On the Women's Problem," August 21–28, 1988.

17. Lynne Atwood, "The New Soviet Man and Woman—Soviet Views on Psychological Sex Differences," in *Soviet Sisterhood,* edited by Barbara Holland.

18. *Tashkentskaya Nedelya,* May 1, 1988.

19. A note on the vast difference between the Soviet and American university systems: Instead of following a general curriculum for two years and being able to wait until their third year to decide which field they will "major" in, young Soviets desiring higher education must decide at age eighteen or so which "faculty" of any given university they wish to apply to—Psychology, Medicine, History, Linguistics, etc. The diploma they receive after five years of university study (and the writing and defense of a dissertation) is a "Candidate of Sciences" degree, whose status stands somewhat higher than our M.A. Only after a decade or more of being employed in any vocation can they start working on their doctoral dissertations, the defense of which earns them a Doctorate of Sciences—an honor scholars seldom receive before they are in their late thirties or forties.

20. Barbara Alpern Engel and Clifford Rosenthal, eds., *Five Sisters: Women Against the Tsar* (New York: Alfred Knopf, 1975).

21. Barbara Alpern Engel, *Mothers and Daughters: Women of the Intelligentsia in 19th Century Russia* (New York: Cambridge University Press, 1983).

22. Linda Harriet Edmondson, *Feminism in Russia, 1900–1917* (London: Heinemann Educational Books, Ltd., 1984).

23. Barbara Evans Clements, *Bolshevik Feminist: The Life of Aleksandra Kollontai* (Bloomington: Indiana University Press, 1979).

24. "Feminism in Russian Literature," in *Modern Encyclopedia of Russian and Soviet Literature*, edited by Harry B. Weber (Gulf Breeze, Fla.: Academic International Press, 1977).

25. *Woman and Russia: First Feminist Samizdat* (London: Sheba Feminist Publishers, 1980). My information on Sergey Paradzhanov and on attitudes toward homosexuality in the U.S.S.R. is drawn from Tatyana Mamonova's *Russian Women's Studies* (Elmsford, N.Y.: Pergamon Press, 1989).

26. *Express-Chronicle*, May 25, 1988.

27. Joanna Hubbs, *Mother Russia* (Bloomington: Indiana University Press, 1988).

28. Nikolay Berdyanev, *The Russian Idea* (Boston: Beacon Press, 1968).

29. Quoted in Engel, *Mothers and Daughters*.

30. Nikolay Berdyaev, *The Russian Idea* (Boston: Beacon Press, 1966).

31. Barbara Heldt, *Terrible Perfection: Women and Russian Literature* (Bloomington: Indiana University Press, 1987). Throughout my research for this chapter, I have also been indebted to the following texts: Edward J. Brown, *Russian Literature Since the Revolution* (Toronto: Collier Books, 1969). Ronald Hingley, *Russian Writers and Soviet Society, 1917–1978* (New York: Random House, 1979). Ruth Crego Brenson, "Two Natashas," in *Women in Tolstoy.* Antonia Glass, "The Formidable Woman: Portrait and Original," in *Russian Literature Tri-Quarterly,* Spring 1974; Xenia Gasiorowska, "Two Decades of Love and Marriage in Soviet Fiction," in *Russian Review,* January 1975.

I am particularly grateful for the insights offered by my friend Vera Sandomirsky Dunham in her admirable essay "The Strong-Woman Motif" (collected in *The Transformation of Russian Society,* edited by Cyril Black (Cambridge, Mass.: Harvard University Press, 1960).

32. I. Grekova, "The Retirement Party," in *The New Soviet Fiction,* edited by Sergei Zalygin (New York: Abbeville Press, 1989).

33. Viktoria Tokareva, "Nothing Special," in *Balancing Acts: Contemporary Stories by Russian Women,* edited by Elena Goscilo (Bloomington: Indiana University Press, 1989).

34. Lyudmila Uvarova, "Be Still, Torments of Passion," *Balancing Acts.*

35. I. Grekova, *Russian Women* (New York: Harcourt Brace Jovanovich, 1983).

36. Nina Katerli, "Between Spring and Summer," *Balancing Acts.*

37. Natalya Baranskaya, "The Kiss," in *The New Soviet Fiction.*

38. Introduction to *Balancing Acts,* E. Goscilo.

39. Julia Voznesenskaya, *Women's Decameron* (New York: Henry Holt & Co., 1987).

40. The name of the victim was Maya Khassanova. The information comes from my taped conversation with eighty-six-year-old Uzbek actress Sara Ishanturaeve of Tashkent, who knew the woman well. (F.G.)

Notes

41. *Pravda,* "Living Torches," April 21, 1988.

42. *Moskovskie Novosti,* "Consumerism and Spiritual Values," August 28–September 4, 1988.

43. *Moskovskie Novosti,* "Up Against the Mafia," April 10–17, 1988.

44. Ibid.

45. *Moskovskie Novosti,* "The Soviet Mafia," August 21–28, 1988.

46. *New York Times,* December 31, 1988.

47. Martin Walker, *The Waking Giant: Gorbachev's Russia* (New York: Random House, 1986).

48. Tatyana Tolstaya, *Collected Short Stories* (New York: Alfred Knopf, 1989).

49. All information and statistics in this chapter on the plight of Soviet orphans are taken from Spring 1988 issues of *Semya.*

50. *Moskovskie Novosti,* "She and We" column, January 8–15, 1989.

51. V. Merezhko, in *Sputnik Kinozritelya,* as quoted in *Moskovskie Novosti,* "On the Women's Problem," August 21–28, 1988.

52. Mikhail S. Gorbachev, *Perestroika* (New York: Harper & Row, Perennial Library edition, 1987).

53. V. I. Lenin, *The Tasks of the Working Women's Movement,* speech made on September 23, 1919. Excerpted in *Not by Politics Alone, the Other Lenin,* edited by Tamara Deutscher.